S0-BJL-393

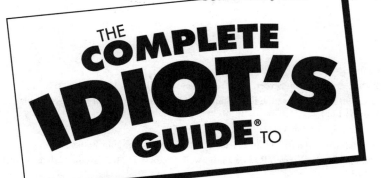

THE
COMPLETE IDIOT'S GUIDE® TO

Framing Basics

Illustrated

by Norman Skanon

ALPHA

A member of Penguin Group (USA) Inc.

ALPHA BOOKS

Published by the Penguin Group

Penguin Group (USA) Inc., 375 Hudson Street, New York, New York 10014, USA

Penguin Group (Canada), 90 Eglinton Avenue East, Suite 700, Toronto, Ontario M4P 2Y3, Canada (a division of Pearson Penguin Canada Inc.)

Penguin Books Ltd, 80 Strand, London WC2R 0RL, England

Penguin Ireland, 25 St. Stephen's Green, Dublin 2, Ireland (a division of Penguin Books Ltd.)

Penguin Group (Australia), 250 Camberwell Road, Camberwell, Victoria 3124, Australia (a division of Pearson Australia Group Pty. Ltd.)

Penguin Books India Pvt. Ltd., 11 Community Centre, Panchsheel Park, New Delhi—110 017, India

Penguin Group (NZ), 67 Apollo Drive, Rosedale, North Shore, Auckland 1311, New Zealand (a division of Pearson New Zealand Ltd.)

Penguin Books (South Africa) (Pty.) Ltd, 24 Sturdee Avenue, Rosebank, Johannesburg 2196, South Africa

Penguin Books Ltd., Registered Offices: 80 Strand, London WC2R 0RL, England

Copyright © 2007 by Norman Skanon

International Standard Book Number: 978-1-59257-668-5
Library of Congress Catalog Card Number: 2007926851

09 08 07   8 7 6 5 4 3 2 1

Interpretation of the printing code: The rightmost number of the first series of numbers is the year of the book's printing; the rightmost number of the second series of numbers is the number of the book's printing. For example, a printing code of 07-1 shows that the first printing occurred in 2007.

Printed in the United States of America

Note: This publication contains the opinions and ideas of its author. It is intended to provide helpful and informative material on the subject matter covered. It is sold with the understanding that the author and publisher are not engaged in rendering professional services in the book. If the reader requires personal assistance or advice, a competent professional should be consulted.

The author and publisher specifically disclaim any responsibility for any liability, loss, or risk, personal or otherwise, which is incurred as a consequence, directly or indirectly, of the use and application of any of the contents of this book.

Most Alpha books are available at special quantity discounts for bulk purchases for sales promotions, premiums, fund-raising, or educational use. Special books, or book excerpts, can also be created to fit specific needs.

For details, write: Special Markets, Alpha Books, 375 Hudson Street, New York, NY 10014.

Publisher: *Marie Butler-Knight*
Editorial Director/Acquiring Editor: *Mike Sanders*
Managing Editor: *Billy Fields*
Development Editor: *Nancy D. Lewis*
Production Editor: *Megan Douglass*
Copy Editor: *Nancy Wagner*

Cartoonist: *Richard King*
Cover Designer: *Becky Harmon*
Book Designer: *Trina Wurst*
Indexer: *Julie Bess*
Layout: *Chad Dressler*
Proofreader: *Mary Hunt*

Contents at a Glance

Contents

Appendixes

Introduction

Some of the best work you can do in your life is with a saw, a hammer, nails, and lumber. Many jobs these days are done indoors, dealing with information, pushing around electrons, or pushing around paper. At the end of the day you go home and you wonder what you accomplished because you can't see it.

But framing is entirely different. Unless you are working inside an existing home, the framing you do is outdoors. You breathe outdoor air, and the wind ruffles your hair. You can play the radio, have all kinds of snacks and drinks, and make jokes with the people you are working with.

But perhaps most importantly, you can see and feel the work you are doing. At the end of the day, you can clearly see what you have done and how the work site has changed. You have put up some walls, put down some floor joists, put up some rafters, or built a gable dormer. Your body might ache at the end of all this, but you have the reward of actually having accomplished something.

When I started framing, I worked during the summer in the country. We started as the sun came up and worked until the sun went down. Drink never was so refreshing; food never tasted so good. A dunk in the river never felt so cool and lovely.

And guys, women appreciate men who can make things with lumber. No kidding! And you may not be into this yet, but children appreciate a dad with construction skills, too. When I built a playhouse for my daughter, she was thrilled.

Carpentry has a long and honorable tradition because people use it to build their homes. A carpenter is a skilled worker whose abilities have always been in demand. Even where homes are masonry, the roofs and floors and porches are made of wood. Somebody has to know how to cut and install the rafters, how to cut and assemble the stairways. Carpenters with their measures, their framing squares, and their saws are the people who do it.

Even if you haven't used a hammer since the plastic one in playschool, you can use this book to go from that to framing a gable roof. I explain what tools you need, how to use them, and what to do with them. I also explain how to keep yourself and others safe, so that whatever you build, at the end of the day, you're ready to enjoy it.

Framing is an ancient skill that has always followed common sense rules. Upright lumber carries weight; where there is a door or window, horizontal lumber distributes the weight left and right. Stairwell openings need to be reinforced with doubled joists and so on. The common sense of centuries is now shaped into rules written into local building codes, which you need to follow for any framing job. In addition, most framing jobs need permits from the local building departments; officials there need to be assured that you are going to follow the building codes so that you, your guests, or future owners of your project are not going to be hurt owing to too few nails or too feeble lumber. Always follow the rules and your project will come out fine.

Now let me tell you what's in store for you in this book.

Parts of the Whole

Part 1, "Tools, Materials and Keeping Safe," covers the basics. I tell you about the tools you will need, from the hand saws and hammers to the levels and electric-powered circular saws. I give you information about the different kinds of nails, their strange terminology (10 penny, 16 penny), and modern framing connectors that more quickly and securely fasten lumber together, such as rafters to the tops of framed walls. I explain about the different kinds of lumber you use when framing, how it is graded, and how it is sized. You also learn about plywood and modern plywood-like products. Part I also has a very important section on safety. I inform you of the cautions and the rules you have to pay attention to. From being up on a ladder to cutting with a circular saw, you must be careful of what you are doing.

Part 2, "Framing Techniques," contains essential information. I start by showing you how to read blueprints (actually black-and-white these days and often called "plans") because you may be working from drawings drafted by a professional architect or designer. And here's where you learn about why walls are designed the way they are, dealing with weight bearing down and wind trying to blow them over. I discuss the fundamentals, too, the proper way to saw and different saw cuts and the best way to nail, along with different nailing techniques.

Part 3, "Framing," starts the real sawing and hammering. This section pretty much follows the steps in building a house, beginning with the first pieces of lumber that attach to a masonry foundation. It lays the first floor, then moves on to building the walls and hammering them in place. It presents the techniques for putting up ceiling joists and shows how to make a roof. It also explains how to construct stairs, from a two- or three-step stair, as from a deck to a patio, to a full flight of stairs from one story in a house to another. There's also a chapter on framing inside existing homes, even, if you care to tackle it, removing part of an existing wall and replacing it with a beam.

Part 4, "Special Framing," takes up some special framing jobs. The first chapter explains how to frame a bay window. Large ones can act as sun rooms, and small ones can shelter window seats—the framing is about the same either way. The next chapter tells how to frame a shed dormer in a gable roof to make a large living space within; it also shows how to frame a gable dormer for a smaller and more intimate space. There's a chapter on framing in basements because many people would like to turn an unfinished basement into a finished one—it's not too hard if you have the basic framing skills. And last, there is a chapter on built-ins. Here you learn how to build a cabinet recessed into a framed wall, floor-to-ceiling book cases, or an alcove bench that has a lid for storage.

The first appendix is an extensive glossary, which contains every technical term defined in the body of the book. If as you're reading along, you encounter one of these terms and have forgotten its meaning, just look it up in the glossary. The second appendix is a listing of resources. These are lumber associations, books, magazines, and websites that are useful to framers.

Sidebars

As you read the text, you'll notice the occasional sidebar. There are three types.

Framer's Lingo

Here I draw attention to technical terms and define them—these terms also appear in the glossary.

Finger Tips

These are little chunks of advice about doing things a little better or in a different way.

Heads!

These items address safety issues. Always read them; always heed them.

Acknowledgments

I wish to take the space here to sincerely thank the following persons and organizations for their kind assistance in the making of this book:

A&A Rental Station, Alexandria, Virginia

APA – The Engineered Wood Association, Tacoma, Washington

Alexandria Lighting and Supply, Inc., Alexandria, Virginia

Butenhoff Construction, Springfield, Virginia

Ivan Chirinos, Fairfax County Public Schools

Rick Dobson, Dobson Building and Remodeling, Fairfax County, Virginia

Steven J. Doebel, Encompass Design Build, Vienna, Virginia

Edison Academy, Fairfax County Public Schools

John Hannah, Burlington, Vermont

James and Darlene Meggesto, Alexandria, Virginia

Jose Pastor Mejia, Encompass Design Build, Vienna, Virginia

Shane Mills, Fairfax County Public Schools

Chris Neumann, Encompass Design Build, Vienna, Virginia

David Olinger, Encompass Design Build, Vienna, Virginia

Peter and Valerie Page, Alexandria, Virginia

Robert Brian Vincent Custom Builders, Damascus, Maryland

Jorge Reyes, Encompass Design Build, Vienna, Virginia

Linda Serabian, SOMA Architects, Alexandria, Virginia

Todd Schneider, Schneider Contracting Corp., Alexandria, Virginia

Robert Stets, Fairfax County Public Schools

Western Wood Products Association, Portland, Oregon

Bill Wiley, Alexandria, Virginia

Mike and Marci Woodgerd, Fairfax County, Virginia

Brian Wright, Encompass Design Build, Vienna, Virginia

Trademarks

In This Part

"I'm just looking for a good-old-fashioned box of nails."

Part 1

Tools, Materials, and Keeping Safe

Framing is fun. You build things. It's satisfying. But no one every strolled out under the sun and started framing. No. They got tools first and materials. When you have and understand the tools and the materials and how to deal with them safely, then you can start framing. That's what this part of the book is all about.

If you already have the tools, fine. If you understand the materials, fine. Skip ahead. But do me a favor. Don't skip the safety chapter. Everyone, from the first-timer to the old-timer, needs to go over the rules again and again until they are second nature. Framing is meant to get you somewhere—onto the couch in the living room of the home you are building, into the bay window you are adding to your dining room—and you want to get there whole and hearty so you can enjoy the fruits of your labor.

In This Chapter

- ◆ Important hammers and saws
- ◆ Tools to help measure and mark
- ◆ Additional hand tools
- ◆ Tool carriers such as belts and buckets
- ◆ Saw horses and workbenches

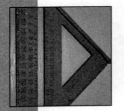

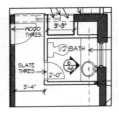

Chapter 1

Hand Tools

One of the benefits of carpentry work is working with hand tools. People have used hand tools for centuries, and the designs of some of these tools can be traced back to the earliest civilizations. Sumarians used hammers; Greeks used saws; Romans used plumb bobs. In fact, the word "plumb" comes from the Latin word for the metal lead, and the word "carpenter" comes from the Latin word for a person who made carriage wheels.

Framing is erecting the wooden "bones"—the joists, studs, and rafters—of a building. It can also encompass fastening the sheathing to those "bones." Sheathing is plywood or similar panels that are nailed to the joists, studs, and rafters.

Hand tools are wonderful and can become like friends. Choose high quality ones; cheaper ones break and then instead of getting the work done you have to drive to the store for a replacement. But if you choose good ones, they will stay with you for life, doing job after job. In this chapter, you learn all about a framing carpenter's most needed and useful hand tools.

Hammers

Hammers are to the framer what cameras are to the photographer; you gotta have them to do what you do. When you start framing, you'll probably want at least two hammers, a *framing hammer* and a *claw hammer*. It's also a good idea to have a *hand sledge hammer*, also called a baby sledge, for driving stakes or "persuading" a piece of framed wall to fit exactly into place.

Framing Hammer

The main hammer for framing, is, ta da, a framing hammer. Models vary, but most framing hammers weigh between 20 to 24 ounces. Generally, the face has a waffle texture so that when it strikes a nail head, it is less likely to slip off but rather drives the nail down truly. The handle can be wood, fiberglass, or steel.

The advantage of using a heavy framing hammer is that, when it strikes a nail, the weight behind it is more likely to drive the nail farther into the wood than would be the case with a lighter hammer. But the drawback to a heavy hammer is that it is more taxing on the muscles and joints. At the end of the day, a framer is likely to be more tired and achy having used a heavier framing hammer. You might be able to choose this way: if you are a small person, choose a lighter hammer. If you are a large person with bulk and muscle, you can likely work all day with a heavier hammer.

A framing hammer normally has a straighter claw than the more severely curved claw of the smaller claw hammer. The straighter claw is good for wedging between two pieces of lumber. Sometimes framing hammers are called ripping hammers because their claws are used to rip pieces of lumber apart.

As to the best handle, it is said that a wooden or fiberglass handle absorbs more shock than one made of steel. A wooden handle is more likely to break than one made of steel, but it is no dinosaur—many framers still prefer the feel of a wooden handle, and wood has served well for centuries. However, a steel handle is practically indestructible. Test any hammer you are about to buy by hefting it in your hand. It should feel comfortable in your grip and not too heavy to your shoulder muscles.

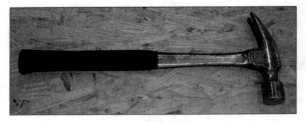

A framing hammer.

Claw Hammer

Claw hammers, smaller than framing hammers, normally weigh 16 ounces. Their handles are generally not as long as those of framing hammers, and they have a more severely curved claw, which works better to pull nails out of boards.

Claw hammers have smooth faces but should not be ultra-smooth. In fact, it's a good idea every now and then to rub some fine sandpaper across the face of a claw hammer. This will remove wood resin and other gunk and roughen the surface slightly so nail heads won't slide away when struck.

Claw hammers also come with wood, fiberglass, and steel handles. Choose the kind that feels best to your hand.

Sometimes claw hammers are called curved claw hammers to distinguish them from framing hammers with their straighter claws.

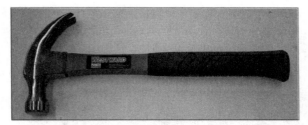

A claw hammer.

Sledge Hammer and Hand Sledge Hammer

A sledge hammer is just a really heavy hammer on a long handle. It can come in very handy to knock (often called "persuade") a piece of framing into place.

Framers sometimes use a hand sledge hammer, sometimes called a "baby sledge," which has a handle not much longer than that of a hammer, but whose head is heavy and shaped like that of a sledge hammer.

A hand sledge hammer.

Saws

Power saws, which are either called circular saws or power miter saws, do much of framing sawing. But a framer always needs a handsaw, either to finish an angled cut started by a power saw or to saw in a place a power saw cannot reach.

Framing carpenters generally use two kinds of hand saws: a *rip saw* and a *crosscut saw*, though a single combination saw combining the properties of each can suffice.

Crosscut Saw

As the name implies, a crosscut saw cuts across the length of wood, that is, across the grain. When you cut a length of 2×4 with a handsaw, you use a crosscut saw.

Crosscut saws have teeth that are slightly beveled, that is, finished to an angle. Some crosscut saws have 8 teeth to the inch and some 10 or 12 teeth to the inch. A good crosscut saw for framing is one with 8 teeth to the inch; 12 teeth per inch is more in line for *trim work*.

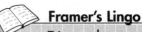
Framer's Lingo

Trim work is carpentry that applies the thinner wood around windows and doors, the baseboard along the floors, and other inside carpentry tasks.

A **crosscut saw** is for cutting across the grain. A **rip saw** is for cutting with the grain. A **combination saw** is for cutting both across and with the grain.

Rip Saw

The teeth of a rip saw are not beveled but straight and are designed to cut better with the grain, which is called a rip cut. Rip saws have fewer teeth per inch than crosscut saws. A good rip saw for framing has 5 teeth per inch.

If you have a circular saw and you're not going to do a lot of framing, you can function well with either a crosscut saw alone or a combination saw alone. Whatever ripping of wood you need, you can carefully do with the circular saw or have your lumber yard make the ripping cuts for you.

Combination Saw

If you are not going to do a lot of framing, buy a combination saw. Its teeth are set to cut both across and with the grain, though not as well as a crosscut or rip saw alone.

A crosscut saw. A rip saw and a combination saw look just about the same; the teeth set them apart.

Short Saw

A *short saw* is sometimes called a toolbox saw because it fits into a tool box. In this capacity, it is right at hand and thus useful for short cuts.

A short saw.

Hack Saw

A *hack saw* cuts metal. You might wonder why you would want such a thing doing framing, which is the cutting and assembling of lumber

and plywood … until, that is, you have to cut a nail or the end of a bolt or something such. Keep a hack saw around the job site because you'll need it from time to time.

A hack saw.

Keyhole Saw

A *keyhole saw* is a narrow blade attached to a wooden handle with the narrowest portion of the blade at the tip. Its main purpose is to begin cutting a piece of wood from somewhere in the middle and not at the edge. Normally a hole is drilled in the wood where the cut is to begin, and then the tip of the saw is inserted into the hole and the sawing begun.

Keyhole saws are also good where a standard hand saw cannot fit. Large keyhole saws are called compass saws.

Framer's Lingo

A **short saw** is for carrying in a tool box. A **hack saw** is for cutting metal. A **keyhole saw** is a narrow saw for cutting from holes.

A keyhole saw.

Measuring and Marking Tools

A framer would be lost without measuring tools. Framing begins with measuring and cutting, and if the measuring is wrong, you're defeated almost before you've begun.

Let's discuss some of the various measuring and marking tools that a framer uses:

- *measuring tape*
- *folding rule*
- *steel tape*
- combination square
- sliding T-bevel
- compass or dividers
- awl
- carpenter's pencil
- framing square
- levels
- chalk line
- plumb bob

Framer's Lingo

A **measuring tape** is a flexible steel tape in a steel body. A **folding rule** has wooden sections that unfold for measuring. A **steel tape** is a tape measure about 50' to 100' long and wound in a steel case.

Measuring Tape

A measuring tape is invaluable for framing. It consists of a marked length of flexible steel tape that extends from a steel case. You can lock the extended section at any length, and it retracts automatically into the case when your finger releases the locking mechanism. A good one for general use is 25' long. Buy one that is ³/₄" wide; the narrower ones are too flimsy. Also choose one that has a clasp on the outside for hooking to a trouser belt or the fold of a tool belt. Make sure the one you buy has special markings every 16" and 24", the normal distance between *joists*, *studs*, and *rafters*. For shorter distances, you can use a folding rule and for longer distances a steel tape (see the following section).

Framer's Lingo

A **joist** is a horizontal piece holding up solid flooring. Often a 2×8, 2×10, or 2×12. A **stud** is a vertical wooden piece in a framed wall, generally a 2×4 but sometimes a 2×6. A **rafter** is a framing piece holding up roof sheathing, often a 2×6 or 2×8.

Be sure any tape you buy has a shifting riveted end. This accounts for the thickness of the turned-down hook itself, about ¹/₁₆". When you hook the hook over the end of a board and pull the tape, the rivet allows for slippage, which means that the 1" mark, for example, is a true 1" from the end of the board. When you use the tape to measure an inside distance, say between two standing studs in a wall, the rivet allows for the hook to move toward the rest of the tape, again allowing for a true measurement.

Measuring tape.

A measuring tape should last years, but you must be careful with it. When a great deal of the tape is extended, don't let it twist or kink because this weakens the metal at the point of the bend. Control the speed of retracting the tape for three reasons. One, a fast-moving, whipping tape may hit and hurt someone; two, a twist or kink in the blade may be made worse; and three, slamming the hook end of the blade at high speed into the body can loosen the rivet holding the hook to the blade, thus hurting the accuracy of later measurements.

> ### Heads!
> A measuring tape's internal spring retracts the blade very quickly if a finger is not on the braking latch controlling the speed. A fast-moving blade, especially one with a twist or a kink, moves erratically and could strike and hurt someone nearby.

Folding Rule

Before the flexible steel measuring tape that retracted into a steel case, a folding rule was the measuring device of choice. A folding rule comprises wooden sections, about 6" long, that are hinged and fold back one on another. A typical one is 6' long when fully extended. Buy one that has a sliding metal piece imbedded in the first section; it comes in handy for measuring small, narrow, or awkward distances.

> ### Finger Tips
> It's difficult to write your name on a folding rule, but carpenters use a trick. Slide out the metal piece imbedded in the first section until the metal piece stops. Write your name on the plain piece of wood that is revealed. If someone thinks your folding rule is his, slide out the metal piece and show him your name.

A folding rule.

Steel Tape

Sometimes called a long tape, a steel tape is 50 to 100' long. You are not likely to need a tape of more than 50' unless you are building a home with a wall longer than this. The end of the tape should have a hook for grasping the end of a piece of wood combined with a loop for hooking over the head of a nail. Expensive ones have an automatic retraction feature, but you can get away with a less expensive one that has a manual rewind.

Steel tape.

Combination Square

A *combination square* is a straight edge, often called the blade, marked in inches fitted to a body that has a section running at a right angle to the straight edge. Another section runs at a 45° angle to the straight edge. A turn screw surrounded by the body loosens to let the blade shift perpendicular to the body, then tightens again to lock the straight edge in place.

You can use a combination square to help make a rip cut. We explain the technique in Chapter Seven.

A combination square.

A *triangular square* is a heavy-duty triangular piece of aluminum or plastic used for marking saw cuts. It has a flange along one side that hooks to the edge of a piece of wood. You can then draw a line along an adjacent edge marking a 90° angle to the edge or a 45° angle. Other markings on a triangular square also make it useful; some note distance in inches from the flange edge; some denote angles other than 90 and 45. A triangular square is also called a Speed Square (T) [Swanson Tool Co.] and a rafter angle square.

Some people use a triangular square as a guide to a power saw during a cut so that they get a straight cut all the way through the wood.

A triangular square.

Sliding T-Bevel

A *sliding t-bevel* is a handle and a sliding piece of steel that you can lock at any angle to the handle. You can set it to an existing angle, lift it, and set it on a piece of wood to be cut; then draw the cut line along the piece cocked at an angle to the handle.

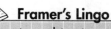
A sliding t-bevel.

Framer's Lingo

A **combination square** is an instrument with a sliding blade for checking and marking right angles and 45° angles. A **triangular square** is a triangle for checking and marking right angles and other angles. A **sliding t-bevel** is an instrument for transferring odd angles.

Compass or Dividers

You called it a *compass* in geometry class. It has a sharp leg on one side and a pencil on the other. What you do with it is called *scribing*, and some carpenters call this tool a scriber. It helps fit a new piece of material snugly against another that has an irregular or curved surface. Hold the piece to be scribed as close as you can to the irregular surface; put the end of the nonpencil leg against the irregular surface and the pencil-end leg against the moveable material. When you pull the compass along, holding the non-pencil end to the irregular surface, the pencil end draws an exact profile along the moveable material. If you then cut along the pencil line, you will end with a profile of the irregular surface. The cut material can then fit snugly to the irregular surface.

You might frame an entire house without using a compass in this way. On the other hand, if you had to fit one piece to another that had an irregular surface, you'd be very hard pressed to do the job without a compass such as this one.

Dividers normally don't have pencils attached but are two pointed metal legs. They are less useful in carpentry than in ship navigation.

A compass.

Framer's Lingo

A **compass** is a two-legged instrument for scribing. One leg ends in a pencil point. If there is no pencil, the instrument name is dividers. **Scribing** is transferring the profile along one surface to another surface.

Awl

An *awl* is a piece of hard, sharp-pointed metal with a handle. It has a couple of handy uses. You can draw the point across a piece of wood, making a grooved line to serve as a cut mark just like a pencil line (though narrower and, therefore, more accurate). You can also make a sharp dimple in a piece of wood that can serve as a starting point for a drill bit, a screw or a nail.

An awl.

Carpenter's Pencil

A *carpenter's pencil* is not like an ordinary pencil because it is not round but flattened and the lead is flattened as well. The shape gives it strength. Ordinary round pencil lead breaks with annoying regularity on framing jobs, and so a carpenter's pencil is the solution. When a wide mark is needed—as to mark Xs on joists or studs—draw the pencil lead along the wide side. When a narrow mark is needed—as to mark for a saw cut—use the narrow dimension.

The shape has two other benefits. One, the pencil won't roll away if set down. And two, it's easy to sharpen with a utility knife without breaking the lead.

A carpenter's pencil.

Framing Square

A *framing square* is a large L of steel or aluminum marked in inches but also with tables for determining angle cuts for rafters. It is essential for work on rafters and stairways and is useful for checking square corners and marking long right angles.

A framing square.

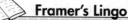

Framer's Lingo

An **awl** has a pointed rod with a handle. A **carpenter's pencil** is a thick, flattened pencil. A **framing square** is a large right-angle square for testing right angles and determining rafter cuts and stair carriage cuts.

Levels

Spirit levels tell framing carpenters what is *plumb* and what is *level*. Framing carpenters need one that is 2' long and one that is 4' long. Both have marked, slightly curved vials of liquid and a bubble. When a level is held exactly plumb, that is, absolutely vertical, the vial showing verticality reveals the bubble exactly in the middle between two marks. Another and similar vial shows the bubble between two marks when the level is exactly level, that is, positioned perfectly horizontal.

Framer's Lingo

Plumb means exactly vertical and **level** means exactly horizontal. A level is an instrument for determining plumb and level.

Levels can also serve as straight edges, along which to draw lines. Some 2' levels have inch marks and so can serve as measuring tools. The 2' levels, being smaller, are handy and fit into tool buckets. The 4' levels must be carried separately, but are more accurate and, therefore essential, for checking the plumb of wall studs.

Finger Tips

Treat levels gently because the vials can break. Avoid leaning them against things; rather hang them on a hook or lay them flat.

A 2' level; 4' level.

Chalk Line

A *chalk line* is essentially a string placed inside a steel or plastic housing that holds chalk dust. The string's end is tied to a hook that grips the edge of a panel of plywood or slips over a nail-head. Use a chalk line to mark a long straight line. Some have strings 50' long and some 100' long; you likely can get by with one 50' long.

> **Framer's Lingo**
>
> **Chalk line** is string in a housing filled with chalk dust that is pulled taut then snapped to mark a straight line.

If you plan to use a chalk line frequently, buy spare chalk. It comes in a bottle with a nozzle so that you can squeeze the chalk powder into the opening of the chalk line housing.

Some chalk line housings are shaped so that the end opposite where the string comes out narrows to a point. Thus you can use it as a rough plumb bob (see plumb bob).

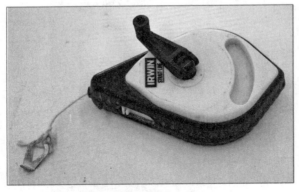

A chalk line.

Plumb Bob

A *plumb bob* is string with a pointed weight at the end. It locates a point directly under another point, say a point on a floor directly below a point on a beam above. You can sometimes use a chalk line as a fairly good plumb bob, but because the chalk line housing is lighter and larger, it can move in a breeze.

> **Framer's Lingo**
>
> A **plumb bob** is a heavy pointed object on a string that shows the position of a point under another point.

A plumb bob.

Miscellaneous Hand Tools

You'll need some other hand tools, too, ones that don't fit into the categories above but that are often needed. Some cut and shape; some undo mistakes; and some do other tasks but all are needed in your tool supply.

You will want to have these various hand tools available:

- rasp
- block plane
- chisel
- screwdriver
- utility knife
- nail set
- flat bar
- cat's paw
- clamps

Rasp

A *rasp* is a hand-held length of steel with rough teeth that is used to shave wood.

A rasp.

Block Plane

A *block plane* is a small plane that you can operate with one hand. It is useful in shaving wood or an edge or surface of wood. You can sometimes use it across the end of a piece as well, if the grain is tight.

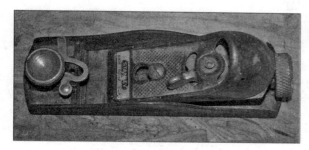

A block plane.

📖 Framer's Lingo

A **rasp** is a strip of metal with rough teeth for shaving and shaping wood. A **block plane** is a small plane for one-hand planning or cutting across the grain.

Chisels

Chisels are used more in finish or trim carpentry than framing carpentry. But you might occasionally need them for framing carpentry to cut notches or trim boards. Normally, ones with blades $1/4$" to 1" suffice. If you are going to do finish or trim carpentry, you might want to

own two sets of chisels, one you would keep in excellent condition for the trim carpentry work and one you would use for the rougher framing carpentry work. Even if you have "rough" and a "fine" set, store chisels in the wrappings they come in from the store—a nicked or dulled chisel is not nearly as good a tool as a clean sharp one.

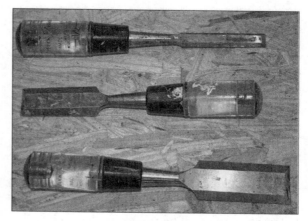

Chisels.

Screwdrivers

Even framing carpenters use screwdrivers. Although you may never use one to set a screw into wood, many of your tools will require screw drivers—a utility knife to open its storage portion, for example. Keep three or four in your tool bucket, some Phillips head ones and some straight ones.

Screwdrivers.

Utility Knife

A *utility knife*, which has a retractable triangular blade, is so often used that your tool belt has a pocket for one just above the loop for your hammer. The handle of a utility knife is a hollow housing for storing spare blades.

A utility knife.

Nail Set

A *nail set* is a cylinder of hardened steel used for driving a nail head to the surface of the piece of wood the shank of the nail is in or even to just below the surface. The tip is dimpled so it will not slip off the nail head and narrowed so that it can drive small nails without making a larger mark on the wood. The end the hammer strikes is squared. Tip size varies. Framing carpenters can use one as large as $5/32$". I always carry a nail set in the pouch next to my utility knife.

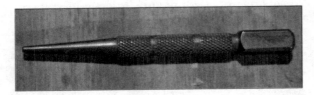

A nail set.

> **Framer's Lingo**
> A **utility knife** is a knife whose blade retracts into its handle. A **nail set** has a hardened steel rod for driving nails to or below the surface of the wood.

Flat Bar

A *flat bar* is a piece of flat steel curved at both ends. There are notches at both ends for hooking under a nail head and then, by prying back the flat bar, extracting the nail from its piece of wood. You can also hammer a flat bar between two pieces of wood joined together to pry them apart.

A flat bar.

Cat's Paw

A *cat's paw* is a short piece of curved bar steel with a notch at one end for gripping nail heads. Use it for extracting nails whose heads have been hammered flush with or below the surface of the wood it is in.

To extract a nail with a cat's paw, point the sharpened edge of the notched end to the area around the nail's head. Wear eye protection. Strike the "heel" of the cat's paw with a hammer, sinking the sharp edges around the nail head. Further hammering should settle the nail—just below its head—into the cat's paw's notch. Then pull back on the handle of the cat's paw, which will pull up the nail. Finish extracting the nail with the claw of a hammer or with a flat bar.

A cat's paw.

Clamps

Clamps come in handy. Light duty ones, such as a *spring clamp*, can hold a straight edge to a piece of plywood to guide your circular saw. They can also apply pressure to small pieces of wood that you are gluing together.

A *hand-grip clamp* can secure a piece of lumber to a work bench or sawhorse for steadying during cutting. It sets quickly by sliding along a bar and then tightening with a hand pumping mechanism. A trip lever quickly releases it.

C-clamps, which come in many sizes, can also secure pieces of wood for cutting or for gluing but are often slower to use than hand-grip clamps.

There are many other kinds of clamps, but they are required more in fine woodworking than in framing carpentry. Buy clamps as needed for special jobs; the spring clamps, hand-grip clamps, and some C-clamps should sustain you through most framing tasks.

Spring clamps can hold a straight edge to a piece of plywood for guiding a circular saw during a cut.

A hand-grip clamp can secure a piece of wood to a sawhorse for cutting or two pieces of wood together for gluing.

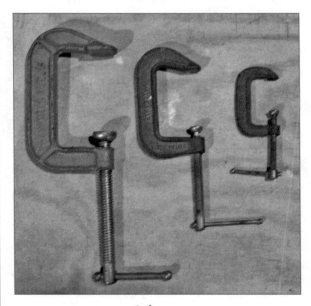

C-clamps.

Carrying Your Tools

A framing carpenter needs a *tool belt*. It's part of the culture. Sure, you could get by with a canvasy *tool apron* that costs a few dollars, and for small jobs this is all right (though a surprising amount of these do not have loops for hammers!).

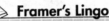

Framer's Lingo

A **tool apron** is a canvas apron for carrying tools. A **tool belt** is a heavy belt, often made of leather, for carrying nails, materials, and hand tools. A **tool bucket** is used for carrying materials and tools.

A tool belt is made of tough leather and costs $25 to $50, but I've had mine for years. A tool belt generally has a holder at the front for a measuring tape, a loop on the right for a hammer, two pouches over each thigh for different kinds of nails or other materials, a sling for a combination square, a pocket for a utility knife, another for a carpenter's pencil, and various places for screwdrivers, chisels, or whatever is needed at the time.

Finger Tips

Tool belts are kind of macho. The guy with the darkest, most beat-up-looking leather of his tool belt is obviously the guy who's been at carpentry the longest, the guy to respect. He's got the longest horns, so don't mess with him. Likely he is the guy who is snapping the chalk line (See the sidebar on chalk line etiquette).

Guys tramp around with their overloaded tool belts like knights used to kalumph about in their iron armor. After a bit, you can see that they have a peculiar type of stepping motion. It's not natural and straightforward; it's more like what an upright cow would look like strolling through the swinging doors of a saloon. Or is that my imagination?

When you buy a tool belt, it will look very clean and new. But don't worry in the least if you spill coffee on it or gouge it with your utility knife. These are marks of honor, and the faster your tool belt turns a darker shade, the more respect you'll get around the framing site.

And by the way, don't mess with a guy's tool belt, as in don't sling it on because you left yours in your basement. He'll resent it tremendously, and besides, it smells like he does.

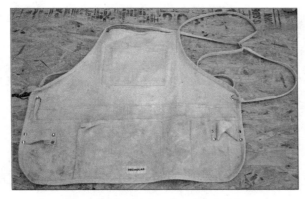

A tool apron (a) and tool belt (b).

You can get yourself a tool bucket in two ways. One is to buy a 5-gallon bucket with a comfortable handle and a nylon liner that fits to the lip of the bucket and has all sorts of pockets on the outside for the likes of screwdrivers, drill bits, pliers, and so forth. Inside the bucket you can keep a drill, pry bar, and other large items. Alternatively, you can buy a bucket and liner together. Most models come with divider trays that fit into the bucket for carrying screws, nails, and other handy items.

Back in the day, carpenters made their own tool boxes with scraps of wood and carried them with pride. Some even carved their initials into them or made other identifying marks. Normally these were long boxes, long enough for a handsaw, with a long thick dowel as a handle. Alas, these have gone the way of the black bag doctors used to carry when they made house visits.

But you still need a way of toting your tools around, the ones you can't cram into your darkening tool belt. This job has now fallen to the humble *tool bucket*.

A tool bucket.

Sawhorses

Every jobsite needs surfaces for sawing. In the old days the job fell to handmade sawhorses. These were made of wood lying about—2×4s and perhaps plywood and boards. They always had angled cuts so the legs could be splayed for stability and often precise angled notches in the top plank to receive the top of the angled legs. Anyone who could make a good sawhorse probably had the skills needed for a framing carpentry job.

You can still make your own sawhorses, and if you are particularly tall or short, you might well want to consider doing so in order to have a work surface that is comfortable for you. If you want to make your own sawhorses, you can find designs in woodworking and carpentry books in the library and on the Internet. Sawhorses should be about 24" high, and, of course, very sturdy.

> **Heads!**
>
> Wobbly sawhorses pose a danger if you are resting material on them for sawing or drilling. If your sawhorse is wobbly, stop your work and tighten the fasteners.

Because making a good sawhorse is moderately difficult, manufacturers have come up with parts you can use to make one quickly and easily or whole saw horses you can buy. As to the former, you can buy either metal or rugged plastic brackets into which you insert the cut ends of 2×4s in order to assemble a sawhorse. If you go this route, at least cut the floor-ends of the legs at an angle so they meet the floor with a whole surface and not just an edge—you want the legs to be as slip-resistant as possible. If you buy saw horses, look for ones with slip-resistant leg ends.

I prefer sawhorses with a top surface at least $3\frac{1}{2}$ inches wide, that is, the wide surface of a 2×4 and not the narrow surface. The wide surface is more accommodating for supporting pieces I am working on. Sawhorses whose top surface is the edge of a 2×4 are best used in pairs, that is, material is laid across two of them or a piece of plywood is supported by two of them and becomes a work surface.

Buying a complete sawhorse is more expensive than buying brackets with which to make one, but they are sturdy and often have tool trays. A sawhorse at a home improvement store can be had for $30 to $50 each.

Sawhorses

Making a sawhorse used to be the measure of a good carpenter. In fact, when a carpenter walked on a jobsite and asked for a job, the foreman would often say, "All right. Let's see you build a sawhorse." The foreman was being crafty. Building a good sawhorse is tricky work, involving cutting lumber at angles so that the sawhorse legs are splayed for stability. And a sawhorse has to be well fastened so it does not wobble. If the applicant carpenter made a sturdy and attractive sawhorse, it demonstrated he had the skills for the job. The foreman would hire him and let him use the sawhorse he had just made. If the applicant failed the test, he could take the sawhorse with him or leave it on the jobsite for the foreman to use or not as he preferred.

Work Benches

In the old days carpenters used to make work benches, too. These offered more work surface than sawhorses, often a foot or so wide and two feet long. Sometimes these were about 20" high and could serve as stools when the carpenter had to gain height for a task. They often had a hole in the top so the carpenter could slip his hand in and carry the bench where he needed it, and sometimes it had a tray between the legs for carrying tools and materials.

You can still build these if you care to, making them out of boards held together with screws. But manufacturers offer you a way out as long as you are willing to part with some of your hard-earned money. For about $100 you can buy a portable work bench with a wooden working surface. These likely have clamps and vices attached for securing material you are working on and nonskid leg bottoms. Such benches might be collapsible for storage and portability. You can get by without one if you have a couple of good sawhorses you can rest a piece of plywood on.

A workbench.

The Least You Need to Know

◆ To do framing, you will need some common hand tools, including hand saws, tools for marking straight lines, and hammers.

◆ Framing hammers come with three different kinds of handles and in different weights.

◆ For carrying tools and materials, buy a tool belt and a tool bucket.

◆ Make or buy a pair of sawhorses. You can make or buy a workbench if you will often need a wide flat work surface.

◆ Buy quality hand tools and they are likely to last you a lifetime.

In This Chapter

◆ Power saws that speed a carpenter's work

◆ Electric drills and bits

◆ Pneumatic nailers, but for big jobs only

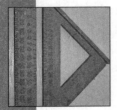 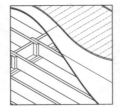    

Chapter 2

Power Tools

When you do framing, hand tools feel good in your hand, and you enjoy a certain pride having them in your tool belt, but a framer has to have power tools. These electric-driven tools make jobs go much faster and in some respects better and more accurate.

For framers, power saws and power drills are the most important power tools. Saws enable the framer to make accurate and swift cuts of 2× lumber. Although drills are used less often, when the need arises, they sure do beat the old hand drills.

In this chapter, you learn about the most useful power tools for a framing carpenter. And like hand tools, with proper care, they can stay with you for a lifetime.

Saws

Framing means wood; wood means cutting; and cutting means saws. We might well add, sawing means power sawing. Once upon a time a carpenter's triceps bulged with the work of pushing and pulling a saw's blade through thick wood. Now those triceps get their workout from lifting a circular saw, or in some cases, a reciprocating saw. They hardly exert themselves at all when using a power miter saw.

Electric saws have been a great boon to framing carpenters, vastly speeding up their work. They are part of every framing carpenter's assemblage of tools.

For information on using a power saw to make particular sawing cuts, see Chapter 8.

Power Saw Safety

Always treat a power saw with extreme respect; a moment's inattention could place some part of you in the path of a blade that has no trouble cutting through tough lumber.

Buy a model with as many safety features as you can, and take the time to read the safety instructions provided with the saw. Never remove or tamper with any of the safety features, including the blade guard, and never attempt to wedge a blade guard to the open position.

Never attempt to change a blade or adjust its angle, without disconnecting the saw from the power source, whether an extension cord or batteries.

Only use a power saw when you have two feet firmly placed on the ground and when the piece you are cutting is firmly set on a work bench or sawhorses. Firmly grip the piece in place either with your nonsaw hand or with a clamp. Never attempt to cut a piece of wood merely held in your hand or propped on your knee.

Wear eye and ear protection when you use a power saw. If sawdust bothers you, wear a dust mask or respirator as well.

Take extra care if you are sawing through old lumber because there may be a nail in it. If you hit a nail and are not using a carbide-tipped blade, you'll ruin the blade, and you may get a nasty kick back that can make you lose your grip or your balance.

Always sharpen or replace a dull blade. When a blade is dull, you have to use greater force to cut the lumber. Doing so can cause your hand or your foot to slip. Sharp blades make your work easier and safer.

When blades become dull, replace them with new ones.

Do not use a power saw in wet conditions, including standing on a wet surface.

Do not operate power saws when you are fatigued, have been drinking alcohol, or are taking medication that makes you drowsy.

And as with most framing tools, keep children away from power saws.

When you are finished with power saws, disconnect them from their power source. Check that they are clean. Then store them in a safe place until you need them again.

Circular Saw

Next to a hammer, a *circular saw* is your best friend. It makes rapid cuts through 2×4s, 2×6s and much else that you as a framer deal with. The blade is normally set so that it cuts at a right angle to the base plate through which the blade descends. But you can tilt the blade with respect to the base plate so that the blade makes a cut through the wood at a different angle. You can also adjust the blade for the depth of the cut.

The common size of circular saw uses a $7^1/_4$" blade. This is large enough, of course, to cut straight through a 2×4 at a right angle. But it is also large enough to cut through at a 45° angle when more of the blade has to extend through the base plate. It can cut through lumber $3^1/_2$" thick (such as 4×4s) in two passes.

You can replace the blade that comes with the saw with ones that cut masonry, plastics, ceramics, and *plywood*. The blade, which comes with the saw, might only last six hours or so of cutting, less if you are using it to cut through plywood or particle board, which contains abrasive glues. When the blade that comes with a new saw dulls, replace it with a carbide-tipped blade. These cost more than standard steel blades but last as much as 50 times longer and never need sharpening. A *carbide-tipped blade* is good for general lumber cutting.

📖 Framer's Lingo

A **circular saw** is a portable electric power saw with a circular blade. **Plywood** has panels of five or seven thin sheets of wood glued together. A **carbide-tipped blade** is a very useful blade for a circular saw with carbide steel tips on the blade teeth. It can cut through nails in the wood and lasts far longer than an ordinary steel blade.

Choose a circular saw that feels comfortable in your hand and not so weighty that it will tire you in the time you allow to framing each day. A lightweight saw—good for must jobs around the house—runs about 10 pounds, a heavier weight 13 pounds. Most circular saws require cords because they draw a good deal of power, but you can buy some that are battery driven and thus cordless.

Also consider how much framing you plan to do. A homeowner's circular saw draws 9 or 10 amperes of electricity; a professional model draws 12 to 13 amperes and thus is more powerful. A professional model can withstand longer and more rugged use.

👆 Finger Tips

When shopping for a circular saw, do not rely on the horsepower rating because it can be misleading. Instead, pay attention to the ampere rating.

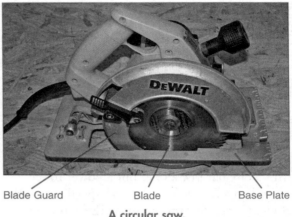

Blade Guard   Blade   Base Plate

A circular saw.

Power Miter Saw

Another good friend of a framing carpenter is the power miter saw, also called a cutoff saw or a chop saw. Essentially, it is a circular saw on a pivot arm stationed above a cutting table. You set the piece you are cutting on the table and steady it with one hand. Turn on the saw with your other hand and lower the teeth through the piece.

A power miter saw was designed to replace a miter box, which uses a hand saw to make angled cuts. A power miter saw can make angled cuts because the arm holding the saw pivots. But you will use it most in framing to make right-angled cross cuts.

You must mount a power miter saw on a firm work surface. Typical is a sheet of thick plywood securely fasted to two saw horses or work benches. Securely fasten the base of the power miter saw to the plywood, and lead the electrical cord away from the user.

A good size for general framing work is a power miter saw that uses a 10" blade.

> ### Framer's Lingo
>
> A power miter saw is a stationary power saw on a pivot arm that cuts by lowering the blade through the piece of wood. A miter box is a metal or wooden box guiding a hand saw through angled cuts.

Strictly speaking you don't need a power miter saw for a framing project; you can get by with a circular saw alone. But a power miter saw set to a firm work table can speed the work along. Generally you can make the cuts a bit faster because you do not have to guide the blade along as with a circular saw. You set the piece to be cut to the mark on the power miter saw table and merely bring the spinning blade down, taking care not to rush the blade.

A power miter saw.

Reciprocating Saw

A *reciprocating saw* is like a keyhole saw with a motor attached. The motor is behind the blade and makes the blade move rapidly forward and back. The blade normally has a narrow tip which allows the blade to be inserted into a hole in a piece of lumber and then made to cut outside the hole, either to enlarge the hole or merely to cut from it to an edge.

> ### Framer's Lingo
>
> A **reciprocating saw** is a portable power saw whose straight blade moves rapidly forward and backward.

Blades are available for cutting metal, plastic, and wood that may have nails in it. Fitted with a metal-cutting blade, the reciprocating saw is like a power hack saw. For cutting wood, choose a blade with 5 to 7 teeth per inch. For cutting nails or wood that may contain nails, choose a bimetal or two-metal blade (one metal is very hard and the other, which is welded to the first, is softer and more flexible).

The blades come in varying length. Generally, you should buy the shortest length you can get away with; 6" is normal.

Shoe or Blade Guard

A reciprocating saw.

A framer can do without a reciprocating saw. But if you are going to be doing your framing indoors, it will come in very handy if you have to do some demolition. Its blade can reach where that of a circular saw cannot, and it can make much more rapid work of wood than your arm with a hand saw.

Reciprocating saws are available in one-speed, two-speed, and variable speed. The variable speed works well because it allows you to begin a cut slowly to first make a groove in the piece being cut. Once you establish the blade in the piece, then you can increase the blade speed to finish the cut.

Power Drills

As a framing carpenter, you will need an electric drill. Sooner or later you are going to have to drill a hole in a stud or joist for an electrical wire or pipe. Or you are going to want to drive a bunch of screws.

Some drills are cordless; some have cords. I prefer one with a cord because I don't have to worry about batteries running low and changing them, but plenty of other framers like cordless ones because they can take them anywhere. Moreover, if you are using a cordless drill, no electrical extension cord is snaking around the worksite. Not only can someone trip or slip on one, but cords are forever getting snagged on something.

You should probably buy what is called a $^3/_8$" drill. The number stands for the size of the maximum opening in the *chuck*, which is the cylindrical piece on the front of the drill that tightens around the shank of a drill bit. There is a $^1/_4$-inch" drill, but this is generally too lightweight for a framer. And there is a $^1/_2$" drill, but this is a size for professionals.

Nearly all $^3/_8$" and $^1/_2$" drills have variable speed and reversible speed features, but check to be sure yours does. Variable speed is very handy when starting a drill bit into material; you can let the bit get a good grip before raising the speed. A slower speed is also welcome when you are drilling large diameter holes. You control the rate of speed by how much pressure you put on the trigger, which is located in the grip.

When a drill bit hangs up in a hole, the reversible speed feature is very handy. A switch built into the body of the drill or near the trigger makes it available.

Cordless drills are ranked by voltage. The higher the voltage rating, the more powerful the drill. A voltage rating of 12 volts is adequate for a framing carpenter.

If you buy a cordless drill, buy two batteries. Keep one charging while the other is fitted to the drill. Then switch the batteries when the one on the drill begins to weaken. That way the drill will always be available to you.

All drills have a chuck and many have a *chuck key*. To fit a drill bit to a drill, use your fingers to rotate the chuck and widen its opening. Insert the shank of the drill bit, and use your fingers to rotate the chuck again, closing the opening on the shank. Tighten as best you can with your fingers. Then tighten with the chuck key, which fits to the chuck grooves and rotates clockwise to tighten. Always remove the chuck key from the chuck before operating the drill. Keep the chuck key attached to the cord or some part of the drill so it is always handy. Often the drill manufacturer includes a short rubbery leash for attaching the key to a part of the drill or cord for this purpose. Some drills don't use a key. You tighten by hand.

A cordless electric drill.

A corded drill.

Drill Safety

To work safely with drills, observe the following:

◆ Wear eye protection. If you prefer, also wear ear protection and a dust mask or respirator.

◆ Secure a drill bit tightly in the chuck; then remove the chuck key from the chuck.

◆ Secure the material you are drilling into. This is not a problem if you are drilling into a stud of a wall. But if you are drilling into a small piece lying on a work bench, clamp the material securely in place. Do not rely on holding it with your hand. If the material were to get loose, it would spin rapidly and hurt anything it struck.

◆ Place both feet firmly on the ground. If you have to use a drill on a ladder, be especially careful. A drill bit can "hang up," that is, get pinched, in the material being drilled. In that case, the body of the drill begins to turn ("kicks back"), and this can throw you off balance.

◆ Use an awl to make a dimple in the material to be drilled. Set the end of the drill bit to the dimple and begin the drill at a moderate speed. Work up to a higher speed. Do not press hard on the drill, but let the drill bit cut at its own pace.

◆ If the material heats up, stop the drill and pull back on the drill to extract the bit. From time to time, pull back on the drill so the bit can clear its grooves of sawdust.

Finger Tips

I've always used a corded drill, but, dog-gone it, sometimes I think there are gremlins out there trying to snag my extension cord. Tool bench legs, radiator legs, a stack of lumber, the gap between the bottom of a door and the floor—all are snares for electrical cords.

If a cord snags, don't tug to free it. That could scrap insulation off the cord, and a frayed extension cord is an unsafe extension cord.

Drill Bits

There are numerous types of drill bits. As a framing carpenter, you are most likely going to need twist bits and spade bits, and maybe masonry bits and auger bits.

Twist bits are the normal drill bits. They come in diameters from $\frac{1}{64}$" to $\frac{1}{2}$". They can be used on wood, metal, and plastic. Spade bits have a cutting face wider than their shanks and come in diameters $\frac{3}{8}$" to 2". Auger bits are very long. Often used to drill holes for electric cable through studs or floor joists, they drill quickly, if roughly, but have a long reach and make the job of drilling many cable holes less tedious and time-consuming.

A framing carpenter might also need masonry bits. These are tipped with carbide steel and can drill into mortar, brick, and concrete. If you have much of this kind of drilling to do, consider renting or buying a *hammer drill*. This is a heavy-duty drill, often with two handles, that vibrates its chuck rapidly forward and backward, hammering the tip of the drill bit into the material being drilled. It can vastly speed drilling into difficult material.

Framer's Lingo

A **hammer drill** is a heavy-duty drill that vibrates its drill bit back and forth; especially used for masonry drilling.

The screwdriver bit is also handy because it converts your variable speed drill to a screw gun. It has a tip that fits to the heads of screws. In fact, with a good screwdriver bit, you can avoid a lot of drilling of pilot holes for screws; you just apply the screw to the wood and drive it in with the screw attachment of the drill. The most useful screwdriver bits are magnetic so screws are less likely to slip off.

Also worth mentioning but not entering much into framing tasks are hole saws and countersink bits. Hole saws have a shank that fits into a drill's chuck but then takes the shape of a circle with teeth. They are for drilling large holes, as for locks in a door. Countersink bits are slender bits that step up in diameter in stages the closer to the drill's chuck. They mimic the profile of different sized wood screws. When you are finished drilling with a countersink bit, the corresponding screw fits perfectly into the hole and its head sits flush—or even below if that is desired—the surface of the wood.

Twist bits.

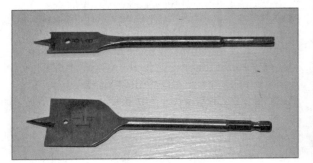

Spade bits.

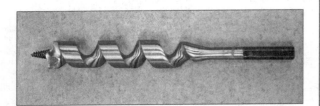

An auger bit.

Masonry bits.

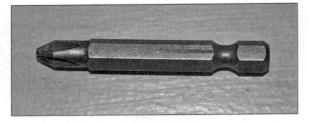

A screwdriver bit.

A hole saw.

A countersink bit.

Pneumatic Nailers

You'll see some professionals using *pneumatic nailers*. These can make much nailing go faster and with less fatigue to the carpenter. But they have lots of drawbacks for the amateur. They require a compressor and a hose, and these, along with the nailer itself, are expensive.

Framer's Lingo

A **pneumatic nailer** is a portable nailing gun powered by compressed air.

They can also be dangerous. Apart from a compressor making noise on the site and a hose snaking around that a person could trip or slip on, there is the danger of hurling a nail into some portion of your body. However, manufacturers build in safety features so that the chances of this are very remote. The nailer cannot "fire" unless the front of the tool is held firmly against a surface and until the trigger is pressed. But nevertheless, persons have been penetrated with the nails propelled by these pneumatic tools.

Such nailers are most welcome where there is nailing or stapling to do hour after hour. This might be for lots of repetitive floor nailing, applying siding to a home, or the like. But unless you face mass nailing or stapling jobs like this, stick with your trusty hammer.

Other pneumatic tools are available: drills, sanders, wrenches and the like, but these are generally for professionals.

A pneumatic nailer.

The Least You Need to Know

- If you have to buy one power saw, buy a handheld $7\frac{1}{4}$" circular saw.
- Observe all the safety measures for using power saws.
- You'll need an electric drill, whether corded or cordless.
- You probably won't need a pneumatic nailer unless you are doing lots of flooring or siding work.

In This Chapter

- ◆ The nuts on nails
- ◆ The skinny on screws
- ◆ Fashionable framing connectors
- ◆ Anchors that hold down a home

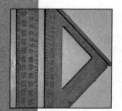
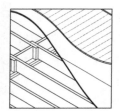

Chapter 3

Fasteners

Experts say that the Great Pyramid and the walls of Machu Pichu were constructed without fasteners, that all the pieces just fit perfectly and tightly together. Well, we don't have the patience for that. In our work, we have to use fasteners. But without good fasteners in the right places, what we put together would eventually fall apart.

So a framing carpenter needs to know about all sorts of fasteners and which ones to use where. After a while you get a sense of what to use for any particular situation, but you also have to be careful. Sometimes building codes are quite specific about what to use at particular joints. These codes can demand a certain number of a certain dimension nail every so many inches. These are called *nailing schedules*. For example, a nailing schedule for plywood flooring might call for 8d (pronounce this "eight-penny" and see the section on nails for further explanation) nails every 6" into the joists along the plywood edges and every 10" into joists between the edges. Pay attention to such nailing schedules, and do as they say or you will fail a building inspection when the building inspector comes around. When in doubt, it's no disgrace to ask. In fact, if you ever have to nail unusual material, copper flashing to a roof say, ask what the manufacturer recommends for nails and distances between nails.

But for framing, you have to know about other kinds of fasteners as well. There are screws, of course. These might come in handy for special joining situations. Then you have what are known as framing connectors. These are stamped metal pieces shaped to help join pieces of lumber together. And there are anchors, generally metal bolts fitting into metal sleeves for fastening lumber to masonry.

Nails

So you want to do framing? Then you're going to use nails, no way around it. So let's learn about different kinds of nails, those extremely useful and extraordinarily common spikes of iron.

These days you can go to a store and buy nails in boxes that tell you the length of the nails inside. But then where in the world did the "penny" designation of nails come from?

Back in Merry Old England, nails used to be sold in bags of 100. Because a bag of 100 large nails had more iron than a bag of 100 small nails, you might pay 16 pennies for the bag of large nails and 8 pennies for the bag of smaller nails. So the larger nails were called 16 penny nails, and the smaller nails were called 8 penny nails.

The abbreviation for penny was "d." because of the word "denarius" in Latin, of course! Denarius was a small coin; a penny was a small coin. So the brilliant merchants abbreviated penny with the letter "d." Clear as mud, right?

Anyway, we are stuck with the nail designation system, so get used to it.

Common Nails

The nails you will use most often for framing are 8-penny *common nails* and 16-penny common nails. These are often indicated 8d and 16d common nails. Confused? Blame it on blokes in England. An 8d nail is $2\frac{1}{2}$" long and a 16d nail is $3\frac{1}{2}$" long. You use 16d nails when joining studs, joists, and other 2× (pronounced two-by) material. You use 8d nails when nailing plywood, boards, siding, and so forth (pieces less than 1" thick) to 2× material.

Framing carpenters use common nails because they have substantial heads so their hammers do not slip off when hitting them and substantial shanks so they do not bend.

Framing carpenters might also use *box nails*, which have a more slender head and a more slender shank than common nails. Carpenters use a box nail when a common nail might split the wood. Although a box nail, being more slender, is more likely to bend, it is less likely to split a piece of wood.

A *cement nail* is another frequently used nail. This nail is simply a common or box nail coated with a resin or vinyl. When you hit it, you'll notice it penetrates the wood fairly easily. The coating liquefies from the heat of friction going in, lubricating the nail in its descent. But once the nail is in the wood and stopped, the coating gels again and holds the nail shank tightly to the wood grain. Cement nails are difficult to remove. Sometimes cement nails are called coated nails, but don't confuse them with galvanized nails. Cement nails are also sometimes known as "sinkers" because a hammer blow sinks them so readily.

When framing structures whose nails are going to be exposed to the elements, carpenters need to use special nails that will not rust. Rusting will weaken the nail and thus the joint it creates, but also will stain the wood. Commonly, these special nails are *galvanized*, meaning a zinc coating covers the iron nail. The coating might be hot-dipped (HDG, for hot-dipped galvanized) or electrogalvanized (EG). The hot-dipped kind has a thicker coating, and sometimes specifications for a job call not just for galvanized nails but hot-dipped galvanized nails. Other nonrusting nails are made of stainless steel, aluminum, and bronze, but these are costly.

Framer's Lingo

A **common nail** is a thick-shanked nail with a large head. A **box nail** is similar to a common nail but with a more slender shank. A **cement nail** is a nail coated with cement or resin for better gripping power. A **galvanized** nail is a nail coated with zinc to keep the nail from rusting.

Common nails larger than 16 penny (they can go to 60d, which are 6" long) are often called spikes.

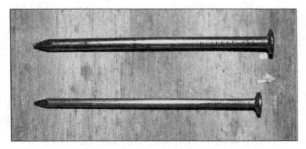

Figure 1 A common nail (top) and a box nail (bottom).

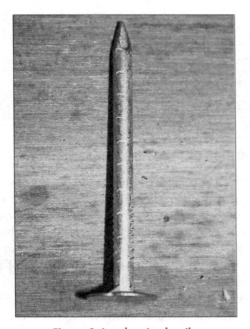

Figure 2 A galvanized nail.

Other Nails

Some other nails are not so common in framing but are worth mentioning either because they are used right after framing (to apply siding or roofing), are used in interior trim work, or are special fasteners.

◆ Finish nails, casing nails, and brads are small nails with heads not much bigger than the shanks. The point of that is to use a nail set to tap the heads below the surface of the wood and then cover the nail with wood putty to disguise it. Finish and casing nails are used on trim, that is, window and door casing, baseboard, crown molding, and the like. Casing nails differ from finish nails in that they have cone-shaped heads rather than slightly bulbous ones. Carpenters prefer these for interior and exterior casing, the large pieces of trim wood around windows and doors.

◆ "Brad" is the name for the smallest nail other than a tack. Brads are used for joining very small or thin pieces of wood.

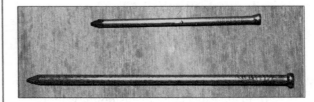

Figure 3 Finish nails.

◆ Duplex, or double-headed nails, are common nails with two heads, one lower on the shank than the other. When you hammer one into wood, the nail stops at the first head. The second head rests above the surface of the wood a quarter inch or so. The point is that you can easily pry one out of its location. Duplex nails are used when you want to disassemble what you have put together, such as scaffolding or a form for concrete.

A duplex or double-headed nail.

- Roofing nails are galvanized nails with wide thin heads used for roofing material. They are normally shorter than regular nails because they are penetrating thin material, such as shingles or roofing felt, before entering the wood.

- Spiral and Ring Nails have shanks with a spiral configuration or rings or grooves on them. They grip better than smooth-shank nails and are often used for flooring.

- Masonry nails are made of hardened steel, and some are wedge shaped. They can be hammered into concrete, mortar, or brick. You must wear eye protection! Even full-face protection with what is known as a full-face protector descending from a grip around the head is not a bad idea when hammering these nails because masonry nails can ricochet back when hit.

- Paneling nails are small nails for fastening paneling to studs. They come in colors to match the paneling.

- Wallboard nails have ringed shanks and are made especially for fastening wallboard to studs.

- Some other specialty nails come with a rubberized color collar; these fasten corrugated fiberglass roofing to the rafters of sheds. The collars stop rain from working through the fiberglass around the nail.

There are also aluminum and copper nails to use when fastening aluminum or copper. You also might use aluminum nails to attach cedar fencing to fence posts.

 Finger Tips

Nails were once looked upon with some degree of covetousness. In early seventeenth-century America iron products were rare. When buildings that were not useful were burned to the ground, the ashes were sifted through to retrieve the nails for reuse.

Screws

Nailing is what a framer does, right? Then what's this screw business about? Well, a framer had better be familiar with the different types of screws, too. Some are preferred when making a deck, and lag screws (almost a kind of bolt, more on this later) are often used when making beams or attaching joists to the outside walls of homes.

Besides, screws have a few advantages over nails. They offer a good grip; they can be applied with a screw gun or screw attachment of a variable speed drill; and they can be "backed out," that is, removed in the way they went in when a nail has to be pulled out like a wisdom tooth.

 Finger Tips

The word "screw" comes from the Latin word for sow, a female pig, perhaps because of the shape of her tail.

Common Screws

Common wood screws are made of soft steel. The threads stop short of the head so there is a smooth portion of the shank. Wood screws, of course, are made for joining wood together, and they are normally used in finish carpentry and cabinet making. The smooth portion of the shank should just about pierce the upper piece of wood and the threaded portion end up nearly totally in the piece to which the upper piece is joined.

Mainly wood screw heads are slotted (there is a straight slot across the head) or Phillips head (two slots cross each other at right angles).

Wood screws are designated by length and by gauge. The gauge notes the diameter of the shank, that is, the diameter of the shank not including the threads. Common gauges are 6 ($^9/_{64}$" across), 8 ($^{11}/_{64}$" across, and 10 ($^3/_{16}$" across).

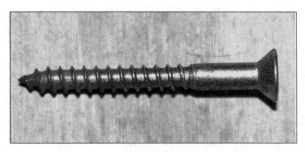

A wood screw.

Finger Tips

When I was a tot, my father taught me that when it looked as if the driving of a screw was going to be particularly tough, coating the screw with soap would make driving the screw easier. He was right; it did. But when I grew up, I learned that father could be wrong. Soap on screw threads is a poor idea because it can deteriorate the wood fiber around the threads and thus weaken the grip of the screw over time.

Drywall Screws

Drywall screws were made to attach drywall, also called wallboard, to studs, but they have become so popular that they are seen on framing sites. They are also called bugle heads, zip screws, drive screws, and general purpose screws. Normally they are black, but ones for outdoors use are silvery. Drywall screws have a bugle-bell shaped head, a slender shank, and widely spaced, thin but sharp threads. Generally they do not need a pilot hole.

You can use drywall screws when attaching plywood to floor joists or where you might have to separate joints after a time because the screws can be backed out.

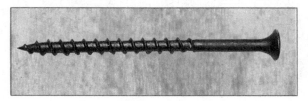

A drywall screw.

Lag Screws

A lag screw, sometimes called a lag bolt, looks like a wood screw but is longer and thicker and has a square or hexagon-shaped head (the latter called a hex head) rather than a slotted or Phillips head. Lag screws are sized by length and the thickness of their shanks, normally $^5/_{16}$", $^3/_8$", and $^1/_2$". Lag screws are used for making beams, attaching large 2× lumber pieces to one another, attaching 2× pieces to posts, and the like. They are turned with a common wrench or socket wrench, also called a ratchet.

Normally the head of a lag screw would rise above the level of the wood, but you can make it sit below or at the same level as the face of the wood if you drill two pilot holes. The first is the countersink hole, which is only as deep as the head is thick, but wide enough to accommodate the socket wrench head. The second is for the shank. This one, in fact, is often done in two stages, a wider one for the smooth portion of the shank and a longer one $^1/_8$" narrower for the threaded portion.

A lag screw.

> **Framer's Lingo**
>
> A **rafter tie** is a framing connector that helps tie a rafter to the top of a wall. A **framing anchor** is a general purpose framing connector for right-angle joists. A **T-strap** is a framing connector for butt joints, and a **truss plate** is a flat framing connector.

Framing Connectors

Someone back in the middle part of the last century sat down and thought he could make money selling ways of joining wood together without using traditional nailing. Thus *framing connectors* were born. The first kind might have been joist hangers. Imagine you want to build a deck off the side of your house. You have to have joists protruding out into the yard on which the flooring of the deck is to rest, so you attach a long piece of wood (called a *ledger*) to the side of the house. Now how are you going to attach the joists to the ledger?

Well, you couldn't go inside the house and hammer long nails through the ledger into the end of the joists. The old way was to *toenail* the joist to the ledger, two or three nails on a side. But truth be told, the connection was not that great. So someone came up with the idea of using a kind of metal saddle with flanges. The flanges were nailed to the ledger and the joist sat in the saddle. It was a terrific solution to the joist-ledger connection.

Now practically any conceivable wood-to-wood connection has a framing connector for it. Some framing connectors, like the *joist hangers*, are very handy and can speed a job along and make a joint stronger. In fact, building codes where hurricanes or earthquakes are prevalent require some kinds of framing connectors.

> **Framer's Lingo**
>
> A **framing connector** is stamped metal, shaped for strengthening joints between two pieces of lumber. A **ledger** is the name given to a wide piece of lumber attached to a house and to which protruding joists are fastened. A **toenail** means nailing though a piece of wood at an angle so the nail goes into the adjoining piece of wood. A **joist hanger** is a framing connector that is U-shaped and holds a joist.

The downside is that framing connectors cost more than nails. So framers do not use them everywhere, only where code requires, where they can speed the work, or where a particularly secure joint is needed.

Framing connectors are pieces of punched steel that make wood-to-wood joints stronger than using nails alone. Although there are many types, I'll cover the most common here and name a few others.

Thicker and shorter nails than commonly used in framing fasten framing connectors to the wood. Use the nails that come with the connectors or that the manufacturer recommends in order to get the best gripping power as well as the best engineering quality out of the joint. Holes for the nails are manufactured into the framing connectors.

The advantages of framing connectors are speed, assured security if attached appropriately, and sometimes easier joinery.

Joist Hanger

A joist hanger is a saddle-shaped framing connector that connects the end of a joist to a similar 2x piece at right angles to it.

A joist hanger.

Rafter Tie or Hurricane Clip

A *rafter tie* or hurricane clip is a piece that twists to make a right angle. It connects a rafter to the top of the wall on which the rafter rests and can be used for other purposes.

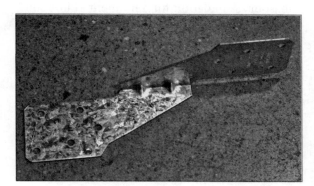

A rafter tie.

Framing Anchor or Right-Angle Clip

A *framing anchor*, also called a right-angle clip, is a general purpose framing connector that is essentially a steel right angle. But halfway down the angle, the pieces are separated and so can be bent to fit different kinds of wood-to-wood joints.

A framing anchor.

T-Straps and Truss Plates

T-straps are flat pieces of steel fastened across the seam between two pieces of wood. You might use a T-strap where a beam rests on a post. And use a *truss plate* where three pieces of wood join. Another sort of flat framing connector is a plain strap. Like other framing connectors it has prefabricated holes and reinforces across a joint where wood meets end to end.

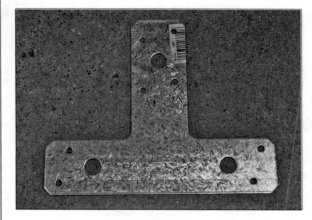

A T-strap.

A truss plate.

Post Caps

A *post cap* is a useful framing connector that fastens a beam to the top of a post and come in different configurations. There are also framing connectors for attaching the bottom of a post to a concrete footing.

A post cap.

Anchors

Carpenters use anchors? You thought they were for sailors, didn't you. Well, yes and no. Anchors are for carpenters, too. Anchors anchor things down.

Technically, framing carpentry of a home begins when you lay the first piece of wood onto the masonry foundation. Because this piece of wood is connected with an *anchor*, framing carpenters have to know about anchors.

And carpenters have to know about anchors at other times. When framing in a basement, carpenters are likely to have to connect some of their lumber to the basement walls, or if framing a deck, they are likely to have to connect to piers of concrete set into or rising above the ground.

But let's go back to the first piece of wood on a masonry foundation for a moment. The foundation is likely made of concrete or cinderblock by foundation contractors, and now it's ready for you, the framer. How do you hold the house to the foundation? Well, typically, you use an anchor called a J-bolt.

J-bolts

J-bolts are shaped like a J. The J end is lowered into fresh concrete, and the straight end has threads and sticks straight up. A *sill plate* is drilled with holes to fit over the vertical threads. Then a washer is slipped over the threads and a nut is threaded on. Tightening the nut anchors the bottom plate to the top of the foundation wall.

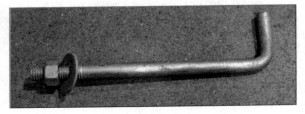

A J-bolt.

Expansion Shields

An *expansion shield* is a two-part anchor. First a hole is drilled in the masonry. Then a soft metal jacket, also called a shield, is pressed into the hole. A lag screw can then be tightened into the shield, which expands and firmly grips the sides of the hole. The lag screw and shield can come in different sizes but often are sold together along with instructions on how large to make the hole.

A wedge anchor.

Expansion shield and lag screw.

Wedge Anchors

Wedge anchors come in several varieties and are considered excellent anchors. A wedge at the bottom of the bolt's sleeve expands as the bolt is tightened. The expanded wedge holds the assembly to the sides of the hole. Several varieties are available, including ones called self-drilling anchors, sleeve anchors, and drop-in anchors.

 Framer's Lingo

A **post cap** is a framing connector that ties the top of a post to a beam. An **anchor** is a piece of steel used for fastening a piece of lumber to masonry. A **sill plate** is the piece of lumber set on top of the foundation wall. **J-bolts** are j-shaped bolts used as anchors at the tops of foundation walls. An **expansion shield** is a soft metal jacket set into holes in masonry for accepting and gripping lag bolt ends. **Wedge anchors** are special anchors whose ends expand in masonry holes when the upper screw or bolt is turned.

The Least You Need to Know

◆ Many kinds of nails exist because different joinery requires different nails.

◆ Screws offer a good grip; they can be applied with a screw gun or screw attachment of a variable speed drill; and they can be removed in the way they went in.

◆ Framing connectors are useful, and often necessary, pieces of metal for reinforcing joints between pieces of lumber.

◆ Anchors are pieces of metal that connect lumber to masonry.

In This Chapter

- ◆ Understanding framing lumber
- ◆ Learning the difference between nominal and actual dimensions
- ◆ Understanding plywood and its different grades
- ◆ Learning about engineered lumber and its uses

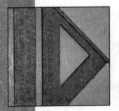
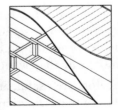

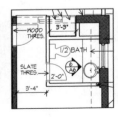

Chapter 4

Working With Wood

One of the delights of being a carpenter is working with wood. It is a wonderful substance, and each piece is different. It's strong but fairly lightweight and has interesting grain patterns. It is easy to work with, is nice to the touch, and can be sanded smooth as silk.

Framing lumber is not as handsome as some other kinds of wood. It is, of course, meant to be covered up. The grains are not as lovely and the color merely plain. It is utilitarian. But it is wood and it has an interest all its own. So it deserves some study. Moreover you have to know something about framing lumber in order to get the best wood for the job at hand and to make yourself understood at the lumberyard.

In this chapter, you learn about how framing lumber is sawn, dried, and graded. You also learn about plywood and panels like plywood and how these are made and graded.

Species of Wood

Trees come in two basic types: *hardwoods* and *softwoods*. Hardwoods are mainly deciduous trees; this means they lose their leaves in autumn. Softwoods are mainly evergreen trees. Examples of hardwoods are maples, oaks, elms, walnuts, and fruit trees. Examples of softwoods are pines, spruces, hemlocks, and firs. Redwoods and cedars are also softwoods.

Hardwoods are slower growing than softwoods. Accordingly they are more expensive. Hardwoods are normally used for furniture and fine flooring. You could frame a home or a closet in oak if you like, but no one is going to see the wood, and you will pay more for it.

Softwoods, on the other hand, are faster growing. They can be sown like farmers' crops and harvested when ready to be cut into lumber.

You should be familiar with two other terms: *sapwood* and *heartwood*. When a tree is young, nearly all the cells in its trunk carry sap, that is, water and nutrients, upward toward the branches and leaves. Any part of the trunk carrying sap is called *sapwood*. As the tree grows older and the trunk thickens, the cellular wood near the middle ceases to carry sap and instead, though still cellular, becomes a tough center that helps to strengthen the tree. The sap is then carried by the cellular wood around this core of heartwood. The heartwood is negligible in a young tree but broadens with age and eventually can be a third or so of the trunk's bulk.

Framer's Lingo

Hardwood is, generally, the wood of deciduous trees. **Softwood** is the wood of evergreen trees. **Heartwood** is the non-living central wood of a tree's trunk. **Sapwood** is sap carrying cells between the heartwood and the bark of a tree.

The heartwood is the strongest part of any log because the grain is often tightest there. When a log is cut, the heartwood is often reserved for pieces of lumber that require the most strength: timbers and beams. The studs used for framing lumber are normally cut from the sapwood of softwood trees.

Framing Lumber

Most framing lumber comes from the sapwood of softwood logs. It is then dried so that it will not shrink appreciably after it has been used to construct a house. Because some of the lumber may have large knots or other imperfections that can affect its strength, it is graded and stamped with its grade. In this way, a framer knows what the piece of wood can do and not put it to a use for which it cannot bear up.

How Lumber Is Sawn

Lumber is sawn from a log in either of two ways: quartersawn and plainsawn. When a log is quartersawn, it is first cut down the middle, and then each half is cut down the middle. Each quarter piece is then cut in such a way that the pieces have their narrow ends pointing in one direction toward what was the center of the original log and in the other direction toward the bark. This means that the grain of such a piece is running perpendicular to the wide face of such a piece. This not only makes for a more attractive piece of wood but also one that is less prone to warpage. The problem with quartersawing is that fewer useful pieces can be cut from the log than with the plainsawn method.

When a log is plainsawn, it is made to produce the most amount of useful wood it can. Many of the pieces produced have the grain running parallel with their faces. Sawing in this manner yields more lumber from a log, but the wood is not as attractive and is more prone to warpage.

Because framing lumber is covered up with drywall on the inside and siding on the outside, no one cares how it looks. But they do care that it is strong enough for the job at hand. They don't want it to be too warped, either. Fortunately, manufacturing methods have pretty well taken care of that problem. Studs and other 2× material you purchase at a lumberyard are straight enough and will remain straight enough to do the jobs they were meant to do.

How Lumber Is Dried

A living tree might have in it more weight by water than cellular matter alone without the water. When it is cut, the logs from it are said to be "green," that is, they still contain a good deal of water. Green wood is unsuitable for building because it will lose quite a bit of this water. In doing so, it shrinks. If you built a structure of green wood, it would groan for a year as the wood shrank and the wall coverings cracked.

So mills make certain that green wood is dried and preshrunk. Lumber suitable for framing contains moisture by weight of 19 percent or less.

Wood is dried in one of two ways. One way is called air drying where it can be set out in a lumberyard and allowed to dry naturally. However, pieces can take months to dry to a 19 percent moisture content. A faster method is kiln-drying. Here lumber is placed in massive kilns and dried under controlled temperatures and humidity. These controlled conditions also help reduce warpage the lumber might tend to if left to dry on its own.

Most framing lumber sold in mills is kiln-dried. Kiln-dried lumber is generally somewhat more expensive than air-dried lumber, but it is more stable and less likely to be warped.

How Lumber Is Sized

Mills must be careful how they cut the lumber because they know it is going to shrink from its green wood state. A hundred years ago 2×4s were cut so they ended up roughly 2" by 4". Over the course of time, engineers determined that 2×4s really didn't have to be as large as they were. They could do their jobs just fine slightly smaller. So these days 2×4s are cut so that when they are dry they are 1 ½" thick and 3 ½" across the face. This is especially important to remember. All measuring in framing takes these dimensions into consideration.

Accordingly, a 2×6 is really 1 ½" by 5 ½", and a 2×8 is 1 ½" by 7 ¼". See Table 4.1 below for the dimensions of common dimensional lumber.

Table 4.1   Nominal and Actual Sizes of 2x Lumber

Nominal Size	Actual Size
2×2	1 ½ × 1 ½
2×4	1 ½ × 3 ½
2×6	1 ½ × 5 ½
2×8	1 ½ × 7 ¼
2×10	1 ½ × 9 ¼
2×12	1 ½ × 11 ¼

Note that for 2×2s, 2×4s, and 2×6s, the wide dimension is ½" less than the nominal designation but that for 2×8s, 2×10s, and 2×12s, the wide dimension falls ¾" short of its nominal dimension.

Very likely you will also be using lumber that is not 2× lumber. These also have their nominal and actual sizes. See Table 4.2 on the following page.

You will notice some sizes of lumber I haven't mentioned before. The 1× ("one-by") material is useful for varying tasks. The 1×2s, 1×3s, and 1×4s can be used as stakes. The 1×8s, 1×10s, and 1×12s are used for shelving and general purpose boards.

The ⁵⁄₄ material is often used for deck flooring. It is stronger than 1x material but not so unnecessarily thick for flooring as 2× material.

The 4×4s and 4×6s are used as posts and beams.

Table 4.2 Nominal and Actual Sizes of 1x, ⁵/₄ and 4x Lumber

Nominal Size	Actual Size
1×2	$^3/_4 \times 1\ ^1/_2$
1×3	$^3/_4 \times 2\ ^1/_2$
1×4	$^3/_4 \times 3\ ^1/_2$
1×6	$^3/_4 \times 5\ ^1/_2$
1×8	$^3/_4 \times 7\ ^1/_4$
1×10	$^3/_4 \times 9\ ^1/_4$
1×12	$^3/_4 \times 11\ ^1/_4$
⁵/₄	$1 \times 3\ ^1/_2$
⁵/₆	$1 \times 5\ ^1/_2$
4×4	$3^1/_2 \times 3^1/_2$
4×6	$3^1/_2 \times 5^1/_2$

How Lumber Is Graded

Every piece of wood is unique. Some is not suited for the work another can do. The size and placement of knots affect strength, as does the slope of the grain. So pieces of lumber are graded in order that customers won't try to put pieces to work at jobs they cannot properly do.

Various associations around the country do *grading* to protect both the consumer and the manufacturer. One of the most prominent is the Western Woods Products Association (WWPA). Another is the Northeastern Lumber Manufacturers Association (NELMA). (See Appendix B for contact information.)

The common grades for a designation named Light Framing are:

◆ Construction
◆ Standard
◆ Utility

Any lumber with any of these designations is suitable for light framing. Most often you will see the *grade stamp* read "STAND" for standard.

Framer's Lingo

Grade is the designation on lumber noting its strength. The **grade stamp** is a stamp on a piece of framing lumber noting, among other things, its moisture content and grade.

A grade outside the three above is "STUD." Wood stamped this way is also good for general use.

A third designation is Structural Light Framing, sometimes written as Select Structural. Any wood so designated is superior to the categories in Light Framing and can bear greater stress.

The grade, along with other information, including the moisture content, is stamped on the lumber before it leaves the mill where it was processed.

Every piece of framing lumber is given a grade stamp at the mill where it was cut and dried. (Thus the stamp is not applied at the lumberyard where you are buying it.)

The grade stamp shows: the manufacturer, the grade, the grading authority, the moisture content, and the species.

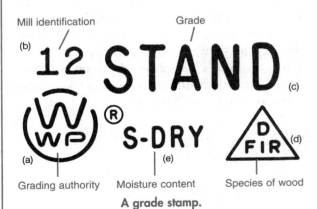

A grade stamp.

The moisture content designations are as follows:

- ◆ KD—Kiln dried means the wood has a moisture content of 19 percent or less.
- ◆ MC-15—The moisture content is 15 percent or less.
- ◆ S-Dry—Stands for surfaced dried and the wood has a moisture content of 19 percent or less.
- ◆ S-Green—The wood has a moisture content of more than 19 percent.

Finger Tips

Although a piece of dimensional lumber is neither as thick nor as wide as its name would suggest, it is nearly always the proper length. If you buy an 8' 2×4 at the lumber yard, it is nearly always cut to exactly 8'. I say nearly because you had better check. In my experience, when you buy 8' or 10' 2×4s, the length is what it says, but if you buy a 10' 1×12, it may be slightly longer. The lumberyards I have dealt with always have erred on the side of the customer. But what you don't want to do is assume, just because you came home with a 2×12 thought to be exactly 12' long, that it is exactly 12' long. So always check.

Pressure-Treated Lumber

Another kind of lumber you should know about is pressure-treated lumber. Generally, you don't want this for framing. Pressure-treated (PT) wood is infused with chemicals under pressure so that it will not rot when exposed to the elements. You'd want that kind of wood for a deck or a wood retaining wall in the garden but not for general construction where the framing is to be covered.

Pressure-treated wood used to be infused with CCA (chromated copper arsenate), but this chemical has been replaced with ones considered friendlier to humans and the environment.

Don't buy pressure treated wood for any project that is going to be for indoors or covered over with siding.

Plywood and Engineered Boards

In the bad old days when it came time to lay flooring, cover the outside of stud walls, or lay a foundation for roof shingles, you nailed on boards. These were normally set at a diagonal to the joists, studs, or rafters to make the whole assembly more stable.

Then someone came up with the idea of making *plywood*, and framing carpentry was forever changed. Plywood is reconstructed wood, somewhat improving on nature. Manufacturers take thin sheets of wood, the plies, (scrolled off logs with very sharp cutters) and glue them together. Adjacent plies have their grains running in different directions so that the whole assembled sheet (normally 4' by 8') is stronger and less prone to warping than any 4×8 sheet of natural wood could be.

Normally plywood has five plies, but there are variations. Indeed, plywood comes in many configurations for quite a number of different uses. And there are plywood-like products built slightly differently, having their own advantages for cost and use.

Framer's Lingo

Plywood is 4' by 8' panels of wood consisting of thin layers (plies), usually five.

Structural Plywood and Equivalents

A framing carpenter mainly deals with structural plywood, as opposed to finish plywood. Structural plywood is used for subflooring, wall sheathing, and roof sheathing. It adds stability to the underlaying framing structure and is meant itself to be covered over. Finish plywood has at least one fairly good surface, which is meant to be seen.

Structural plywood comes in thicknesses $3/16"$ to $3/4"$. Like dimensional lumber, it is graded according to its strength and suitability to certain applications. You don't want to buy plywood that is more expensive than you need for a certain job.

Plywood can come as *square-edged* or *tongue-and-groove*. Square edge means the edges are square and flat. Tongue-and-groove means that one long edge has a groove in it and the other has a tongue protruding from it such that it can slip into the groove of a similar and adjoining panel. In addition, one end has a groove and one edge has a tongue. If you make a floor or roof sheathing of tongue-and-groove panels, the panels all interlock and so make a more cohesive whole than if you were merely using square-edge panels. Tongue-and-groove panels create a stronger structure and one less likely to movement over time.

Member mills of APA—The Engineered Wood Association—grade and label most plywood. The figure that follows is a typical structural plywood grade stamp.

> **Framer's Lingo**
>
> **Square-edged plywood** consists of plywood panels with smooth solid edges.
> **Tongue-and-groove plywood** consists of plywood panels whose edges are either grooves or the tongues that fit into grooves.

A plywood grade stamp.

Courtesy of APA—The Engineered Wood Association.

Structural grades are as follows:

◆ Sturd-I-Floor. This designation is for plywood that can serve as subfloor and underlayment together for a flooring system. Subflooring is nailed to the floor joists. Underlayment goes on top to make a stronger and smoother surface for such flooring as tile and vinyl and is not always necessary. This can come as tongue-and-groove or square edged.

◆ Sheathing. This is made specifically for subflooring, wall sheathing, and roof sheathing.

◆ Siding. This is made for exterior siding. Some come with surface grooves that make them attractive siding by themselves and do not have to be covered with any other material.

Other grading specifications stamped on the plywood are as follows:

◆ Span Ratings. The grade stamp shows a span rating. Ratings for sheathing often appear as two numbers separated with a slash (/). The first indicates the maximum spacing between rafters if the wood is to be used as roof sheathing; the second indicates the maximum spacing between joists if the wood is to be used for subflooring. Sturd-I-Floor and Siding plywood normally come with only one number, the maximum spacing between joists or studs to which the plywood can be nailed.

◆ Thickness. The grade stamp indicates the thickness of the plywood.

◆ Tongue-and-groove. The grade stamp will indicate if the edges are tongue-and-groove with the abbreviation "T&G". If the plywood does not have tongue-and-groove edges, there will be no designation.

◆ Exposure classification. Low on the grade stamp is the exposure rating. "Exterior" means the plywood can be subjected to

the elements without covering. "Exposure 1" means the plywood is suitable where some moisture will be present. "Exposure 2" means that the plywood should be protected. Plywood rated "Interior" should only be used indoors.

◆ Other kinds of structural plywood. You can use other kinds of manufactured panels in place of plywood as long as building codes allow it and the grading stamp allows the usage.

Finger Tips

Which plywood or panel should you choose?

If you are having house, shed, or closet plans drawn up, have the architect or designer designate on the plans what grade of plywood or panels to use for any particular situation. If you aren't using a professional, you still may have to take some drawn plans to your local building department for approval. If so, they can designate the grades to use for specific purposes.

As a last resort, go to the lumberyard and tell the clerk what you are going to use the plywood for. Then he goes, "Oh, yeah. You want 24-inch Sturd-I-Floor Exposure 1 panels. I'll tell Tony."

◆ Oriented Strand Board (OSB). Oriented Strand Board is made of layers of wood chips or strands of wood oriented in a single direction. Layers of chips aligned in different directions are alternated to make the panel. The chips are visible both along the top and bottom surfaces. OSB can be as strong as plywood and is used for wall sheathing, subflooring, and roof sheathing. Manufacturers often have their own names for such products.

◆ Waferboard. Waferboard is like Oriented Strand Board, but the chips and strands are not directionally oriented. Thus it is not as strong as OSB.

Veneer Plywood

Plywood that is not especially manufactured and marked for Sturd-I-Floor, Sheathing, and Siding grades has another designation, one for the appearance of the top and bottom faces. The highest grade, meaning the best-looking finish, is called N (for "natural finish") with very few repairs and would be good looking even with a transparent stain. The order then goes from best to worst A, B, C Plugged, C, and D. "A" means smooth and paintable and has had minor repairs made to it at the mill. "B" is a solid smooth surface that has had repairs made to it. "C Plugged" likely has repairs as well as very small splits and holes. "C" can have knotholes up to 1" across. "D" can have knotholes up to 3" across.

If the plywood you are going to use is not going to show, a D surface is acceptable. If you are going to use plywood to make a window seat bench or shelving, you'd probably want no worse than a C Plugged surface to show.

Many plywood panels are sold as C-D or B-C, meaning one face is better than another.

Heads!

Some plywoods and similar manufactured sheathing products are made with urea-formaldehyde glues, which give off gases for a considerable period after being installed. If you react adversely to urea-formaldehyde, you may not want to use scores of these boards for subflooring, sheathing, and the like in a new home. Ask at the lumberyard for alternatives.

Engineered Lumber

Plywood is not the only invention of modern manufacturing meant to make life easier for framing carpenters. Someone also came up with the idea of premade beams and premade trusses, which serve for rafters. There are also manufactured joists, which are lighter in weight than solid wood joists.

In some respects, this *engineered lumber* is for professional home builders. They get good prices on premade joists, trusses, and beams and can build more quickly with them. Amateurs can do just fine with solid dimensional lumber, as they have since corn began to grow. But you would do well to know a bit about engineered lumber and how some of it is applied. Your lumber yard might have some available and recommend it for your situation.

Trusses

Modern trusses take the place of solid rafters. But where a rafter might have to be made of a very long 2×8, a truss can be made mostly out of relatively short pieces of 2×4. The trick is in making what is called *webbing*, the interior portion of the truss. Most trusses resemble a triangle, the longest and lowest piece forming the base and called a *lower chord*. The *upper chords* form the top sides of the triangle. Then within the triangle are connecting pieces of 2×4 called web members.

The configuration of the web and chords give the truss its strength in bearing the roof overhead. The chords and *web members* are not nailed or glued together or joined with fancy wood joinery. Rather *gussets* hold them together. These are flat pieces of metal or plywood fastened to the separate pieces and holding them together.

Framer's Lingo

Engineered lumber are pieces made of lumber products to imitate solid lumber. A **truss** is an engineered piece used to hold up a roof. **Webbing** is the interior pieces of a truss. A **lower chord** is the low, horizontal piece of a truss, and the **upper chord** is the piece along the top of a truss. **Web members** are pieces of a truss's webbing. The **gusset** is steel or plywood plate which fastens pieces of a truss together.

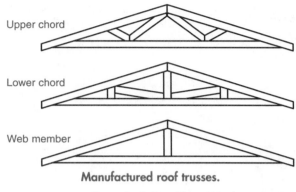

Manufactured roof trusses.

(Copyright © Ivan Chirinos)

Beams and Joists

There isn't much point in going into the different kinds of engineered lumber that make up beams and joists. Beams might be made of pieces of wood built up one on top of another; these are called veneered beams. Some might be made of chips and strands of wood all glued together. Some look like steel I-beams except that each of the parts is made of particles of wood and adhesive. The beams can be heavier than their solid wood counterparts, and for the most part they are not as attractive.

The advantages of engineered beams and joists are that they are stronger than solid wood, straighter than long lengths of solid wood, and less likely to shrink or warp once in place.

Another advantage is that some types have openings designed into them so that you can run plumbing pipes and electrical wire through them without drilling or notching holes.

A disadvantage is that they can be more expensive. And some cannot be drilled or notched for pipes and wires.

The Least You Need to Know

- Framing lumber is made out of softwoods, such as pines, firs, and spruces.
- Framing lumber has a nominal dimension and an actual dimension, which is always smaller. You call it a 2×4, but it actually is $1^{1}/_{2}$" by $3^{1}/_{2}$".
- Framing lumber is graded for the jobs it can perform and also whether it is dry or "green." Always use dry lumber.
- Plywood is a useful material and is graded for the jobs it can perform. Some are graded according to the appearance of the top and bottom surfaces.
- Another type of framing lumber is engineered lumber, which can take the place of rafters or solid wood beams and joists.

In This Chapter

- ◆ Be alert and you will be safe
- ◆ Attitude is key: don't let troubles distract you
- ◆ Keep a first aid kit on the site
- ◆ Observe all safety precautions with electricity
- ◆ Do not tamper with safety guards on power tools
- ◆ Use safety equipment

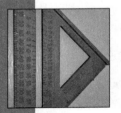
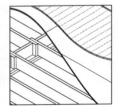

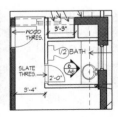

Chapter 5

General Safety

Unfortunately, framing puts you in harm's way of injury. There are any number of ways to hurt yourself, and both professionals and amateurs have done so. Nearly every framing carpenter has put a splinter into his hand, or at one time or another hit one of his fingers with a hammer. More serious injury also lurks: grit in your eyes, a cut from a power tool, or a fall from a ladder.

Remember that no matter what your goal is in framing—from a house to a closet—safety is what you really want. It's nice to have a newly framed closet or a newly framed house, but you want to enjoy it in good health. A new closet or a new house is not much solace if you are in bed or bandaged.

In this chapter, we review safety rules and equipment. Always remember the rules, and wear the equipment at the proper times. Then you'll arrive unscratched at the end of your labors.

General Safety

Before doing any framing, you should be well rested. Little sleep the night before or fatigue from some other activity is an ingredient to a recipe for injury.

Similarly, you should never do framing after or while drinking alcohol or taking drugs that make you drowsy.

For that matter you should never do framing when you are angry about something or otherwise emotionally or mentally distracted. Power tools are wonderful, but they can injure quicker than you can jerk back a finger. A fall from a ladder occurs faster than you can reach out to grasp something to hold you up. Under conditions like these, you really have no margin for error.

Heads!

Injury can happen in a split second, faster than you can jerk a finger away from a saw's blade. At all times you must have a sense of where every part of you is, how you are balanced, and what the tool is doing.

Being alert also means being alert to your surroundings. Not only must you have a good sense of where your fingers, arms, and legs are at any second and how you are balanced, but also you must know what framing parts are where and who might be around you. When you build things, you put into place parts that were not in those places moments before. You are erecting parts of walls or parts of ceilings, and, if the job is moderately big, so are other people. If you're not careful, you might finish some work, then raise your head and hit a part that wasn't there five minutes ago.

In addition, you must be alert to where persons working around you are and know what they are doing. You can't carry a 2×4 around a corner unless you know that anyone who had been working there is safely away. You have to be alert to anyone bringing new supplies onto the worksite; someone carrying plywood might not see you and bump you when you are using a power tool.

Also be careful about playing loud music on a worksite. If it's so loud that you can't hear warning shouts or even a worker's footsteps bringing plywood or joists, it's too loud and distracting.

Follow these other important safety practices to assure you get the job done and not a medical bill instead.

◆ Watch out for other workers. Try to know where they are, what they are doing, and where they might be going.

◆ Keep the worksite clean. Wood scraps, piles of sawdust, scattered nails, and screwdrivers left on the floor are just ambushes waiting to strike. Tidy up for your sake and for the sake of those working with you. Don't leave anything laying around that a person could trip on or that could roll under someone's shoe.

◆ Keep extension cords under control. Too many curves and loops of these around the site are a nuisance and a hazard. Don't use extension cords that are too long for the work in any case because long ones deliver less electricity (and thus power) to power tools.

◆ Look where you walk. See that you are not about to step on a 2×4 scrap or put your heel on a portion of extension cord. At the same time, keep your eyes elevated a bit so you won't run into a piece of lumber that wasn't there a few minutes ago.

◆ If you see protruding nails that could snag someone, hammer them in or pull them out and throw them away.

◆ Work at a steady and deliberate pace. Don't get overly tired. A weary mind is one about to walk into an accident. Take breaks from your work to rest your muscles and recharge your mind.

◆ Stay refreshed and comfortable. Don't work hungry or thirsty. Drink enough fluids; this is especially important working outside in the sun or on a warm day.

Lighting

Avoid doing framing work at night. Even with bright lighting, the shadows are different than in the day. You see differently under these conditions, and your perception of distance is altered. So keep outdoor framing a daytime activity.

Attitude

All sorts of safety equipment are out there to protect your various parts—eye protectors for eyes, gloves for fingers, hard hats for tops of heads. But there is a big gap here. Most injuries happen because someone wasn't paying attention. No piece of safety equipment can protect your heart and your mind from wandering to something other than what you are doing.

Heads!

It's no coincidence that so many slapstick movies were set in construction situations. Buster Keaton, the Three Stooges, and other luminaries of the silent and black-and-white eras of movie making, chose construction as the mayhem for pratfalls. Larry carries floor joists around a corner and smacks Moe with the front of his load. Buster Keaton steps in a bucket and hobbles around until he falls over. Someone opens a door and walks into a ladder. Someone else steps into a sheet of plywood being carried by another and falls flat on his back. Curly teeters precariously on a ladder, swaying back and forth on it.

Construction materials and maneuvers are rich veins for mining such situations, and filmmakers took full advantage in the early days of movies. Audiences were meant to double over laughing.

But all these situations stem from inattention of some sort—not thinking about where the bucket was, not knowing who might be approaching from around the corner, not understanding how you are balanced on a ladder.

The slapstick artists were fools to be laughed at because with only the smallest bit of attention they could have avoided their injurious ways. But they didn't and so they were ludicrous.

Don't join them. Stay alert to your surroundings, what you are doing and where your comrades are.

Any number of distractions can crop up. Everyone from time to time has heartaches, a lost loved one, a sick child, too many bills to pay. If you can't concentrate on what you are doing—if something is going to distract your mind or heart while you want to do framing, it's best to put the framing off until your troubles pass.

Safety equipment is fine, but you have to start with an untroubled mind.

Lifting Heavy Materials

Framing often requires lifting heavy materials. Most often this is not like lifting a rock by squatting down, keeping your back straight, and lifting with your legs. More often, it is lifting along your side, as in lifting to carry lumber, a heavy tool bucket, or a power tool. So the rules are slightly different.

First, you should be in fairly good shape before you do any heavy lifting. If you have spent most the winter in inactivity, your first effort of the spring should not be hauling heavy lumber to a worksite. Do some exercising first and work up to it. Even if you are in fairly good shape or you have been active, it is a good idea to do some stretching exercises before lifting so your muscles and tendons are flexed and warmed for the work.

When you lift heavy loads to carry along your side, descend as much as you can with your legs. Grasp the load firmly. Keep your back as straight as you can make it with your head up. I often repeat to myself "Eyes to the sky" to remind me to look up. When I do, my spine is straighter than when I am looking at the ground. Lift as much as you can with your legs, the rest with muscles on the side opposite the load so you end up standing straight.

If you are going to be doing a lot of lifting, consider buying and using a lifting belt. These help support the middle body muscles that are strained during lifts.

Clothing, Jewelry, and Hair

Wear clothing that is not too tight or too loose. Avoid cuffs on pant legs—they are more likely to snag on a nail or corner. If you unbutton sleeves, roll them up tight to your arm; don't let sleeve ends hang about or they might snag on a nail or a power saw's blade.

Don't do any framing with neck chains or any sort of loose jewelry that might become caught in power tools. Some professional carpenters remove their wristwatches and rings before they work, which is not a bad idea at all.

If you have long hair, bundle it up or keep it under a hat.

Electrical Safety

Using power tools means you are working with electricity, and you must follow a number of rules and precautions to assure your safety.

Weather and Wetness

If you are working outside, call it quits when a rain comes. Electricity and moisture are a deadly combination. Even if you are working with no power tools and there is no electrical conductor around, rain makes lumber slippery. You can much more easily lose your footing on wet plywood than on dry.

And call it quits if you hear thunder. Lighting can strike miles ahead of a storm, long before the rain comes, and miles behind a storm. If you hear thunder, get off ladders, get off an outdoor worksite, and get indoors.

Outlets

Any outlet you use for power tools outdoors must be protected with what is called a *Ground Fault Circuit Interrupter, or GFCI* for short. All homes built within the last several decades

should have them on outdoor circuits, so if your home is new, you're covered. If your home is older, you better check.

And here's how. Look at the outlet itself. If it has a "test button" and a "reset button" then it has a GFCI. In fact, you're looking at it. The GFCI is right there at the outlet.

All outdoor electrical circuits must be protected by a Ground Fault Circuit Interrupter (GFCI) either at the outlet or in the circuit breaker box. One is shown here in an outdoor outlet.

If you don't see a "test button" or "reset button" but instead a regular outlet, it may be protected and it may not. You have to check at the *electrical panel* inside your home, usually in the basement. The electrical panel is often called the circuit breaker panel or the fuse box.

Open up the electrical panel. If you see fuses, you don't have a GFCI on any of the circuits. You'll have to install one at the outlet (this is not an impossible task for a homeowner but out of the scope of this book) or use an extension cord that contains a built-in GFCI.

If you see a circuit breaker with a test button, this is a GFCI circuit breaker.

📖 Framer's Lingo

A **Ground Fault Circuit Interrupter (GFCI)** is a device on an electrical circuit that stops electricity in a fraction of a second to prevent electric shock. An **electrical panel**, also called a circuit breaker panel or fuse box, is the place in the house where the electrical circuit breakers—or fuses—are located for controlling electricity to a circuit.

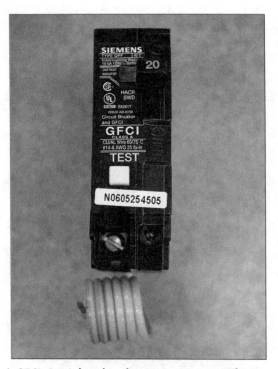

A GFCI circuit breaker that protects an outside outlet is sufficient protection when using power tools outside. In fact, it probably controls other outlets that may be outside.

But how do you tell if a GFCI circuit breaker controls the circuit you want to use? It's simple. Turn the switch on the GFCI circuit breaker to off. (You might want to warn children playing video games, spouses cooking dinner, and guests in bathrooms that you are about to do this because you might be turning off a circuit controlling their televisions, microwave ovens, or bathroom lights). Then go outside, plug something into the circuit you are planning to use, and see if it works. If it doesn't, then the GFCI is controlling that circuit, and you can use it with outside power tools.

If you see no GFCI circuit breakers in the electrical panel or if ones in the electrical panel do not control the circuit you want to use, you have two options. You can buy a GFCI to plug into the outlet. Or you can buy an extension cord for outdoor use that contains a built-in GFCI. These come in short lengths, about 9', and in long lengths, up to 100'. Unfortunately, these are on the expensive side, and you're better off with a GFCI at the outlet or in the electrical panel.

⛑ Heads!

Don't be fooled into thinking that because a circuit is grounded (has three prong holes—all modern circuits are grounded), it is safe for outdoor use and not in need of a GFCI. A grounded circuit can blow a fuse and trip a circuit breaker when the circuit malfunctions, but a GFCI can do it far faster and when the leakage of current is far less. Persons have been seriously injured by electricity on a grounded circuit not protected by a GFCI. The GFCI makes for a far more safe electrical environment.

Extension Cords

Only use extension cords meant for outdoors use. These are always three-prong ones—the male end has three prongs, two that are straight and one that is round. The two straight ones connect to wires in the extension cord cable that carry the electricity to a power tool and back again. The round prong connects to a ground wire. Under normal conditions the ground prong and the ground wire do not carry any electricity at all. But if the power tool you are using malfunctions and electricity reaches the casing of the tool, then the electricity will travel back in its loop through the ground wire rather than, first, through your hand and then through your body to the ground, which you never want to happen! When electricity travels through the ground wire, the GFCI detects this non-normal current and shuts down the circuit.

So never cut off the round prong from any extension cord or any electrical appliance. It is there to save you from injury should something go wrong with the appliance.

There can be another sort of short circuit. Say the extension cord gets caught on something, wedged under a rock or a tool chest, and you give it a big yank. If the insulation comes off the extension cord and off of one of the current-carrying wires in it, the electricity is going to want to flow out of that wire to the ground. A circuit breaker, fuse, or—very quickly—a GFCI detects this non-normal flow of current and shuts down the circuit. It's good to have these safety features, but don't yank extension cords when they get caught up on something! Take a few seconds to find where the trouble is, and fix it that way.

Safety Equipment

What's the most important thing about you? Your health, of course. Without it, you're not much good at all. Safety equipment is made so you can keep this most precious health. So use safety equipment.

And use it properly. In many cases, you have to do more than put something on. You must read the instructions that come with the equipment so you can use it properly; otherwise you may not be protecting yourself adequately. Reading the instructions only takes a minute or two, and remember what you are protecting!

Eye Protection

Your eyes are certainly one of the most important parts of you, and you won't do much more framing if you put your eyes out of action either temporarily or permanently. Framing has a number of ways of being dangerous to eyes. Sawdust flies out of power tools, and persons carrying 2x4s or other equipment can hit your eyes. It's just better to be protected. And use eye protectors that have side projections as well.

Wear eye protection any time you are operating a power tool. And try to get used to wearing it at other times; it may save you a trip to the emergency room.

But don't take the view that regular eye glasses are enough protection. They are not designed to protect your eyes, and they do not have side projections.

Eye protectors.

Dust Masks/Respirators

Sawing and sanding creates sawdust, which is best kept out of your lungs. Some people are allergic to sawdust. When you are sawing, sanding, sweeping, or otherwise swirling wood grit into the air, at least wear a dust mask. This should have reinforcing ribs across the bridge of the nose, which you can bend downward to make for a tighter fit.

Respirators with filters do a better job and keep out finer dust. Wear one of these if you are sawing lumber pressure treated with preservative chemicals, if you are sanding wood coated with paint, or if you are doing some demolition before beginning your framing. And remember to change the filter when it gets dirty.

Note that a respirator's ordinary particulate filter does not block fumes and vapors. If you are going to be applying solvents or working with paint strippers, wear a high-grade respirator that has a cartridge-type carbon filter that absorbs fumes.

A dust mask and respirator.

Ear Protection

Framing activity can be hard on the ears. Power saws and power sanders kick up some pretty good doses of decibels. Even the constant whack of hammers on iron nails around you can be a stressor on eardrums.

To deal with this noise, you can easily press foam ear plugs into your ear canals. These inexpensive plugs are available at home improvement stores.

If you want to leave your hearing unimpaired except when using a power tool, consider muff-style ear protectors. You can easily put these on when you are power sawing, power sanding, and the like.

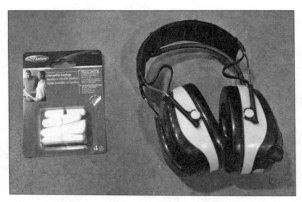

Ear plugs and muff-type ear protectors.

Safety Guards

Power tools often have safety guards. For example, a circular saw has a guard that shelters the saw's blade. Read about the safety features of the tools you buy. Keep them clean and in good working order. Do not tamper with safety guards in any way, attempt to prop them in an open position, or remove them. They are there to protect you.

Fire Extinguisher

Always keep a fire extinguisher nearby, and keep it fully charged. When you are framing, it's not like you are creating lots of heat, but there is a lot of dry wood and sawdust around, and sometimes flammable solvents, dry paper, and the like. A spark could set solvents off, and fire could spread rapidly. It's best to nip this in the bud with a fire extinguisher.

Owing to the power tools, there is a danger of electrical fire. So when choosing a fire extinguisher, buy one that is rated "ABC," for (a) wood, (b) liquids, such as gasoline and grease, and (c) electrical. Most fire extinguishers are now rated ABC.

First Aid Kit

No one likes to think about injury, but in framing, it happens. Splinters, smashed fingers, and cuts are most common. So be prepared. Keep a first aid kit nearby with these items in it.

Have tweezers for pulling out splinters; blunt-nosed scissors for cutting away clothing; cotton swabs; adhesive bandages; sterile gauze pads; rolled bandages for sprains; cold compresses for injuries to fingers or muscles; antiseptic ointment; antiseptic wipes or solution; sterile eye wash (or a saline solution for using as an eye wash); and sterile gloves, because it is better to treat a cut with a sterile surface than with dirty hands.

Read up on first aid techniques so that you know how to use any of the items in your first aid kit and treat the most common forms of construction injuries. These would be cuts; abrasions; fingers, bones, or muscles hit with a hammer; and debris in the eyes or ears.

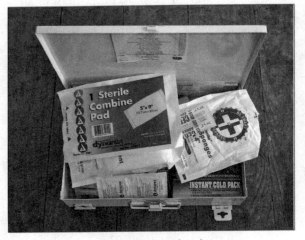

Elements for a safety kit.

Gloves

Framing can be pretty rough on the hands. The next time you meet a professional carpenter, look at his hands. The fingers are larger than normal, roughed up, and reddish. That comes from a lifetime of abrading the skin against wood, acting like a pincushion for splinters, and taking countless hammer whacks. (Of course, those hands are in some respects as sensitive as an artist's. They can tell by the feel of a piece of wood just how close a nail can go to its end without splitting it, how close to a right angle one edge is to another, and scores of other characteristics.)

Leather gloves are good for hauling lumber and plywood. They keep the splinters and rough scrapes at bay, so keep a pair handy. They are not so good when you hold a nail to a 2×4. But they are essential if instead you are hammering against something metal, if for example you are hammering against a pry bar to separate two pieces of lumber.

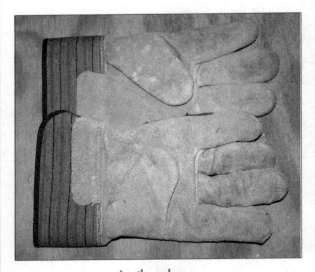

Leather gloves.

Hard Hat

It's always handy to have a hard hat around. If you are in an area where people are working above you, wear a hard hat because people are likely to drop things—tools, lumber, cut ends of lumber, soda cans, you name it. Or if you are working in a confined area or where there is a low ceiling such as a basement, you are always likely to turn your head quickly and conk your noggin. Wearing a hard hat saves you from seeing stars and planets swirling in front of your eyes.

When you wear a hard hat, firm up the inner straps. You are often going to lower your head—to operate a saw, hammer a nail, or pick up a scrap of wood—and it's darned inconvenient to have to swish up a hand when you do so to hold the hard hat in place.

A hard hat.

Knee Pads

When I first started swinging a hammer, I never saw the likes of these. How I could have used them! I was always up and down, up and down on my knees always on hard plywood. And when going down, I had to brace myself and slow down to lessen the impact on my kneecaps. It was hard enough on the knee joints just bending them so much in a day, but to bash them against inflexible plywood was a positive insult.

So if you are doing a lot of getting on your knees, consider these useful items. They look a bit silly, though not so silly as in the days before roller blading, but they really help comfort the knee caps.

If you won't be bending too much or if you are going to be on your knees a great deal but just shuffling along for a period, as in nailing plywood to joists, consider a flat moveable knee pad. These are thick comfortable pieces of foam, sometimes sold to gardeners, which really make a difference on your kneecaps.

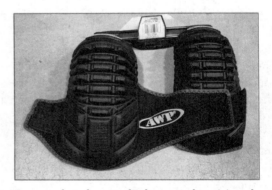

Knee pads to be attached to your legs (a) and an independent, moveable knee pad (b).

Sun Screening

Sunscreen is not thought of as safety equipment; nor are hats and long sleeves. But they can all prevent damage to skin over the long term. If you are working outside, even on cloudy days, you must be aware of the radiation slamming your skin. If you are not wearing a hard hat, consider a broad-brimmed hat when you are in direct sun. Apply sunscreen lotion on a sunny day to block the sun's ultraviolet radiation. Wear long sleeves and pants if you don't.

Heads!

The key to safety is being alert to what you are doing, what might go wrong, and how to make sure nothing does go wrong.

Shoes/Boots

Wear sturdy shoes with good treads. There's always a temptation to wear your oldest shoes, but these are also the ones most likely to be worn smooth under the ball of the foot. Smooth is bad because it can slip, especially when wet, and slipping is bad.

Many professionals wear work boots, and you can, too. They have good treads, and they offer more protection to the upper foot against dropped 2x6s than do common running and walking shoes. If you are working around heavy items that might frequently be dropped, use boots with a built-in curved steel plate across the toe.

But remember you are likely to get down on your knees quite a bit. That means the soles of your boots or shoes need to be flexible. After safety, you want to think comfort.

Work boots.

Ladders

As a framer, you are going to need ladders. Likely the most useful will be a step ladder, especially if you are going to be doing your framing in existing buildings. Framing normally requires working no more than 8' off the floor. Of course, if your framing is going to take you to nailing on house siding or working on the roof, you will need an extension ladder.

When choosing a step ladder, buy one that is sturdy and has wide rungs. Aluminum ones are lighter than wooden ones, and do not suffer the splinters or splits wooden ones do. Make sure the feet of the ladder are skid-resistant, and read the safety instructions for your ladder. Do not use the top or the next-to-the-highest step.

Folding ladders, also made of aluminum, but available in fiberglass, are handy because you can configure them into step ladders, straight ladders, and an M or U shape to support planks you can walk on as scaffolding.

Heads!

Working from a ladder can be dangerous. Always observe these safety measures:

1) Do not carry or place ladders near overhead electrical power lines.

2) Do not stand on a step ladder's top or next-to-the-top step.

3) When on a ladder, do not lean out farther than your belt buckle.

4) Do not carry tools in your hand when climbing a ladder. Put them in your tool belt or in a sack that you can pull up with a rope.

5) Place ladder legs on firm, nonskid, and level ground or flooring.

6) An extension ladder's legs should be out from the wall $\frac{1}{4}$ the distance the ladder is high.

Extension ladders are good for reaching heights outside.

Ladders are rated Type I, IA, II, and III. I and IA are the highest and industrial grades. Type II is fine for commercial and home use.

Ladder Jacks, Pump Jacks, and Exterior Scaffolding

If you are installing insulation board or siding over a framed wall, you may be in need of ladder jacks, pump jacks, or exterior scaffolding.

Ladder jacks are brackets that hook to the rungs of extension ladders and onto which 2×10 planks are set. Instead of 2×10 planks, you can lay an extension ladder with grillwork covering the rungs on the horizontal portions of the ladder jacks.

You need two extension ladders and two ladder jacks, one for each end of the planks. Ladder jacks are like scaffolding in that they allow you to work on an exterior wall without having to stand on a ladder and to store your tools and materials convenient to where you are working. And they are less expensive than scaffolding. Ladder jacks may be rented or bought.

Pump jacks are similar to ladder jacks but connect to 4x4s rising parallel to the outside of a house wall. The 4x4s are connected to the wall with bracing. The pump jacks are metal brackets that hold 2×10 planks, forming a platform for working and materials storage. They rise along the 4x4s by a pumping action with your foot; they lower with a hand crank. Pump jacks may be rented or bought.

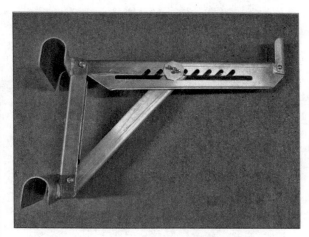

A ladder jack attaches to the rungs of an extension ladder. It adjusts for the slant of the ladder to make a level holding area. Ladder jacks on adjacent ladders hold planks to work from.

Exterior metal *scaffolding* is composed of tubular metal end pieces held together by cross pieces. Planking is set on the rungs of the end pieces. The scaffolding is set on base plates and can be adjusted to level with screw legs. You can rent this kind of scaffolding, which makes for a more permanent and accommodating work platform. But it takes time to set up and take down, and the rental fees are higher than for ladder jacks and screw jacks.

Framer's Lingo

Ladder jacks are metal brackets that attach to extension ladders allowing a pair of extension ladders to support 2×10 planks on which workers can work and store materials. **Pump jacks** are brackets that attach to 4×4 posts rising alongside a house wall. They are raised along the 4×4s by pumping with a foot and lower by hand cranking. **Scaffolding** are temporary structures on which workers can work and store materials off the floor or ground.

Pump jacks.

Scaffolding.

The Least You Need to Know

◆ The most important product of your work is getting you to the end of it safe and healthy.

◆ Being alert is the most important element in safety. When doing framing, you cannot let outside events or thoughts distract or upset you. Instead you have to concentrate on your work.

◆ Work slowly and steadily; a fatigued mind and body opens the door to injury.

◆ Observe all safety and electrical safety precautions.

◆ Use safety equipment to protect parts of your body. Read the instructions, and use the safety equipment properly.

◆ Use ladders properly, following safety procedures. Do not lean out from ladders father than your belt buckle.

In This Part

"Maybe we should take a step back, Ron."

Part 2

Framing Techniques

So you know the tools and the materials, and you know how to be safe. Do you start building the house? You could, but you ought to command some skills before you do. These are the skills that are going to see you though a successful framing project.

You ought to know how to read blueprints, what building codes are, and how your local building department is going to deal with your project. You ought to understand something about the physical forces that try to tear a framing job apart. And you should be skilled in measuring, cutting, and joining lumber. This part deals with these things.

In This Chapter

- ◆ Reading "blueprints" or plans
- ◆ Different kinds of plans
- ◆ Ways plans help with framing
- ◆ Purposes and effects of building codes

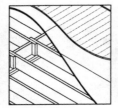

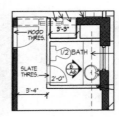

Chapter 6

Reading Plans

Plans used to be called blueprints. But no one uses blue anymore, so they had to come up with a different name. Plans is it, though you still hear the term blueprints from time to time. Blueprints were blue because of the way they were created and copied. These days, better reproduction methods allow for white paper with dark lines.

You can frame without plans, and many people do. But you may also be framing a large and complex structure, and for these you will likely welcome plans. In addition, in order to even start your project, you may need permission from your city or county building department. They will want to see at least a sketch of what you are constructing to make sure it meets the local building codes (refer to the last section of this chapter). They may require extensive plans, or for complex projects, professional drawings of an architect or engineer. Thus you may be working from professional drawings, so you better know how to read and interpret them.

In this chapter, you learn the basics of reading architect's plans, what the symbols mean and how to work from them. You also learn how building codes are going to affect your building project.

Plans

When using plans, look first at the title block. You should see the scale the drawing is using. If you don't see the scale indicator there, look at the bottom of the individual drawings.

A common scale is $\frac{1}{4}$" equals 1'. But there can be other scales, so take care, and a set of plans showing a house is likely to have drawings with different scales. A detail, for example, of one part of the construction will probably have a larger scale than the floorplan. If you were to take a ruler and measure a dimension on a plan, you could then do the multiplication and determine the dimension of the true object. But doing so is risky. It is too easy to misread a scale on a ruler, and the drawer of the plan may have erred. It is better to observe a written dimension on a plan.

Draftsmen used to draw plans, but these days plans are more likely to be rendered on a computer using architectural drawing software.

In addition, plans have different kinds of lines, each with a different meaning.

Lines

Plans have plenty of lines, and they are not all alike. To understand plans properly, you must know what the different kinds of lines mean.

There are six basic kinds of lines:

- *Object lines* are broad and solid. They outline an object, such as a house or room perimeter.
- *Dimension lines* are solid but thinner than object lines. They terminate in arrows, dots, or slashes and show how long, high, or thick an object is.
- *Centerlines* are fine interrupted lines of long and short dashes. Often along their length is a symbol of a capital C and a capital L written together. Centerlines show the center points of objects or areas.
- *Section lines* are often a broad solid line interrupted by two short dashes. They identify a section drawing (see the figure that follows) that illustrates a different view from the one crossed by the section

line. Section lines normally have a right angle in them and end in an arrow.

- *Break lines* are thin and display one or more lightning-like spikes. They indicate that the object continues unchanged although the drawing stops in order to save space.
- *Leader lines* are fine thin lines ending with an arrow. They identify objects or draw your attention to a note.

Framer's Lingo

Object lines show the outline of an object. **Dimension lines** show the length, width, or thickness of an object. **Centerlines** show where the center of an object or area is, while **section lines** identify section drawings. **Break lines** show a break in the drawing to save space. **Leader lines** identify an object or call attention to a note about it.

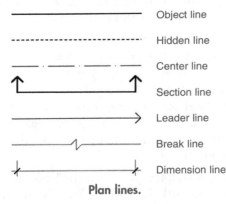

Plan lines.

(Copyright © John Hannah)

Floorplans

Floorplans present an overview of a house section, showing the exterior walls, partition walls, dimensions of the house, and various areas within it, often identifying the rooms. The view is from above. It is as if the building were sliced through 3' up from the floor and the upper part tossed away.

Floorplans have abbreviations and symbols, most of which are self-explanatory. If there are any you don't understand, ask the person who made the drawings. Or at any library you can check out a large book called *Architectural Graphic Standards* (published in many editions by John Wiley & Sons), which lists all the commonly accepted abbreviations and symbols.

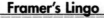

Framer's Lingo

A **floorplan** shows the general layout of the construction from overhead. A **framing plan** shows studs, joists, or rafters. The **elevation** shows the exterior of a construction, usually finished. **Section** shows a slice through an element of the construction. **Detail** shows a close-up of a part of the construction. The **trade drawing** shows the positions or plan of the electrical work, plumbing and heating and cooling.

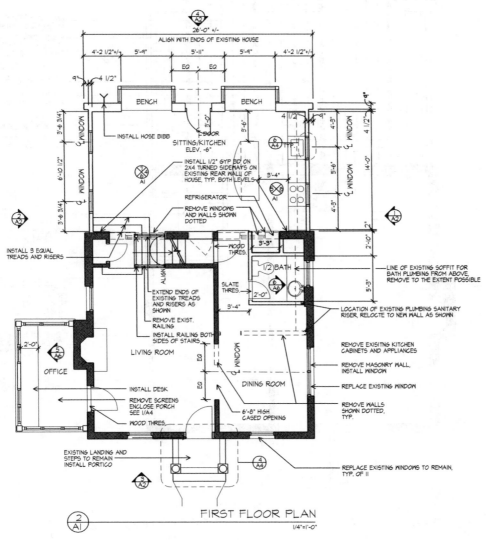

A sample floorplan

(Copyright © Linda Serabian, SOMA Architects)

Framing Plans

Framing plans are a framer's friend. Rather than showing the house or room layout as floorplans do, framing plans show the individual joists, studs, or rafters and exactly where they go.

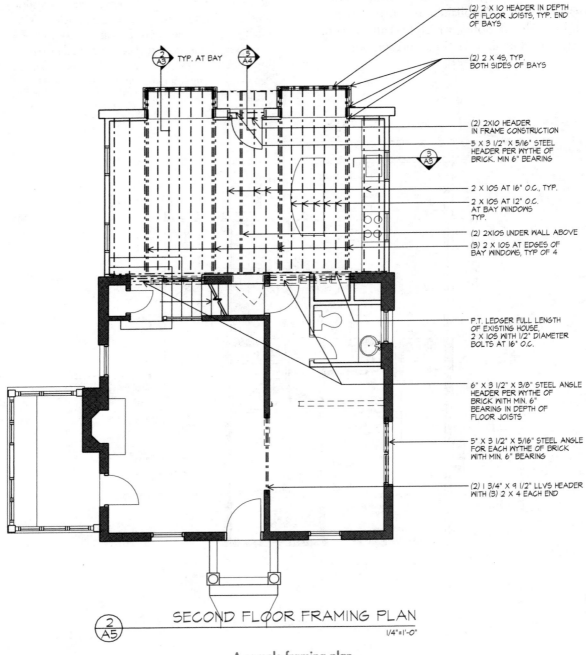

(2) 2 X 10 HEADER IN DEPTH OF FLOOR JOISTS, TYP. END OF BAYS

(2) 2 X 4S, TYP. BOTH SIDES OF BAYS

(2) 2X10 HEADER IN FRAME CONSTRUCTION

5 X 3 1/2" X 5/16" STEEL HEADER PER WYTHE OF BRICK. MIN 6" BEARING

2 X 10S AT 16" O.C., TYP.

2 X 10S AT 12" O.C. AT BAY WINDOWS TYP.

(2) 2X10S UNDER WALL ABOVE

(3) 2 X 10S AT EDGES OF BAY WINDOWS, TYP OF 4

P.T. LEDGER FULL LENGTH OF EXISTING HOUSE, 2 X 10S WITH 1/2" DIAMETER BOLTS AT 16" O.C.

6" X 3 1/2" X 3/8" STEEL ANGLE HEADER PER WYTHE OF BRICK WITH MIN. 6" BEARING IN DEPTH OF FLOOR JOISTS

5" X 3 1/2" X 5/16" STEEL ANGLE FOR EACH WYTHE OF BRICK WITH MIN. 6" BEARING

(2) 1 3/4" X 9 1/2" LLVS HEADER WITH (3) 2 X 4 EACH END

SECOND FLOOR FRAMING PLAN

1/4"=1'-0"

A sample framing plan.

(Copyright © Linda Serabian, SOMA Architects)

Elevations

Elevations are drawings that show a structure from the outside. Generally they show the finished work with its siding, roof, windows, and so forth in place. There can be framing elevations, which show the studs of a wall.

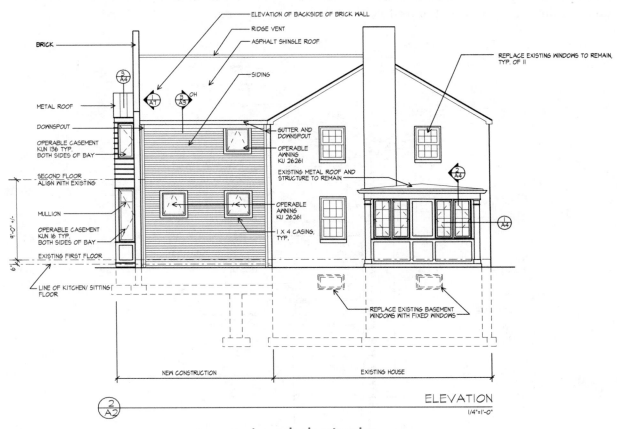

A sample elevation plan.

(Copyright© Linda Serabian, SOMA Architects)

Sections

Section drawings are also very helpful to framers. Sections show the cutaway of elements in other drawings, generally floorplans. A section, for example, might show how a vertical wall is to be constructed. The floorplan would indicate a section drawing with a section line plus a notation. The arrow of the section line would show the point of view of the section drawing. You then use the notation (usually letters, A, B, and so forth) to find the section drawing.

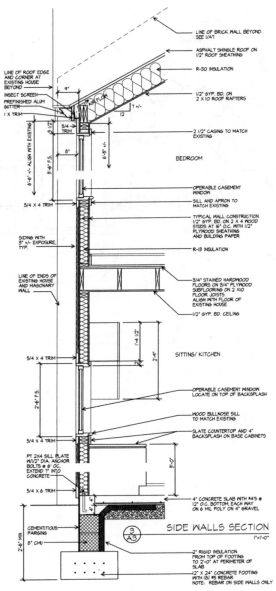

A sample section drawing.

(Copyright © Linda Serabian, SOMA Architects)

Detail Drawing

A *detail* drawing shows a particular object in greater detail, for example, how a rafter fits to the top of a wall. Normally, the scale is larger. Detail drawings are very helpful to you as a framer because you are the one making the lumber cuts and fitting everything together.

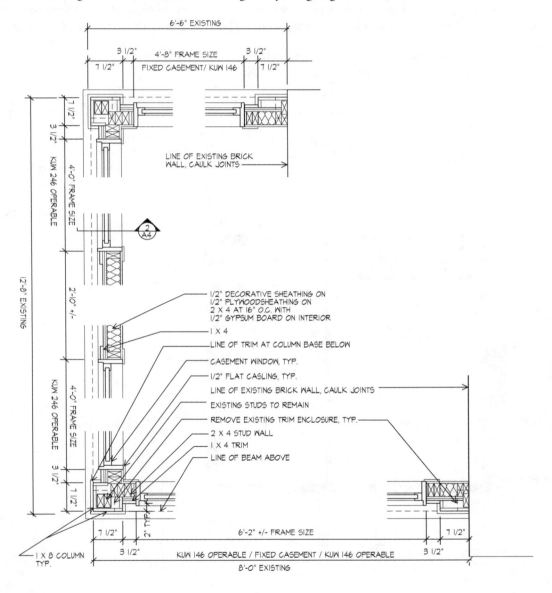

PLAN @ OFFICE
1"=1'-0"

Detail drawing.

(Copyright © Linda Serabian, SOMA Architects)

Trade Drawings

Plumbing, electrical wiring, and heating and cooling installing are three of what we call *trades*, short for "building trades." When a project involves these, additional floorplans are drawn that show where the elements of these utilities are meant to go. Most often they only show where the fixtures are to be placed and leave it up to the electrician or plumber to determine exactly where the pipes are to run. An exception is the heating and cooling drawing, which normally shows the location of air ducts.

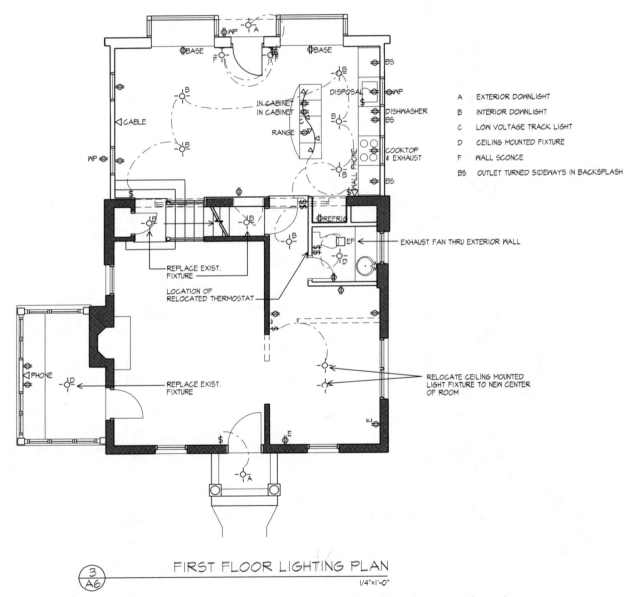

A EXTERIOR DOWNLIGHT
B INTERIOR DOWNLIGHT
C LOW VOLTAGE TRACK LIGHT
D CEILING MOUNTED FIXTURE
F WALL SCONCE
BS OUTLET TURNED SIDEWAYS IN BACKSPLASH

FIRST FLOOR LIGHTING PLAN

1/4"=1'-0"

A sample electrical drawing showing the location of light fixtures and switches.

(Copyright © Linda Serabian, SOMA Architects)

Codes

We could not go much further without a word about *building codes*. These city or county ordinances describe the minimum standards for construction. They assure that a roof is not going to fly off in a high wind and that a floor is not going to collapse. They vary community to community—a roof in Florida has to have stronger connections where the roof meets the exterior walls than a roof in Maine, where hurricanes are not seasonal events. Building codes dictate the size of beams, the dimensions of rafters, and the thickness of subflooring. They dictate the minimum size window in bedrooms (generally large enough for a firefighter to enter with an oxygen tank on his back) and that a fire-resistant door is needed between an attached garage and the rest of the house. They protect everyone. They assure that your project when built will be safe for you and that if you ever sell your property, that the construction will be safe for the new owner, as well.

If you are going to build anything that will be visible outside or that will be new inside, you need for the work to conform to the local building codes. The method for doing so is to take drawings of the project to the local building department. They will want to know where the project will be, how you are going to construct it, and approximately how much it will cost. They will examine your submission. If an architect has done the drawings, very likely the building department will see that the proposal meets the building codes and grant you a *building permit* once you pay a fee, which is normally linked to the estimated cost of the project.

When you receive your permit, the building department gives you a large stiff card that you must post where the project is to be built and which can be seen from the street. The card will have your name on it and the nature of the construction work. It is principally there to help inspectors find the project in order to do their *building inspections*.

> ### Framer's Lingo
> **Building codes**, or codes for short, are ordinances adopted by your city or county describing standards that construction must meet. Plumbers, electricians and heating and cooling installers have their own codes to meet. Once the local building department is satisfied the plans meet the building codes and you have paid a fee, it will grant you a **building permit**, or permit for short. A **building inspection** is an inspection performed by a building inspector to assure that the construction meets the standards of the building code.

Several aspects of the construction must be inspected, and in a certain order. The more complex the project, the more inspections. For example, before you can build foundation walls, an inspector has to inspect the footings to assure that they are below the local frost line. Before you can cover a stud wall with a finished wall covering, it has to be inspected to assure that it is made of 2×4s and not 2×2s. If an inspector sees something that is not up to code, he will make you do it over. If he sees that everything is up to code, you pass that inspection, and he gives you a paper to keep for proof. He files another copy at the building department. If an inspector sees that you have covered something over before he has inspected it, he can make you uncover it so he can see it. So don't make the mistake of going past the point of an inspection!

If electricians, plumbers, and heating and cooling installers will be working on your project, they will have to file for their own permits and call for inspections of their own work.

When you file for a permit, ask the building department what inspections they require and at what stage of the construction you are required to call for them. When you are certain that your work is up to code and ready for inspection, call the building department and schedule one. Sometimes this takes a couple of days, so call in advance.

The Least You Need to Know

◆ Framing is best done with a competent set of drawings, called plans.

◆ Plans have their own sign language, which framers should understand.

◆ Different kinds of plans show different aspects of the construction and can be very helpful to a framer.

◆ Building codes are requirements that construction has to meet.

◆ Building permits are required from the local building department before you can do any framing.

◆ Building inspections by building department inspectors are required to assure that the construction meets building codes.

In This Chapter

◆ Framing with different loads in mind

◆ Bearing and nonbearing walls

◆ Beams and joists versus rafters

◆ Notching and drilling joists and studs

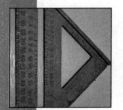

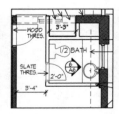

Chapter 7

Framing Engineering

Framing has to stand up to certain forces, called loads. If they did not, the building would sag or fall down. To understand why framing is designed the way it is, you should understand something about these forces. Also important to framing is the concept of bearing walls and nonbearing walls. The first type bears some portion of the weight of the building while the second does not, and these two are framed differently.

Joists, rafters, and beams can only span so far, depending on their depth, species, and grade. If you have had plans made by an architect or engineer, he or she has already made certain the spans meet the building code. But if you are making a design yourself, you need to find out what sizes of lumber or beams can span the distance you have in mind.

And last, you are going to be sorely tempted to make notches and holes in joists and studs. And that's all right, but you are limited to the size and location. In this chapter, you learn about loads, bearing and nonbearing walls, spans, notches, and holes. And you'll be a safer and better framer for it.

Different Kinds of Loads

If you are going to do framing, you're going to hear about loads, a general term for the stress, including weight, placed on a building and its structures. If a building's framing does not deal adequately with the loads, the framing is going to bend or sag; in the worse case, the building could collapse.

There are five kinds of loads:

- *Dead load* is the weight of the building empty, in other words the weight of the framing members, nails, shingles, siding, flooring, and so forth. It bears down on the framing members to the ground.

- *Live load* is the weight of persons in the building plus anything they bring in, that is, all the furniture, books, appliances, televisions, and so forth. Deck builders especially have to worry about live load for the time a homeowner might throw a party and have lots of people on that deck.

- *Shear load* is the force of the wind against the building attempting to move it off its foundation. Shear load might also be a force during an earthquake trying to move the house laterally.

- *Point load* is the weight of an especially heavy object, a refrigerator or hot tub, for example, on the flooring and framing just below.

- *Spread load* is the force attempting to push the walls apart and is caused by the rafters. The weight of the roof—and any snow that might build up on it—presses on the rafters, which then press outward on the tops of the walls upon which they rest. This force has to be countered with framing that assures the walls will not deflect outward.

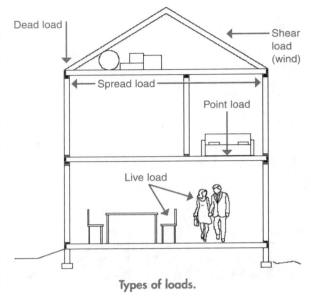

Types of loads.

(Copyright Ivan Chirinos)

Bearing and Nonbearing Walls

The framing of the building deals with these various loads mainly with the construction of the *bearing walls*. As the name implies, these walls bear the weight of the building and the things in it. Bearing walls are ones on which rafters rest or are walls that support beams or joists.

Nonbearing walls do not carry the weight of the building but merely divide space.

Framer's Lingo

Dead load is the weight of an empty building bearing down through its structure to the ground. **Live load** is the weight of objects brought into the house, including people. **Shear load** is the force of wind or earthquake trying to move the house laterally. **Point load** is the weight of a heavy object on the floor and framing below. **Spread load** is the force of the rafters pressing outward on the tops of the walls on which they rest.

Framer's Lingo

Bearing wall is a wall that bears the weight of the building toward the ground. A **nonbearing wall** is a wall that bears no more weight than itself and merely divides space.

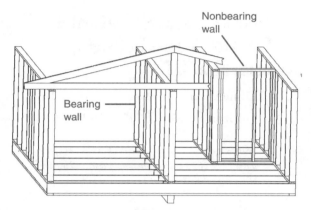

Bearing and nonbearing walls.

(Copyright Ivan Chirinos)

Sometimes it is difficult to determine if a wall is a bearing one or not. The walls at the end of a home on which only two rafters rest (think the end of a gable barn) are not bearing walls. They are not really bearing the weight of the roof; it is the exterior walls running between these two end walls that are bearing walls.

If a column or post in the basement supports a beam and a wall runs on the floor directly above the beam, that is a bearing wall.

Knowing whether a wall is a bearing one or not affects its framing. A bearing wall must have stronger framing over door and window openings to transfer the weight around these openings. If you are framing a new structure, the architect or engineer has figured this out for you, and the local building department has checked and approved his or her calculations for dealing with the loads of the house. You do not have to determine what is a bearing wall and what is not, and the framing plans will show you what pieces of lumber you need over doors and windows.

Knowing the difference between bearing and nonbearing walls when doing renovation work is critical. A nonbearing wall can be removed without worry. A bearing wall cannot be removed unless something just as strong is put in its place, a new beam, for example.

Beam, Joist, and Rafter Spans

Beams and joists hold up the house; rafters hold up the roof. Each of these spans distances, but the longer the distance the beefier the beam, joist, or rafter must be. Framing lumber has been analyzed and tested for a long time, and engineers have developed charts that show what to use under what circumstances. The charts are many and varied, segmented by load, species of wood, and grade of wood.

Owing to the importance of joist-supporting beams and of the complexity in determining what is sufficient in any circumstance, we'll forego specifics here. Suffice it to say that three 2×12s glued and nailed together to make a 6×12 beam can span a distance of about 10 $\frac{1}{2}$' under a bearing wall in a one-story home, 9' in a one-and-a-half-story home. If you are planning to use a beam to support a floor, consult your building department, architect, or engineer to assure that you are using one large enough for the job you have in mind.

Floor Joists

Determining floor joist size and spans is not as complicated as determining beam size and spans. The table that follows is a general guideline. But it is for grade #2 of one species of wood (Douglas Fir—South). Some grades of wood are stronger, some weaker. Consult your lumber yard to determine what they have available and your building department to determine exactly what dimension you can use for the spans you have in mind. The table presumes the joists will be set at 16" on center (O.C.) If you were to set them further apart, they would be limited to shorter spans.

Note also, that the spans in the table are the distances between the near sides of the supports. The joists themselves will have to be longer in order to have at least 1$\frac{1}{2}$" bearing on the post tops or sill plates upon which they are going to rest.

Table 7.1 Suitable Spans for Douglas Fir (South) Grade #2 16"O.C.

Dimension	2×8	2×10	2×12
Span	11'8"	14'11"	17'7"

Assuming a live load of 40 pounds per square foot and a dead load of 10 pounds per square foot.

(Source: Western Wood Products Association)

Table 7.2 Suitable Horizontal Spans for Douglas Fir (South) Grade #2 16"O.C.

Dimension	2×8	2×10	2×12
Horizontal Span	13'4"	16'3"	18'10"

Assuming a snow load of 40 pounds per square foot, a dead load of 10 pounds per square foot, and a pitch of no more than 3' rise in 12' horizontal.

(Source: Western Wood Products Association)

Rafters

Just as joists, rafters have to span distances and carry loads above them, though for rafters the load is the weight of the roof plus any snow that might pile up on it. Obviously, rafters in Colorado must be larger and span shorter distances than ones in Louisiana. Following is a general idea of what grade #2 Douglas Fir—South—lumber can span when used as rafters. The table assumes the rafters will be placed 16" O.C. It also presumes a fairly flat roof, one that rises less than 3' feet for every 12' of horizontal distance. The steeper the roof, the longer the permissible span for any given dimension of rafter.

Again, for your own particular location, roof pitch, available species of lumber, and spacing between rafters, consult your building department, architect, or engineer. And remember that the rafters will be longer than the horizontal span noted in the table. They will be extending at an angle, and thus need to be longer, and in most cases they also extend over and beyond the wall that supports their lower portion.

Notching and Drilling Limitations for Joists

Invariably, joists are notched. Sometimes they are notched even before they are hammered into place. For example, an architect or engineer may have called for the joist ends to be notched as they fit onto beams or sill plates.

After you put the joists into place, some of them are likely to be notched again or drilled with large holes. These are to accommodate pipes, ducts, or cables of some sort. But you have strict limitations on where you can place notches and holes and how large they can be. Violating these limitations will overly weaken the joist. In hole and notch limitation language, the broad dimension of the joist is called its "depth." The limitations here are general; your local building codes may have other specifications, so check before making holes and notches.

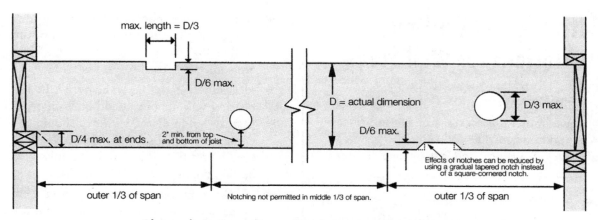

Observe limitations when making holes or notches in joists.

(Used Courtesy of Western Wood Products Association)

◆ A notch at an end of a joist where it rests on a beam cannot exceed $\frac{1}{4}$ of the joist depth.

◆ A hole cannot have a diameter larger than $\frac{1}{3}$ the joist depth.

◆ The edge of any hole cannot be closer than 2" to the upper or lower edge of the joist.

◆ Notches and holes are not permitted in the middle third of the length of a joist. This is where the joist is under the greatest stress.

◆ A notch cannot be longer than $\frac{1}{3}$ of the length of the joist.

◆ A notch not at an end cannot be deeper than $\frac{1}{6}$ of the depth of the joist.

Notching and Drilling Limitations for Wall Studs

Wall studs, like joists, are often notched or drilled through with holes. And, as with joists, you have limitations on the size and location of holes and notches. The following are general guidelines. Your local codes may have different limitations.

◆ A notch in an exterior or bearing wall stud can be no more than $1/4$ the width of the stud ($7/8$" for a 2×4, $1 3/8$" for a 2×6, which are sometimes used in exterior walls)

◆ A notch in a nonbearing wall can by no more than 40 percent of the width of the stud ($1 7/16$" for a 2×4, 1" for a 2×3, which are sometimes used for nonbearing walls)

◆ Holes in 2×4s should be centered. In a bearing wall, a hole should be no more than $1 7/16$" in diameter. They should come no closer than $5/8$" to an edge. A hole larger than this may be permissible in certain conditions; check your local codes.

◆ Nonbearing walls can have holes in them up to $2 1/8$" in diameter, centered and no closer than $5/8$" to an edge.

◆ If a stud has a hole, it cannot have a notch at the same height.

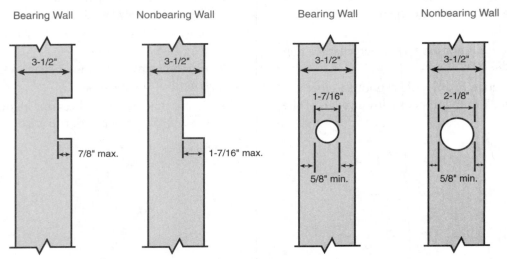

Observe limitations when making notches or holes in studs.

(Used Courtesy of Western Wood Products Association)

The Least You Need to Know

◆ Structures have to withstand different kinds of forces, called loads. Proper framing allows the structure to do so.

◆ The principal weight of a building is carried by bearing walls. Nonbearing walls do not carry weight from above and merely divide space.

◆ Joists, rafters, and beams are sized to span specific distances. Building codes specify those distances.

◆ You may cut notches and holes in joists and studs, but only in certain locations and only up to specified dimensions.

In This Chapter

- ◆ The need to make good marks for cuts
- ◆ Using measuring tools to mark for cuts
- ◆ The proper use of hand saws
- ◆ Using circular saws for various kinds of cuts
- ◆ Using a power miter saw

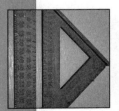
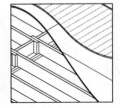

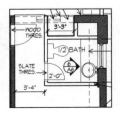

Chapter **8**

Measuring and Sawing

Framing begins with measuring and marking. Then it moves to sawing. That's what this chapter is all about. You must make the correct measurements, mark them correctly, and saw along them accurately. Only then will you get the pieces that will properly create the bones of the structure you are going to build.

There's a good old carpenter's saying: "Measure twice, cut once." When you make a wrong cut, you'll understand the wisdom of this statement. Take the time to measure properly, mark accurately, and then cut once. You'll be a happier framer.

Marking and Measuring

I like to think of framing as a kind of geometry project and also a kind of puzzle project. It is geometry in the sense that each straight line must have an exact length. It is a puzzle project in that all the parts must fit together perfectly for the whole to work.

This is where marking and measuring come in. Being sloppy at either is going to cause problems. If a window opening is not framed properly, its angles might not be right angles and then a window will not fit properly. Construction is a skill of exactitude.

Making Your Mark

Mainly framing carpenters mark with pencils. But a pencil line has thickness, and so do saw blades. You must take both into account. The mark of a carpenter's pencil may be $1/16$" across, and a heavy-duty saw blade may be $1/8$" across.

When you mark for sawing, mark on what is called the waste side of the wood.

Good side | Waste side

Making a pencil mark.

When you make the saw cut, run the blade up through the pencil line, keeping all of the thickness of the blade on the waste side.

Good side | Waste side

Cutting along a mark.

When you are marking for another line, for example, a mark 16" down from the end of a 2×4, do not make a single line to designate the spot.

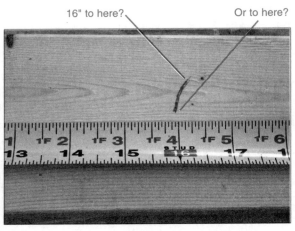

16" to here? | Or to here?

Do not mark with a single slanted line.

When making a mark for a distance, mark a V rather than a single line. The tip of the V shows the true distance you want.

Use a V when marking for distance.

Accurate Measuring

Measuring is critical to framing carpentry. If two studs are meant to hold up the piece of wood across a window opening and one is $1/8$" shorter than the other, the shorter one is not doing its job. In fact, it is not doing a job at all. In carpentry, even the smallest distances are critical.

Use your measuring tool accurately. And mark accurately. These are the beginnings of good framing projects.

Using a Folding Rule

To measure an inside distance with a folding rule, unfold enough sections until within 6" of the inside distance. Hold the rule to one side of the distance to be measured, then slide the metal insert all the way out to the other side. Read the measure where the metal insert meets the end of the folding rule. Add this distance to the distance from the end of the folding rule back to the where it is touching the other side.

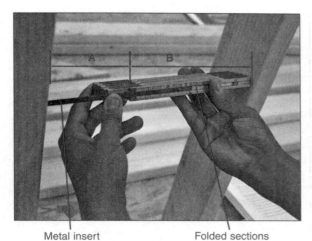

Metal insert   Folded sections

Measuring an inside distance with a folding rule.

Using a Measuring Tape

To measure along a piece of lumber with a measuring tape, hook the end hook at the end of the lumber piece and draw back the measuring tape's case, extracting the tape; the locking mechanism that keeps the tape extended is automatically engaged. Hold the case with one hand to keep tension along the tape toward the case—this is to make sure the hook is firmly against the end of the piece of lumber and that the rivets there have allowed the tape to shift the thickness of the hook toward the case. Designate the measurement with a V mark.

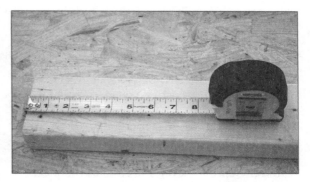

How to use a measuring tape for a proper measurement on lumber.

To use a measuring tape for an inside distance, hold the far side of the case end against one end of the interior space. Extend the tape to the other end. Make sure the hook is firmly against the other end of the space so that the hook has shifted along the rivets toward the case; this accounts for the thickness of the hook. The interior distance is the reading on the tape at the opening of the case plus the length of the case. This length is normally marked on the lower edge of the case itself and for a 25' measuring tape is usually 3".

How to use a measuring tape for a proper inside measurement on lumber. Add A and B to get the right measurement.

Finger Tips

Sometimes the hook does not want to stay in place, and you don't have a helper to hold it. A remedy is to press the point of an awl through a hole in the end hook to keep it in place.

To measure from an upright piece of lumber, catch the end hook on one edge of the piece and pull the case away, keeping tension on the end hook so it will not fall down. If you find it difficult keeping the end hook there and you do not have a helper to hold it, keep it in place with an awl.

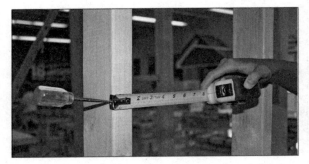

To hold the end of a measuring tape where it might otherwise fall, press the point of an awl through a hole in the hook.

Using a Chalk Line

To use a chalk line, hook the metal end over the edge of whatever you are marking, and, holding the chalk line housing, walk away from the end. The string is drawn out of the housing covered with chalk, usually blue, but sometimes yellow or white. When you reach the mark for the other end of the straight line you want to establish, pull the string taut and hold your end to the mark. Have someone about halfway between the two ends pull the middle of the string straight up then let it go. The string flies down and marks the wood with a straight chalk mark.

Finger Tips

When I was first shown how to use a chalk line, I was asked to be the person to press his thumb on the far end of the string to the correct mark. This was not difficult, but I took some pride in my accomplishment while I waited for someone else to snap the string. But rather than observing the closest person to the middle of the string merely lift it up and let it go, a series of calls and turnings of necks ensued. "Henry! Chalk line's ready!" Whereupon Henry turned to look at it and said, "No, let Chet do it." This was followed by, "Chet! Chalk line's ready!" Whereupon Chet put down his hammer and strolled over to look at the string. He looked all around, and then when satisfied that all was ready, he snapped the string, and everyone went back to work.

The running joke is that the senior member of the team, the "boss," has the honor of snapping the string if he is close. He can do it or delegate the task. It's all a bunch of nonsense, of course, but it does make for an excuse to take a 20-second break to get the senior carpenter over to do the snapping.

When using a chalk line, don't let the line touch the surface before someone snaps it. If you are careless, you'll end up with a number of lines and a mess of chalk on the surface that is meant to have one clear and straight line of chalk.

Also when you are ready to snap the chalk line, be careful to pull the string perpendicular to the surface you are marking. Pulling it and letting it go at a slant could result in a bowed or smeared line. Both are bad.

Using a Steel Tape

To measure with a steel tape from the end of a piece of lumber, hook the end of the tape to the end of the piece of lumber. Then back up with the case until you expose enough steel tape to make the measurement.

To measure from the surface of a board, hook the end of the steel tape over a nail. Set the nail so that the far end of the loop rests on the line from which the measurement is to begin. And slant the nail away from the direction of the measurement so the hook does not ride up the nail; it would have the tendency to do this if the nail is at ground level and you walk away from the nail with the case at the height of your hip.

When beginning a measurement along a board, slip the loop over a nail. Set the nail so that the far end of the loop aligns with the mark that is the beginning of the measurement. Slant the nail so that the loop does not ride up it.

Using a Combination Square

A combination, square is useful for a number of functions. To measure a distance from the edge of a piece of lumber, shift the blade so that one of its inch marks aligns with the long straight edge of the body. Position the long straight edge of the body against the edge of the piece of lumber. Use the aligned inch mark as a Zero Mark and measure from it to the distance you want to measure. Make a V mark there.

Use a combination square to mark a piece of lumber for a rip cut. Imagine you want to rip a 4"-wide board exactly 2" from one edge. Move the blade of the combination square until the 2" mark aligns with the edge of the body. This means that the end of the blade would be exactly 2" out from the body. Place the body alongside the edge of the board and hold a pencil alongside the end of the blade. With one hand, draw the body down the edge of the board, and with the other, hold the pencil firmly against the end of the blade. The result is a straight line down the board exactly 2" away from the edge along with the body moved.

This technique can be a little difficult to get used to because you must hold the body firmly against the edge of the board while still drawing it along, and you have to hold the pencil end firmly against the end of the blade while the blade is moving. In addition, you must be sure that the board does not move. For the latter, if you cannot do it any other way, clamp it to a work surface.

To use a combination square for marking for a rip cut, set the blade so that its end is exactly as far from the body edge as the rip cut mark is meant to be from the board edge. Draw the body of the combination square along the board edge while holding a pencil to the blade end.

Cross Cuts

To mark lumber for cross cuts, that is, across their lengths, use a combination square or a triangular square. Hold the body of the combination square or the lipped edge of the triangular square to the edge of the piece of lumber to be cut. Shift the combination square edge or triangular square edge to the point of your V mark. Hold the combination square or triangular square steady with one hand, and draw a line down the edge through the V mark with the other.

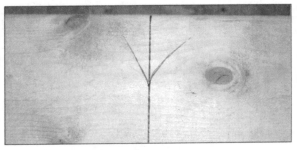

A line drawn with a combination square or triangular square directly through the point of a V mark for a cross cut.

Making Saw Cuts

Framing carpenters normally cut lumber to length, and these cuts are called cross cuts. But we framers must be familiar with several other cuts because they do come up. So onward we go.

◆ *Rip cut.* I have explained a rip cut before. This cut is made along the length of a board or piece of lumber to make it skinnier than it was originally. In some respects this cut is a pain, especially if you are making a long rip cut with a hand saw. A rip cut is best handled by a power saw. But you must firmly secure the piece being cut to a work surface.

◆ *Miter cut.* A miter cut is one cutting at an angle across the face.

◆ *Bevel cut.* A bevel cut is one cutting across the board at an angle to the edge.

◆ *Combination cut.* A combination cut combines a miter cut and a bevel cut in one cut.

◆ *Pocket cut.* A pocket cut cuts through the edge of a board to make a notch.

Framer's Lingo

A **miter cut** is a cut angled across the face of the wood. A **bevel cut** is a cut angled across the edge of the wood. A **combination cut** is a cut that is both a miter cut and a bevel cut. A **pocket cut** is a cut that creates a notch.

A rip cut.

A miter cut.

A bevel cut.

A combination cut.

A pocket cut.

Using a Hand Saw to Make a Cross Cut

Even though framers have power saws, they end up doing a lot of hand sawing. Sometimes the pieces are too small to cut with a power saw. Sometimes the power saw is being used by someone else. In any event, you have to learn to do hand sawing right.

So let me tell you how to make a simple cross cut with a hand saw. Then I'll describe how to make more complicated cuts, for which you'll want to use the power saws.

Heads!

Never try to wedge the blade guard of a circular saw into the open position. As you move the blade forward cutting through a piece of lumber, the blade guard naturally retracts. But it is meant to spring back into place nearly covering all of the blade's teeth when the cut is finished. The quick retracting action is meant not only to protect your fingers and any other part of your body but also to allow you to place the saw down on a flat surface without having the teeth touch that surface.

To set up a cross cut, do the following:

1. Set the piece of wood firmly on a work surface. The wood must have enough support so that it won't move or shift.

2. Mark the piece of wood for a cross cut as described in the previous section on "Marking and Measuring." Check the piece of wood for steadiness. If you think it might shift during cutting, clamp it to the work surface.

3. Align the teeth of the saw to cut along the marked line so that the cut made by the teeth of the saw are all on the "waste side" of the wood, that is, so that when the waste piece falls away, the remaining "good piece" will be exactly the length you want it to be.

4. Create a starter *kerf* along the edge of the wood. A kerf is a small groove made by the saw's teeth. One way to do this accurately is to hold a piece of 2×4 with sharp right-angled edges along the marking line, press down on the 2×4 piece, and place the saw blade against the 2×4 piece.

Framer's Lingo

A **kerf** is the groove made by a saw blade.

The 2×4 piece, of course, is meant to be a guide. It steadies the saw teeth on the measuring line, and its right-angle thickness rising above the surface of the board to be cut is a guide to holding the saw blade perfectly vertical.

Some carpenters dispense with the 2×4 scrap and use the end of their thumb or the knuckle of their thumb to steady the blade of the saw at this stage. But the technique is risky. As you draw the blade back in the first couple of strokes, the blade can jump out of the kerf you make and cut into your thumb.

5. Draw the blade of the saw back slowly to make a small kerf. Lift the blade off the board, reposition it as before, and draw it back again. Do this about five times to make a deep kerf in the edge of the board. Then you can dispense with the 2×4 guide.

6. Place your free hand on the piece to be cut and begin sawing in earnest. Use long strokes. Do the cutting on the down stroke. Check that you are holding the blade perfectly vertical. You should not have to use a lot of pressure; a sharp saw cuts without much effort.

7. When you approach the end of the cut, there is a danger the waste portion will fall away, tearing with it a portion from the underside of the good piece. Reach across the top of the saw to grip the waste piece and support it until the cut is done.

If the board you are cutting has a good face and a bad face, place the good face upward. This is because a handsaw creates more splintered wood on the bottom face of the wood it is cutting than on the top face. If you are cutting studs, joists, or rafters that no one will see, this is of no concern, but if you are cutting door or window trim, you need to follow these instructions.

Hold a piece of 2x4 to the measuring line. Hold the saw at a 45-degree angle to the board to be cut.

Note that when you use a circular saw, you do the opposite. A circular saw produces cuts into the wood at the bottom face and does more splintering where it comes out on the upper face. When using a circular saw, place a "good face" down.

Using a Circular Saw

Besides his hammer, a circular saw is a framing carpenter's best friend; it slices rapidly and at a right angle through 2× lumber. Note that a circular saw blade's teeth face forward; they cut on the upstroke from the bottom of the piece being cut.

Before using a circular saw, carefully read the owner's manual. Follow all the safety guidelines. Familiarize yourself with the tool's safety features and other parts.

Heads!

Make sure that the blade you are using is fit for the job. For example, do not use a plywood blade to cut solid lumber.

When you change a blade, always unplug the saw. The blade goes onto a piece called the arbor. A wrench, sometimes supplied with the circular saw, tightens and loosens the retaining bolt over the blade and onto the arbor. The blade and arbor are held stationary while you do this by means of a braking mechanism you push with your fingers. When you put on a new blade, make sure the teeth are facing forward. When you are finished, the blade should be flat and tight against the arbor.

When tightening a circular saw blade, hold the arbor braking mechanism so the blade and arbor cannot move.

Straight Cuts

To make a straight cut with a circular saw blade, follow these instructions:

1. Begin with the saw unplugged. Check that the base plate is exactly at a right angle to the blade. An indicator mark on the base plate shows this. When the mark aligns with its counterpart on the body of the saw, tighten the angle adjustment knob, which secures the position of the base plate to the body. If you are concerned the mark may be inaccurate, turn the saw over, hold a triangular square to the base plate and blade to check if they are at a true right angle.

Angle adjustment knob   Base plate   "Right angle" mark

If you are going to make a straight cross cut, check that the base plate "right angle" mark aligns with its corresponding mark on the body. Tighten the angle adjustment knob that secures the angle position of the base plate.

2. Pull back on the blade guard—using the small handle that allows you to do this. Place the saw so that the base plate rests on the face of the piece of lumber you are about to cut and that the blade descends along the edge of the piece. Adjust the height of the base plate—another knob, generally at the back, allows you to do this—so that the lowest point of the blade is about $1/4$" lower than the bottom face of the piece you are about to cut. This is the optimal depth for the blade. Tighten the knob that adjusts the height of the base plate.

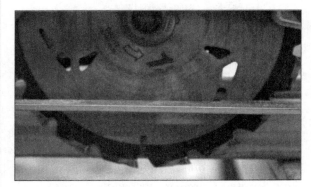

To check the depth of the blade, retract the blade guard and hold the saw so that the blade descends alongside the edge of the piece about to be cut. The optimal depth for the blade is for its lowest point to descend about $1/4$" below the surface of the wood.

3. Mark the piece of lumber for the cut. Place the piece on a firm work surface and make sure that it is steady. Clamp it if your nonsaw hand is not going to be able to adequately secure it. Plug in the saw's cord. Put on eye protection. Use ear protection if you want.

4. Set the front of the base plate on the piece of lumber to be cut. Look over the body of the saw and align the front of the blade with the cut mark, but do not let the blade touch the wood.

Align the blade with the cut line.

5. Turn on the saw—sometimes it takes two actions to do this, pressing a button with your thumb and pulling back on a trigger with your index finger. When the blade reaches full speed, move it into the wood. As you do so, the blade guard will retract automatically. Move the saw forward at a reasonable speed; too fast will jam the blade and possibly cause a kickback, too slowly and the blade will merely rub against the head of the cut, overheating and getting dull.

Finger Tips

As with a hand saw, there is a danger as the saw nears the end of the cut that the waste piece will fall away, taking with it a thick splinter of the good piece. To avoid this, slow down just before the end of the cut; then speed up to cut quickly through the remainder. This cuts the last fraction of an inch so fast that the waste piece does not have a chance to pull away some of the good piece.

6. Release the trigger. The blade should stop very quickly. Lift the saw away, and the blade guard should descend again, covering most of the teeth of the blade. When the blade is stopped and the blade guard is down, set the saw down on a work surface.

Some carpenters like to use a triangular square when they make a cross cut with a circular saw. It steadies the blade of the saw and assures a straight cut. To make a cut in this way, align the blade of the circular saw with the cut mark on the piece you are cutting. With your other hand, slide a triangular square until its straight edge touches the base plate of the saw. Keep the triangular square in place by pressing forward on it; the lip on your side will keep it in position. Turn on the saw, and move it forward making sure the edge of the base plate stays in contact with the triangular square.

Using a triangular square to make a cross cut with a circular saw.

If a piece of wood does not have the proper support during a cut, one or both parts will sag. The result will be a bind on the blade of the saw. If it is a power saw and the blade slows or stops, the force of the motor will try to jerk the body of the saw back against your hand. This is called *kickback*.

Ideally, a piece to be cut will have little waste. Fully support it on a sawhorse or work surface and allow the small waste section to hang slightly out over the sawhorse end or work surface edge.

Under no circumstances should you support a work piece between two sawhorses and cut between them because the work piece will sag and bind the blade. Or, if the saw horses are close together and the work piece long, as the piece is almost cut through, the two pieces will want to fall on the far sides of the sawhorses, rising where the blade is and binding it in this fashion.

If you are cutting a plywood panel and the waste piece is very large, have a helper support the far side of the waste piece—keeping his fingers well clear of the saw—once you are halfway finished with the cut.

Framer's Lingo

Kickback is the motion against a power saw's housing when the blade binds in the wood. The motion is sudden, often powerful, and back toward the user. Kickback also occurs when a drill's bit binds in the hole it is drilling; the drill housing jerks in a twist in the user's hand.

Rip Cuts

Rip cuts are cuts along a piece of lumber's length. You can mark for a rip cut using a combination square.

Rip cuts of more than a few inches are tedious with a hand saw and tricky using a circular saw because you must support the length of the piece you are cutting. You can have a lumber yard do the cut for you, or do the rip cut on a table saw if you have one.

To make a rip cut with a circular saw blade, do the following:

1. Secure the piece firmly to a work surface. Clamping it is the best way.

2. Check that the circular saw blade protrudes no more than $1/4$" below the thickness of the piece you are cutting.

3. Proceed as with a cross cut.

You may have a guide on your circular saw base plate that assists in rip cuts, or sometimes you can buy one to fit your base plate. The guide adjusts for the width of the cut. An outer piece rides along the outer edge of the piece being cut, keeping the spinning blade a constant distance away. Secure the guide firmly in place, and then keep moderate pressure away from the outer piece so it holds continually to the edge of the piece you are cutting.

Panel Cuts

When you want to cut a piece of plywood or other panel, you are likely cutting through 4' or 8' at a time. You can do this by snapping a chalk line on the plywood, supporting it well on two sawhorses, and cutting freehand, that is, guiding the blade along the cut line just by eye. Normally, this gives a straight enough cut for framing purposes.

Alternatively, you can clamp a piece of straight wood to the plywood such that the blade aligns with and cuts along the cut line. Some carpenters who do lots of panel cuts go farther than this and make a simple jig that makes the job simpler; the jig is sometimes called a shooter board. For a 4' jig:

1. Take 10" of plywood or similar material with one 4' long straight edge. Glue or nail on top a 4' piece that is 2" wide so that the 10" piece is exposed on one side slightly wider than the width of your saw's base plate.

2. Clamp the combined piece to a work surface.

3. Set the motor side of the circular saw up against the narrow piece and saw off the excess of the lower piece. There should be enough of the original 10" on the other side of the 2" piece to allow for clamping.

4. Now, when you have to cut across 4' of panel, clamp the jig so that the "blade side" of the jig aligns with the cut line. Then place the circular saw on the jig and make the cut.

For a panel cut, mark a clear line and make sure the work piece is not going to move. Use a jig if you have one to make a more accurate and swifter cut.

Miter Cuts

To make a miter cut, do the following:

1. Draw the cut line across the face of the work piece.

2. Secure the work piece to a work surface so the waste piece can fall free.

3. Align the circular saw as for a cross cut. Owing to the angle at which the blade will meet the work piece, the blade guard may not rise as it does for a cross cut.

4. As you begin the cut, reach for the blade guard handle, and gently pull it up as the blade enters the wood. Release the blade guard handle as soon as the blade is most of the way into the wood.

Heads!

When using a power miter saw, make sure the blade guard is operating smoothly and properly. Do not cross your arms across the blade; that is, do not hold a piece on the right side of the blade with your left hand. If the piece you are cutting is so long that it wants to dip at the far end and rise where the saw blade is, support it at the far end with blocks of wood. Always hold the piece you are cutting firmly against the back fence of the saw so the piece cannot move. Keep your hands well away from the blade.

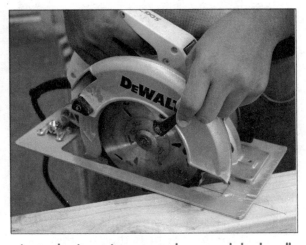

As you begin a miter cut, reach over and slowly pull up the blade guard as the blade enters the wood. Release the blade guard when the blade has about halfway entered the wood.

Bevel Cuts

A bevel cut saws through the wood at an angle to the edge. To do this with a circular saw, you have to tilt the base plate.

To do this, complete the following steps:

1. Unplug the saw. Loosen the base plate thumb screw. Tilt the base plate to the angle you want. A crude angle scale is attached to the base plate. The scale normally has markings for 15, 30, and 45 degrees, but the base plate can be set to any angle between 0 and 45 degrees (0 on the scale means a right angle between the blade and the base plate). For fine adjustments, set a T-bevel to the proper angle you want, and use it to set the proper angle by holding it to the blade and the base plate at the same time. You can see why you have to unplug the saw for this!

Adjust the base plate to the angle for the cut. Adjust the depth of the blade through the base plate. Plug in the saw and make the cut.

2. When you have the proper angle set, tighten the base plate thumb screw. Because the blade will be cutting through the work piece at an angle, more of the blade has to be exposed below the base plate in order to cut all the way through the wood. The same rule applies: the blade should protrude no more than about $\frac{1}{4}$" beyond the bottom of the work piece.

3. Hold the saw up to the end of the work piece. Use the thumb screw on the back of the circular saw to adjust the depth the blade passes through the base plate; then tighten the thumb screw.

4. Clamp the work piece to a work surface. Plug in the saw. Line up the cut as for a cross cut. Take care that the blade aligns with the pencil mark; owing to the slant of the blade, the alignment is slightly different as seen against the base plate. Some circular saws have a point on the base plate that is meant to align with the pencil mark for a 45° bevel cut.

5. When you have made the proper adjustment, proceed to make the cut as if it were a cross cut.

For a bevel cut, align the blade with the pencil mark. Then make the cut as for a cross cut.

Combination Cuts

Combination cuts combine an angle cut and a bevel cut:

1. Draw the pencil mark cut line across the face of the work piece.

2. Set the saw as if for a bevel cut.

3. Make the cut.

Plunge Cuts

Sometimes you might have to cut a hole in plywood or similar panel, say for ducting or something that has to pass through the plywood. For this, you make a *plunge cut* with a circular saw:

Framer's Lingo

A **plunge cut** is a cut with a circular saw through the middle of a plywood panel.

1. Mark the cut lines. Properly secure the work piece so it will not move. With the saw unplugged, adjust the base plate so the blade will cut no more than 1/4" through the work piece. Plug in the saw.

2. Set the front of the base plate on the work piece so that the blade aligns over the cut line. Turn on the saw.

3. Pull up slowly on the blade guard while pivoting the saw downward. As the blade begins to cut into the wood, move the saw forward along the cut line. Lower the saw until the whole base plate is on the work piece. Cut along the cut line. When you approach a corner, stop the blade before you lift up the saw.

Making a plunge cut.

A portion of the cut line will not be cut. Don't back up a saw to do this. Complete one portion of the cut; stop the saw; draw it out; and then realign it for the portion not cut previously. Even doing this, there may be small portions near the corners that you will have to finish with a hand saw.

Power Miter Saw Cuts

Power miter saw cuts are pretty straight forward:

1. Hold the work piece firmly against the back fence, aligning the cut mark with the blade above it.

2. Turn on the saw, and bring it down, slicing through the work piece.

3. If the work piece is so long that it wants to drop at the far end and rise under the saw blade, support it at the far end with a block of wood or with a helper.

Miter saw blades can pivot to make miter cuts. Some can tilt on their pivot arms to make bevel cuts.

The Least You Need to Know

◆ Measure cuts so that the pencil line is on the "waste side" of the wood you are cutting.

◆ Do not mark a distance with a single line but rather with a V mark, the point of the V being the exact distance measured.

◆ Use folding rules or measuring tapes to measure inside distances.

◆ Use a combination square to mark for rip cuts.

◆ Become familiar with all the parts of a circular saw. Read and observe the safety rules.

◆ Consider making a jig for long panel cuts.

In This Chapter

- ◆ Techniques for effective nailing
- ◆ Ways framers join wood
- ◆ Using glue
- ◆ Taking joints apart

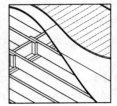

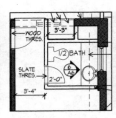

Chapter **9**

Joining

Once you've finished the measuring, marking, and sawing, it's time to put the pieces together. For framers, that means nailing. Everyone thinks he knows how to hammer a nail, but it's actually a skill you get better at the more you do it. After years on the job, framers hold their hammers in a certain way and hammer their nails with a special efficiency and grace. They also have some techniques for making toenailing—sometimes a frustrating chore—go right the first time.

In this chapter, we also look at other ways wood can be joined, including using construction adhesive from a caulking gun. And we look, too, at how to take joints apart because sometimes it's just gotta happen.

Nailing Techniques

Remember your first hammer? It was probably a child's plastic toy, and you used it to hammer squares through square holes and triangles through triangular holes in a little plastic work bench. This taught shape recognition and hand-eye coordination. Maybe you learned how to hold a hammer and drive a nail in 4H club or Scouts. So what's to hammering—it's not rocket science. No it's not. But neither is driving a car, and from a distance all that looks like is a person sitting in a seat and holding a steering wheel.

Actually hammering is somewhat complicated, and, believe it or not, the longer you do it, the better you get. If you don't believe me, go to a construction site and watch a carpenter hit nails. It's like watching a pianist—anyone can bang the keys, but a pianist knows just where to make the motion and just how much pressure to apply. Good nailing is more a matter of coordination than of power or strength.

Of course, nailing begins with a hammer. As mentioned in Chapter 1, you should buy a hammer that is comfortable for you, not too light, not too heavy, and with a comfortable grip. Grasp the hammer handle at the end, but not higher because you lose leverage that way. Wrap your fingers and thumb all the way around the handle.

Look around so you won't hit anyone or anything, and take a light swing. Hammering is a coordinated motion of the shoulder, the arm, and the wrist; the last is a quick rotation of the wrist that is meant to land the face of the hammer squarely on the head of the nail. You want to learn how to do it so that you can pound plenty of nails in an hour and not feel fatigued by it. No one is born knowing how to correctly swing a hammer. You must practice over and over until you get the right feel for it and the right motion.

Heads!

When you are nailing, wear eye protection. An imperfectly hit nail can go flying.

Face Nailing

Face nailing is the easiest and most common form of nailing. The object is to hit the nail head flat on. If you hit at an angle, you risk having the hammer head slip off and bending the nail.

To start a nail, hold it between your fingers, and give it enough of a tap so it can stand on its own in the wood. Hold it near the head rather than the point so if the nail slips out of your grip, the hammer will cause less pain to your fingers. After the nail is standing on its own in the wood, touch the hammer face to the nail head. This gives your muscles "memory"; they'll want to come back to the same place for your swing and guide the hammer face to the correct position. Make your first strike a light one and succeeding ones stronger until you ease up when the nail head is near the surface of the wood.

Professionals can drive a nail in just a couple of blows. You can be less ambitious. Using five swings to drive a nail is fine; it's the pulling out of bent nails that takes up time.

In trim, or finish, carpentry, it's a sin to leave a mark on the wood from the head of the hammer. In framing carpentry, who cares—no one's going to see it. But when you leave marks, it means you are not coming down squarely on the nail head or you are using too much force on the last blow.

A good way to practice face nailing is to take a box of nails and hammer them into an old tree stump. If you don't have an old tree stump in the backyard, then take some scraps of lumber, place them flat, and practice on those.

It may happen that you have to start a nail with one hand or in an awkward location. Don't worry; I have a remedy for this situation. Place the head of the nail against the flat side of the hammer's head. Hold it there with your hand wrapped around this part of the hammer. Then swing the nail point toward the wood. This should stick it into the wood enough that it can stay there on its own. Pull the hammer away, turn the head's face to the nail, and give the nail head a tap. Then give heavier blows to drive the nail home.

Hit the nail squarely on the head.

Hold the nail head against the flat portion of the hammer head below the striking face. With the point of the nail aimed at the wood, swing the hammer and nail forward, sticking the nail into the wood.

Toenailing

Toenailing is nailing near the end of one board into an adjoining board. It normally happens when you cannot nail through the face of the adjoining board into the end of the first—that would be face nailing. Toenailing gets its name on account of nailing near the end—the toe—of one board. As it happens, a lot of toenailing occurs down around your own toes, too.

Framer's Lingo

Face nailing is driving a nail perpendicular to the wood. **Toenailing** is driving a nail at an angle near the end of one piece of wood into a second piece of wood.

Let's say you have to toenail a stud to a 2×4 on the floor. To toenail, tap the nail in about $^3/_4$" up from the end of the stud and angle it between 30° and 45° from vertical. Then hammer down on the nail sending it at its angle through the bottom of the stud into the horizontal 2×4.

You've probably already spotted some difficulties. One is that the stud is vertical, and it's hard to start a nail on a vertical surface. True. One way around this is to create a sort of "frown" dent where you want the nail point to go. Make this with a blow from the hammer face.

Another way to start a nail for toe nailing is to tap it in perpendicular as if for face nailing. Then you cock it upward to the correct angle. It takes a bit of experience to know how far to tap it in—too shallow and it will come out when you cock it upward; too deep and it is too hard to pry upward at all.

For toenailing, angle the nail at about a 30-degree angle.

Another bane of toenailers is the fact that when the nail is tapped in and you give the head a whack or two, the board into which it is tapped shifts off line, which is not surprising because the nail has not penetrated to the second piece of wood yet. You need a way to hold the first piece in place. There are a couple methods for solving this problem. One is to have a helper hold the piece. A second is to go to the other side of the piece, where you are likely to have to drive another toenail in any case, and angle in a temporary nail where the two pieces meet but mostly into the lower piece. This nail stops the lateral movement of the first piece. Once the first toenail is completely hammered in, the angled nail can be removed, or in fact, shifted up $3/4$" and used as the toenail on that side.

When toenailing studs, stop the motion of the studs away from the toenailing by using a temporary spacer block you move from space to space.

Clinching

Framers are sometimes required to join two boards without any possibility of slipping. This may occur when making scaffolding or building a form for concrete. A means of joining in this manner is called clinching. The nails are hammered all the way through both pieces so that the shanks protrude an inch or more. Then these protruding shanks are hammered flat.

To stop the motion of a piece being toenailed, set a temporary nail opposite where the first toenail will be placed. The nail is set into the lower piece but angles up to stop any motion by the upper piece.

A third method is good where you are toenailing studs along a wall. After you have one stud in place, cut a piece of 2×4 the exact distance meant for the spacing between studs. Set it down against the first stud, and it blocks movement of the second stud.

To clinch two pieces of wood, hammer nails all the way through both boards; then hammer over the protruding portions.

Other Nailing Tips

When nailing near the end of a piece of wood, do not place two nails into the same grain because they might split the wood. Instead stagger them.

When nailing near the end of a board, stagger nails so that the board does not split.

When nailing into end grain, do not nail straight in. Rather, make the nails go in at a slight angle which will make the joint stronger.

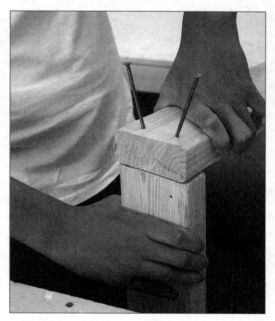

Nails going into end grain should be nailed in slanted.

Sometimes you won't want to risk splitting a piece of wood you are about to nail into. This might be because you do not have other pieces like it, you are nailing near the end, or you are nailing near a small split to begin with and fear the nail will make it worse.

One way to avoid making a split is to haul out the trusty drill, place a drill bit in the chuck that is slightly smaller in diameter than the nail shank, and drill a pilot hole. Then you can put the nail in smoothly without thrusting aside wood and risking a split.

Another and faster method is to blunt the tip of the nail. A blunt tip crushes the wood grain as it penetrates the wood rather than forcing apart the grain. Without the forcing apart action, there is less likely to be a split. To blunt the tip of the nail, merely turn it point up on a solid surface (whose face you don't particularly care about because it is likely to become marred) and strike the point a few taps with the hammer.

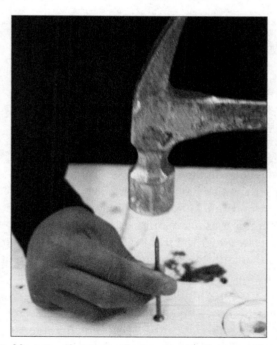

To blunt a nail point, strike it a couple of times with a hammer. A blunt nail will less likely split wood when it is driven in.

Removing Nails

Unfortunately, carpenters sometimes have to remove nails. This can be a tough job, but there are ways.

If a nail has not gone all the way into the wood, use the claw of the hammer to grip under the nail head and pull back. If the nail head is high, place a piece of wood under the hammer head.

To remove a nail set at the surface of the wood, use a cat's paw to dig under it and raise it above the level of the wood.

You can also remove a nail with a pry bar. Once the nail head is above the surface of the wood, grip it with the slot in the curved end of the pry bar. Extracting nails with a pry bar is easier than using the claw of a hammer.

When the nail head is high off the surface of the wood, use a block of wood to elevate the claw and get better leverage to extract the nail.

If the nail head is flush or even below the surface of the wood, use a cat's paw to begin the extraction. Wear eye protection. To use a cat's paw, set the sharp claws at about a 30-degree angle to the surface of the wood and in front of the nail head. Strike the curve of the cat's paw smartly with a hammer. The claw will penetrate the wood and work its way under the nail head. Hammer it as many times as needed to work the claw under the nail head. Then pull back on the shank of the cat's paw, leveraging up the nail head. Either complete the extraction with the cat's paw or with the claw of a hammer.

This method, of course, does considerable damage to the surface of the wood. For framing work, this is of no concern, but for finish work it is.

Once the nail head is above the surface of the wood, you can extract the rest with a pry bar.

Nailing Schedule

Different nailing situations call for different nails and different nail patterns. Use two 16d nails, for example, to nail through the horizontal 2×4 called a top plate into the ends of the vertical 2×4s called studs when framing a 2×4 wall. Use 10d and 8d nails when doing most toenailing. Plywood panel manufacturers will tell you what nails and nailing pattern to use for their panels. Below is a sample *nailing schedule* which gives a general idea of what one is like. Your local building code has one that is more detailed which you need to conform to.

For purposes of the table, OC means "on center," (or, really, "apart," because who measures to the center of a nail head?); W means "in a

W-like pattern;" and FC means "framing connector." Remember nail sizes: 8d nails are 2 ½" long; 10d nails are 3" long; and 16d nails are 3 ½" long.

Framer's Lingo

A **nailing schedule** lists the recommended types of nails and spacing between nails for a specific joining situation.

Nailing Schedule

Task	Joining	Size and Pattern
Band joist to sill	toenail	10d 16"OC
Band joist to band joist	face nail	3 16d
Band joist to regular joist	face nail	3 16d
Joists to top of a beam	toenail	2 10d
Joist to joist lapping at a beam	face nail	4 16d
Subfloor panels to joists		
edges	face nail	8d 6" OC
interior	face nail	8d 8" OC
Sole or top plate into a stud end	face nail	2 16d / stud
Stud toenailed to a plate	toenail	4 8d
Jack stud to king stud	face nail	10d 16"OC, W
Cap plate to top plate	face nail	16d 16"OC, W
Double headers	face nail	2 10d at ends; 12"OC & W from both sides
Ceiling joist to cap plate	toenail	3 8d
Rafter to cap plate	toenail	2 8d or FC
Ridge beam to a rafter end	face nail	3 10d

OC = On Center

W = nail in a W pattern, that is, one nail near one edge, the next nail near the opposite edge and so forth

FC = Framing Connector

8d nails are 2 ½" long

10d nails are 3" long

16d nails are 3 ½" long

*This nailing schedule is presented as a general guideline only. The nailing schedule in your location is controlled by building codes and may differ. Check with your local building department.

Sources: Rick Peters, Framing Basics, Sterling 2000 and Jack P. Jones, House Framing, McGraw-Hill, 1995

Joints

In this chapter discussion, I am going to "cover" two types of joints, butt joints and scabbed joints. There are other kinds of joints in carpentry, but mainly they are for trim carpentry and are not used in framing.

There might be plenty of butt jokes on a carpentry site, as when a carpenter bends over with his heavy tool belt tugging at the waist of his pants, but this is not one of those. A butt joint is the standard framing connection. One piece ends at a right angle and it is placed up against another piece. Sometimes the joinery is by face nailing through the second piece into the end (the butt) of the first; sometimes when face nailing is not possible, the first piece is toenailed through its butt into the second piece.

A butt joint.

When two pieces of lumber join at their ends, they are not easily fastened. The solution is called a scabbed joint. A third piece of lumber (the scab) is laid over the joint. Then nails are face nailed through the scab into the two pieces below. The nails should be slightly less long than the thickness of the scab and underlying wood together. This joint is not attractive, but it is strong.

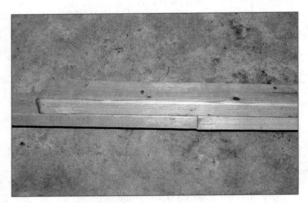

When two pieces join end to end, consider a scabbed joint. You use a "scab" overlying the joint and fasten through the scab into the two pieces below.

Gluing

Glue is sometimes called for in framing joints. On construction sites, glue is also called adhesive and mastic. Its most common use is in applying subfloor panels to floor joists. The glue makes the joint stronger and less likely to squeak. Gluing is also used when building a beam out of two, three, or four pieces of 2× lumber.

Use a cartridge in a caulking gun to dispense the glue. Apply it in a wavy pattern, making the bead about $1/4$" wide.

Unfortunately, applying glue like this to floor joists requires walking backward on a piece of lumber only 1 $1/2$" wide while bending over and concentrating on what the bead of glue looks like. A fall between the joists can be 8' to 10' down to concrete or hard wood. It's not for the faint of heart.

When applying glue to floor joists, lay it down in a wavy fashion.

Disassembling Joints

Think no one ever made a mistake framing walls and floors? Ha! You'll learn. Sometimes framers have to take joints apart. Sometimes it rains, too.

If two pieces have been face nailed together, use a pry bar to pry them apart. Set the short bend of the pry bar into the joint and drive it in with a hammer. Once the bend is all the way in, twist it to pry the two pieces apart. If the pry bar cannot finish the job, use a longer wrecking bar, which is like a long cat's paw.

To pry apart two nailed boards, drive in the short bend of a pry bar. When it has penetrated to its full depth, twist it to pry the two pieces of wood apart.

The Least You Need to Know

- The more nailing you do, the better you become.
- Toenailing is easier if there is a nail or block of wood holding the toenailed piece in place.
- Clinching makes a strong joint. The nails go all the way through both pieces of wood and the ends hammered over flat.
- Nailing schedules tell you what size of nail to use for a certain joint and how frequently to place them.
- Gluing makes for stronger floors and beams.
- Cat's paws and pry bars are good for extracting nails and prying apart joints.

In This Part

"Was there a door in the plans?"

Part 3

Framing

Now get your saws and hammers ready. We really begin to make things in this section: floor framing, walls, rafter arrangements, stairs, and more. The saws will be buzzing and the hammers pounding.

We assume that someone else has built the foundation. The real framing begins when the foundation is ready for beams and the first pieces of solid lumber to go on top.

In This Chapter

- ◆ Understanding foundations
- ◆ Checking accuracy of foundation
- ◆ Attaching to a foundation
- ◆ Beams help support the floor

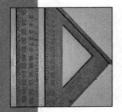
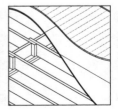

Chapter 10

Foundations and Attaching to Them

House framing actually begins at the top of the foundation. Below is masonry; above is lumber. But as a framer, you should know something about foundation building, and you may even be hammering before placing the first piece of lumber on top of the foundation walls.

In this chapter, you learn about foundations and what you'll likely encounter when the foundation builders have scooted out in their pickup trucks. This can mean leaving the work of making a beam up to you. But don't worry, we cover that here, too.

How Foundations Are Built

Foundation varieties abound. The simplest is a slab of concrete on the ground. Somewhat fancier is a crawl space foundation, which allows a few feet between the crawl space floor—dirt—and the underside of the framed floor of the building. The most expensive is the full basement foundation, with masonry walls 6 or more feet high.

Except for the slab basement, the foundation walls and peers are set on *footings*, or *footers*. These are concrete pads that support foundation walls. They are wider than and constructed separately from the walls. Normally, they are made out of poured concrete. A building inspector needs to inspect these footers before you construct the walls. He will make sure the footings are wide and thick enough for their job and set below the *frost line*, which is the depth in the soil not normally reached by freezing temperatures and is deeper in Wisconsin than in South Carolina. Freezing temperatures will turn moisture in the soil to ice and heave or move it. Any footing not set below the frost line of a locality risks being moved by the forces of freezing, thus the restriction on setting them below the frost line.

> ### Framer's Lingo
>
> The **footing** or **footer** is a concrete pad set below the frost line and on which rests a foundation wall or expanse of concrete underlying a post. The **frost line** is the depth in the soil below which freezing temperature does not normally penetrate.

The walls, which might be concrete block, cinderblock, or poured concrete, are built upon the footings. Some foundations are now built with panels of pressure-treated wood. Others are made by lowering prefabricated concrete panels into place. But many full basement foundations are made of poured concrete. To make these, masons build forms of steel or wood on top of the footings. The forms essentially are two parallel walls between which is poured the concrete and which are removed when the concrete is properly cured. The forms are held parallel with braces both inside and out (the inside ones remain in the poured concrete walls).

Once the forms are removed, a poured concrete wall is ready to work on.

Checking a Foundation for Accuracy

Now you're about to do lots of framing on top of foundation walls, and you want your corners to be right angles and your floors to be level. So the foundation you are given had better have right angles and be level. But how can you tell if it is?

Well, hopefully you hired a foundation contractor with a good reputation and didn't give this job to a moonlighter or first-timer. You looked

at his forms—if he was building a poured concrete wall—and at least eyeballed them for straight. If your foundation maker built with block, at least you checked that the blocks went up straight.

As you might imagine, once the foundation is complete, it's darn hard to do anything about it. But you need to assure yourself that you have a good foundation from which to work, and if you don't, you have to get the foundation contractor to make corrections.

Eyeball the walls to make sure there are no wiggles or bulges. Measure them across to make sure they are parallel. Lay levels on the foundation tops. You can also make the contractor show you with his own instruments that the walls are level.

Lastly, check that the right angles are really right angles. There are two ways of doing this; one is the *equal-diameters method* and the other is the *3-4-5 triangle method*.

If the foundation is a rectangle, its diagonals will be equal. Use a steel tape to measure from one opposite corner to the other. That distance should be exactly equal to the distance between the other pair of opposite corners. The foundation contractor should have done this with his forms or the block masons as their walls were rising.

The other method is the 3-4-5 triangle method, which is based on the Pythagorean Theorem (but does not require computation on your part!). A corner is a true right angle if you can measure out 3' from it on one side and 4' out from it on the other and have the distance between the 3' mark and the 4' mark be exactly 5'. If the distance is less, the angle is less than 90° and if the distance is greater then the angle is greater than 90°.

Greater accuracy on long walls is determined if you can measure out in multiples of 3-4-5. Measure 6-8-10, if you can, or better yet, 9-12-15, or better yet 12-16-20.

If your foundations walls are out $1/2$", you can probably shift around your first pieces of lumber, called *sill plates* or sole plates, to correct the error. If the foundation walls are out by more than this, the contractor delivered bad goods. Have him fix it.

> **Framer's Lingo**
>
> The **equal-diameters method** is a means of checking to see if a rectangle has right angles at the corners. If it does, the diagonals between opposite corners will be equal distances. The **3-4-5 triangle method** is a means of checking to see if a right angle is exact. It is if the distance between the end of one leg from the point of the angle 3' long and the end of another 4' long is exactly 5'. A **sill plate** is the piece of lumber set horizontally on the foundation wall for support of the ends of joists.

If the tops of the foundation wall are not level with one another, you can make small adjustments with shims made of pressure-treated wood. If they are off by more than $1/2$", have the contractor make a correction.

Posts

Once the foundation contractor has driven off into the sunset, you are likely to have the tops of masonry walls 6" across with the tops of threaded bolts sticking up toward the sky. You may also have broad notches in the walls—these *pockets* are for beams. And you may have steel posts rising from the concrete floor to help support a beam that possibly you will make.

Posts can also be made out of 4×4 lumber. In this case, the foundation contractor will have left a raised pedestal for the bottom of the 4×4 and a framing connector partly imbedded in the concrete foundation floor with which to attach the post.

> **Framer's Lingo**
>
> A **pocket** is a notch in the foundation wall into which fit the ends of a beam.

A basement post.

Making Beams

Beams generally run from foundation wall to foundation wall and are supported in between with posts. A beam, in turn, supports floor joists, which support the subfloor. Framing carpenters often make beams by gluing and hammering together large 2× material. Sometimes an architect calls instead for a steel I-beam, often called a girder. In this case, you are better off having your foundation contractor install the steel for you.

If you are making a wooden beam, do not guess at the size. Have an architect or structural engineer determine this for you. For a house foundation, a beam is likely to be made up of several 2×10s or 2×12s.

When you have the architect's or engineer's specifications, note these precautions in constructing the beam. A beam should be long enough to rest at least 4" inside a beam pocket in a foundation wall. Each 2×10 or 2×12 of a beam should have its *crown* up. If you sight down the edge of a piece of lumber, you are likely to see that the edge rises slightly or dips slightly. The rising edge is called the crown, and if the piece of lumber is to be horizontal and on edge, it should always be set in place with the crown up.

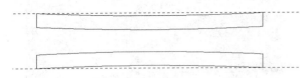

An example of crown.

Likely the 2×10s or 2×12s will not be long enough to run from one beam pocket to the other. If three thicknesses of the lumber suffice for the beam, as is usual, have two thicknesses, but not three, meet directly over the post, which is a technique called *staggering the joints*. It also puts joints, which are a weakness in the beam, directly over vertical support.

Framer's Lingo

A **crown** is the edge of a piece of lumber that rises. **Staggering the joints** is a technique of avoiding joints between pieces of wood next to or near one another. By staggering joints, the whole structure is stronger.

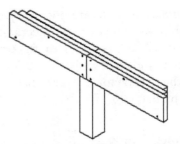

Have one or more, but not all, butt joints of beam lumber directly over posts.

Finger Tips

Beam pockets are often made wider and deeper than a beam's end. Often the pocket is 1" wider so that there is $1/2$" on either side of the beam for air circulation. And the pocket is often deeper because it assumes shimming in order to raise the top of the beam to its proper height.

When assembling the beam, apply construction adhesive in a wavy pattern to one piece before nailing on the next. Remember to keep all the crowns up.

After you have applied the glue, press on the adjacent board—ends staggered—and nail as prescribed by the architect or engineer. This is likely to be something on the order of 16d nails every 32" in two lines high and low on the beam, with three nails at the ends. Note that your architect or engineer may call for a different nailing pattern.

This is not the only kind of beam. Your architect may call for an engineered, or pre-manufactured, beam.

Use adhesive glue in a wavy pattern when assembling beam parts.

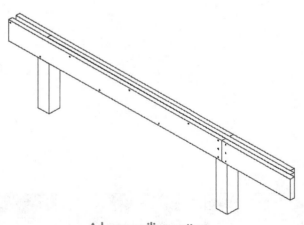

A beam nailing pattern.

Hoisting a beam into place is no joke. Get plenty of help. First hoist one end onto the top of the foundation wall near the beam pocket but not in it. Then lift the other end and set it into its beam pocket. Now go back to the other end and gently shift it to its beam pocket, taking care that it also rests down gently on the center of any intervening posts.

Fasten the beam to posts using framing connectors or bolt holes in the post top.

Now you have the beam in place. The foundation walls, and the beam, are ready for the first pieces of lumber that will support the first floor. You are about to begin the real framing.

The Least You Need to Know

◆ Foundations walls are built on footings that you must have inspected by a building inspector before you build the walls.

◆ A foundation builder needs to leave you a foundation that is square at all corners and completely level.

◆ Follow your designer's specifications if you are making a beam.

◆ Always stagger joints in a built-up beam, and place some of the joists over posts for further support.

In This Chapter

- ◆ Attaching the sill plate to the foundation
- ◆ Setting the joists for a floor
- ◆ Blocking and bridging to make the floor sturdy
- ◆ Creating openings in the framing for a stairwell
- ◆ Fastening the plywood subfloor to the joists

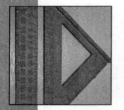
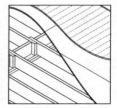

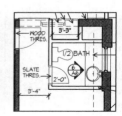

Chapter 11

Floor Framing

Floor framing begins with attaching the sill plates, which should be pressure-treated lumber, to the tops of the foundation walls. Fastening the sill plates exactly is important because on top of them go the outside joists, which define the outer limits of the floors. If the sill plates are not in the proper position, then the joists and the floor above will not be either.

Floor framing also involves making openings for stairs which require doubled joists for strength.

On top of the joists go the subflooring. As this is done, the jobsite begins to take on the appearance of a house about to rise. It is a good moment in the course of the construction.

Regular Floor Framing

Note there are two general types of house framing. One is called *platform framing*, or western framing, and the other is called *balloon framing*. In this book we stick with platform framing. In platform framing, the walls of each story are built on top of the first floor and second floor as these floors are built. In balloon framing, the exterior wall studs rise from the foundation's sill plate two full stories. The second floor is supported by joists resting on blocking secured to the studs half way up their lengths. Balloon framing is an older style and not used much today, but remodelers encounter it in older homes.

Making Holes for the Foundation J-Bolts

Choose pressure-treated 2×6s that are straight and not warped in any way. Check the plans to see if there are any details or sections that show information about the sill plates. There may be information about how the sills are to meet at the corners. Normally, these are butt joints, one sill merely ends at the edge of the other. Check also to see how the sill is meant to lie on the foundation wall. Often the outer edge of the sill plate is meant to align with the outer edge of the foundation wall. But not always. Sometimes, the sill plate is meant to be moved inward somewhat to allow for the thickness of sheathing and siding that will be the outside of the exterior wall.

Because the simplest is when the outer edge of the sill plate is meant to align with the outer edge of the foundation wall, I'll deal with this example first.

The foundation contactor has left you with connectors protruding from the tops of the foundation wall.

Jay bolt threads stick up from the foundation wall.

Now perform the following steps:

1. Cut the pressure-treated 2×6s you are using as the sill plates to length. Hold a sill plate on the top of the wall and up against the connectors, here the tops of J-bolts. Make sure that the sill plate is exactly where it is meant to be in terms of right and left (that is, along its length).

2. With a straight edge, draw lines across the sill plate from both sides of a J-bolt top. Do this for all the J-bolt tops.

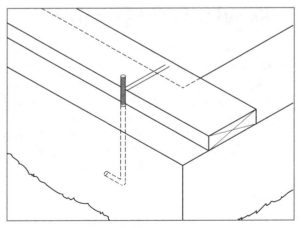

Mark the locations of J-bolt sides.

(Copyright: John Hannah)

3. To determine the location of the J-bolt from the edge of the sill plate, measure the distance from the edge of the foundation wall to center of the bolt. Mark this distance from the outside edge of the sill plate inward to the marks that show the sides of the J-bolts. Where the first mark meets the center point between the other two represents the center of the hole you will drill for the J-bolt top.

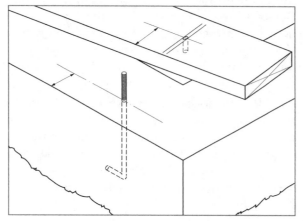

Transfer the distance from the edge of the foundation wall to the edge of the sill to the sill itself.

Copyright: John Hannah

If the edge of the sill is not meant to align with the edge of the foundation wall (this is called *flush* in carpenter talk), determine from the architect's drawings how far from the outer edge of the foundation wall it is meant to go. Snap a chalk line at this distance from one end of the foundation wall to the other. Proceed as above but instead of measuring in from the edge of the foundation wall to the center of the J-bolt when the sill is up against the J-bolts, measure in from the chalk line.

Framer's Lingo

Flush is aligned with or one exactly atop another.

Finger Tips

Do not presume that each J-bolt is the same distance from the edge of the foundation wall. Measure and mark for each individually.

Attaching the Sill Plate

Now perform the following steps to attach the sill plate:

1. Remove the sill plate from the foundation wall and drill a hole for each J-bolt. Make the hole $1/4$" in diameter larger than the diameter of the bolt.

2. Place caulking or other sealing material on top of the foundation wall where the sill plate is to rest. The caulking or other sealing material (it could be strips of insulation) seals out wind, moisture, and insects.

3. Set the sill plate in place over the J-bolts and on top of the caulking or sealing material. Place washers over the J-bolt tops, and then tighten down with nuts. In this manner, install all the sill plates around the foundation walls.

A bolted sill plate.

Anatomy of Floor Framing

The principal ingredients of floor framing are joists. Most of the joists span open areas below. If the open area is long enough, the joists must be supported in the middle with a beam. Thus one set of joists runs from one sill plate to the beam, and another runs from an opposite sill plate to the beam from the other direction. There are different ways of having the joists meet at the beam and be supported by the beam. A traditional way, and the one demonstrated here, is to have the joists coming from opposite directions lap at the beam rather than meet end to end. In this way you can face nail the lapping joists together.

Traditionally, the joists rest on top of the beam. But some designers like to have the beam higher to give better head room below. In this case the joist tops can be flush with the beam tops and attached to the beam with joist hangers. There are other variations as well.

Not all of the joists span open areas. Some joists rest on the sill plates. These are called *band joists* or *rim joists*. Some of these run parallel to the spanning joists, and some run perpendicular to the spanning joists. Ones that run perpendicular to the spanning joists are sometimes called *header joists*.

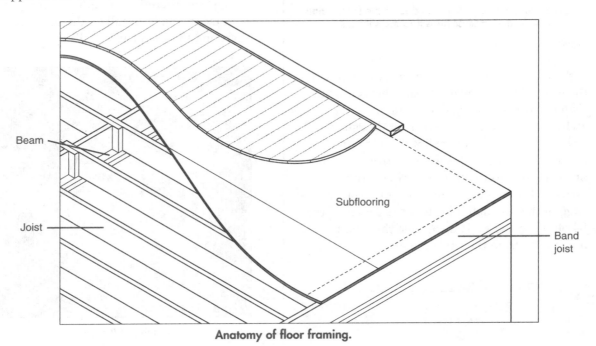

Beam

Subflooring

Joist

Band joist

Anatomy of floor framing.

(Copyright: John Hannah)

Mark the Sill Plates for Joists

Once the sill plates are down, it's time to mark them for the joists that will go on top of them. A first step is determining which way the spanning floor joists are going to run by checking the framing plan. Obviously, if there is a beam in the basement, the joists are going to run from the sill plate to the beam. Most likely there will be two sets, one running to the beam from one side and one running to the beam from the other side. They meet on top of the beam and lap each other, that is, they do not meet each other in a butt joint, but their end portions run alongside each other for a distance over the beam.

Mark the sill plate where the joists are going to go. This is called laying out the sill plates. In this example, let's call one sill plate A and the one perpendicular to it sill plate B. The joists will run parallel to sill plate A and perpendicular to sill plate B. The band joist to be set on top of sill plate A we will call joist #1. The band joist to be set on sill plate B we will call the header band joist.

Generally joists are set 16" apart. We will call them joist #2, joist #3, joist #4, and so on. Joist #2 will not be 16" away from joist #1. Instead its edge closest to joist #1 will $15\frac{1}{4}$" away from the outside edge of joist #1.

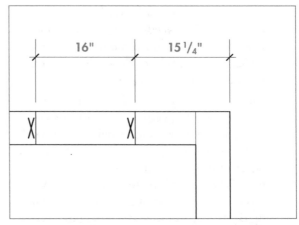

Measure $15\frac{1}{4}$" from the outside of the sill plate to the closest edge for joist #2.

(Copyright: John Hannah)

The reason for this is that plywood or other engineered subflooring comes in panels exactly 48×96". By setting joist #2 $15\frac{1}{4}$" from the outside edge of the sill plate (and thus the band joist on top of it), followed by a spacing of 16" thereafter, the 48" edge falls exactly along the middle of joist #4, or the 96" edge falls exactly along the middle of joist #7. That way, the edge of such joists can serve to support two plywood panels, and every edge has support without adding extra lumber.

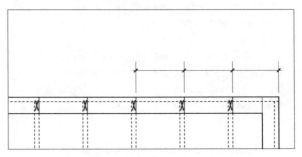

By spacing the second joist $15\frac{1}{4}$" from the first (the band joist, or joist #1), a plywood panel's 4' or 8' edge falls exactly down the middle of joist #4 or joist #7.

(Copyright: John Hannah)

1. Mark sill plate B for joist #2. Draw a perpendicular line across the sill plate, and then mark an X on the side of the line on which the joist will rest—in this example, on the far side of the line.

2. Mark sill plate B every 16" from the line for joist #2. A speedy way to do this is using a steel tape. Tack a nail into the sill plate at the line for joist #2. Loop the steel tape's end over the nail, and pull the steel tape down the sill plate. The steel tape has prominent markings every 16". Make marks there. Remove the steel tape, and make lines across the sill plate at each 16" mark. Place an X on the far side of each of these lines to show on which side of the lines the joists will go.

☞ Finger Tips

A frequent term in framing is *on center*. It is abbreviated O.C., even on plans. You will frequently see an instruction *16" O.C.* This means you should place the joists or studs or rafters so their centers are exactly 16" apart.

But because marking one piece of lumber at a point where another's center is going to go is going to cover the mark, you mark for the edge and not the center. Then you set the edge of the joist, stud, or rafter down on the edge mark. Of course, if the edges are 16" part, the centers will also be 16" apart.

16 O.C. is not the only spacing framers encounter. Some framing members have to be 12 O.C.; others can be 24 O.C. These will be specified in the plans.

3. Duplicate the marks on sill plate B on the central beam. Make the lines and same Xs the same distances from the outside edge of sill plate A.

If your floor is going to be supported by two sets of joists meeting at a central beam, note that the joists probably are not designed to meet end to end. They will likely lap at the beam, meaning one is set off from another the width of a joist, or $1\frac{1}{2}$". Remember this when you lay out the sill plate opposite sill plate B. Plywood will not fit perfectly there; however, you can trim the plywood on that side to make the fit.

Setting the Band Joists

Look at your framing plans to see how the band joists are meant to join at the corners. Check to see if there are any sections or details in the plans about the band joists.

Now select the band joists, which will sit up on edge on top of the sill plates. When you select band joists from the many pieces of joist lumber you have on hand, make sure they are straight, not warped in any way and with few or small knots.

1. Cut band joists to length. Take one, hold it on edge, and sight along it with one eye. If the middle appears higher than the ends, this means that the piece is "crown up." This is the way you want it to be.

2. Hold the first joist in position, upright, on edge, crown up, and flush with the edge of the sill plate. Toenail it to the sill plate. A typical nailing schedule is 16d toenails every 16", but check your approved plans. Add the other band joists, all with their crowns up. At the corners, face nail three 16d nails through one band joist into the other.

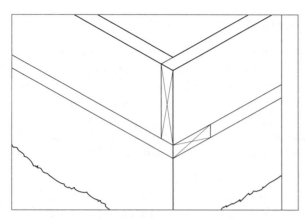

Toenail the first band joist into place. Face nail through the second into the first.

(Copyright: John Hannah)

Setting the Joists

Once the band joists are in place, it's time to set the spanning joists. Pretty soon people are going to see a floor taking shape.

1. Select lumber for the spanning joists. Set aside any pieces that are warped or have large knots; you can saw them into smaller pieces for other tasks. Cut all of the joists to length. Normally joists must lap a beam by at least 4 ".

Heads!

If you are installing the floor joists over a full basement, you will be working from ladders or scaffolding to set them in place. If you will be working from ladders, review the safety precautions for working from ladders in Chapter 5.

2. Set joist #2 into position, crown up, one end overlapping the beam and the other butt jointed up against the header band joist. Make sure the joist is exactly over the X and its edge along the marking line; then face nail three 16d nails through the band joist into the end of joist #2. You do not have to nail the part of the joist at the beam just yet. Toenail the joist into the sill plate with 10d nails.

3. Nail subsequent joists to the band joist and the sill plate in the same way, all with their crowns up.

4. Go back to the beam. Hold each joist edge on the mark for it, and toenail each to the beam.

Heads!

Leave joists flat until they are nailed. If some were to be on edge unnailed, an unsuspecting person might step on one thinking it was nailed and secured. It would collapse under his foot and cause a fall.

5. Set the joists coming from the other direction in the same manner. Face nail them to the band joist, and toenail them to the sill plate. Set them on their marks on the beam; their ends at the beam should lap the ends of the joists coming from the other direction.

Toenail these joists to the beam. Fasten overlapping joists to each other by face nailing through each into the other using two 16(d) nails from each side.

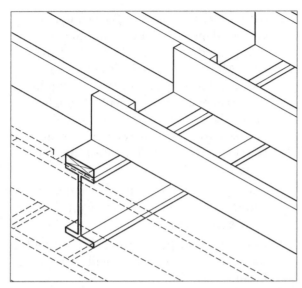

Toenail each joist to the beam. Face nail from each side through one joist into the other.

(Copyright: John Hannah)

Blocking and Bridging

Many codes call for *blocking* and *bridging* between the floor joists. Blocking is made from joist stock and is nailed between joists. Blocks keep the joists from twisting and stabilize the floor. In addition, if flames from a fire were ever to move into a gap between joists, the blocking would at least temporarily stop them from moving from one side of the blocking to the other. Bridging is composed of smaller pieces of wood, or of steel, placed on diagonals between joists. They help stabilize the floor.

Framer's Lingo

Blocking are pieces as deep as joists, which are set between joists to stabilize the floor. **Bridging** are slender pieces of wood or steel set at an angle joist to joist to stabilize the floor.

Blocking

If your plans call for blocking between joists where they lap over a beam, use the same stock of lumber you did for creating the joists. Likely, however, here you can use the pieces of joist stock that were slightly warped or had large knots. You merely cut up the previously unused joist stock into the blocking, as follows:

1. Cut blocking to fit between the joists. If joists meet at the beam and are nailed together, the proper length for a piece of blocking will be 13", that is, 16" minus the thicknesses of two $1\frac{1}{2}$"-thick joists. Cut as many of these as you need. Note that the blocking next to the band joist will be different than the rest because joist #2 is less than 16" away. Cut this blocking $13\frac{3}{4}$".

Consult your floor framing plan. The designer may have called for the bridging to be all in a straight line so that the edges of subfloor plywood sheets might have a continuous support. Install them this way if this is what the plans call for, and install them exactly where the edge of the plywood sheets would fall upon their centers.

But there are instances where staggered blocking is preferred. One is when the joists run all the way from one foundation wall to the other, and there are not two sets of joists meeting in a lap at the beam. In this instance, it is easier for nailing if the blocking is staggered, that is, offset one after another $1\frac{1}{2}$". In that way, you can face nail through each joist into the end grain of each piece of blocking. A similar situation arises when blocking is called for not over a beam but rather over open space.

In any event, the blocking should fit snugly but never force a joist out of its true position. Rather the blocking should help to maintain joists in their proper positions.

Staggered blocking not at a beam.

2. Set the first blocking in position on top of the beam between the band joist and joist #2. Nail through the band joist into the end grain of the blocking. Toenail through joist #2 into the blocking at the other end of the blocking. Near joist #2 toenail the blocking into the beam.

3. Continue with the remaining blocks, nailing them to the joists and the beam either in staggered fashion or all in a straight line.

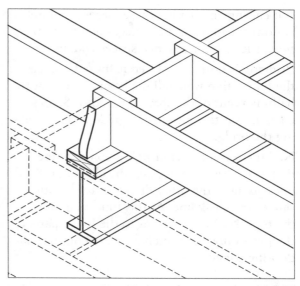

Floor bridging along a beam.

(Copyright: John Hannah)

Bridging

Bridging material was traditionally wood and consisted of 1x3s cut at a bevel on the both ends. Two of these where nailed into every joist space alongside one anther so that they formed an X (see the figure that follows).

Wooden bridging.

But cutting and nailing these pieces accurately is slower than using steel pieces bought to the proper length for the joist spaces you have.

Bridging is normally placed halfway between the foundation wall and the beam, that is, at the halfway point of the span of the joist. Snap a chalk line at this location to guide you in locating the bridging.

Nail the tops of steel bridging going in one direction to joists alongside the chalk line. Nail ones going in the other direction to the other side of the chalk line. At this time, nail only the tops. Nail the bottoms to the lower parts of the joists only after you have nailed on the subflooring panels.

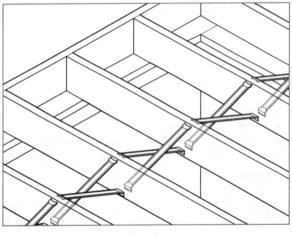

Steel bridging.

(Copyright: John Hannah)

The bridging can also be solid, as along the beam. In fact, if two joists have to be close together (see next section) the bridging normally is solid because it's more difficult to cut special short 1×3 diagonal bridging or to find steel pieces that fit.

> ☞ **Finger Tips**
>
> The reason why you do not nail the bridging to the lower parts of the joists until after the subfloor is on is that nailing the lower portions first could thrust up or maintain a joist in an elevated position, thus creating an uneven floor. If you wait, the subfloor panels help to even out the level of the joists, and then the bridging helps to maintain that evenness.

Framing for Floor Openings

You may have noticed that the floor assembled in the previous section did not have openings in it for the likes of stairways, chimneys, and so forth. So let's handle that now.

Openings are handled by what are called *trimmer joists*, *header joists*,, and *tail joists*. Trimmer joists are joists that run alongside an opening and are parallel to regular joists. Normally they are paired, also called doubled. Header joists are pieces of joist material that run alongside an opening but are perpendicular to the regular joists. Header joists are often paired or doubled also. Tail joists are short joists that run from header joists parallel to regular joists back to either the sill plate or a beam.

Your floor framing plan will show the trimmer joists, header joists, and tail joists. These are actually nailed into place *before* the regular joists, which makes the nailing somewhat easier. We bring up this topic after the instructions of setting regular joists because that gives the basics of joist installation while this goes into the special cases.

So look to your floor framing plan to find the dimensions and locations of the floor openings.

To begin an opening in floor framing as for a stairwell:

1. Nail in place the inside trimmer joists. These are full-length joists that define two sides of the opening. Mark the top edges of these trimmer joists for the header joists at both ends of the opening. Normally these will be two at each end, but there are possible exceptions. Draw vertical lines down the insides of the trimmer joists to mark the edges of the header joists.

Framer's Lingo

A **trimmer joist** is a joist that defines a side of a floor opening and runs parallel to regular joists. A **header joist** is a joist that defines a side of a floor opening and runs perpendicular to regular joists. A **tail joist** is a joist that runs from a header joist to a beam or sill plate.

2. Measure for the length of two header joists. Do not do this between the joists where they are to be installed; though you may not see it, the joists may be warped there and not be the intended distance apart. Instead, use the plans or measure between the trimmer joists where they lie on the sill plate or beam.

   Assuming each end of the opening is going to have two header joists, install the "back ones" first, that is, the ones that are not going to be at the very edge of the opening. Face nail these in place with three nails through each trimmer joist into the ends of the header joists.

3. Now add the tail joists. These are joists running from the "back" header joists to the sill plate and beam. Cut them to length. They are set on the sill plate and beam in the location they would be if they were full length joists, that is, in the posi-

tions 16" O.C. where they would be if they were full length joists.

Face nail through the header joists into the ends of the tail joists. Toenail the tail joists to the sill plate and beam, and face nail through the band joist into the foundation-wall end of any tail joist.

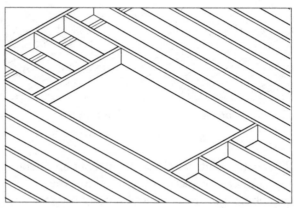

Install the inside trimmer joists, "back" header joists, and tail joists first.

(Copyright: John Hannah)

4. Nail the inside header joists in place. Nail through the trimmer joists into the ends of the inside header joists. Face nail through the inside header joist into the back header joists.

5. Add outsider trimmer joists to the inside trimmer joists. These are identical to the trimmer joists to which they will be attached and rest on both the sill plate and the beam. To fasten them to the first trimmer joists, face nail through them into the first trimmer joists using 16d nails every 16" alternating near the upper and lower edges as for making a beam (See Chapter 10). An alternative for nailing is using 10d nails every 12" from each side and two from each side at the ends.

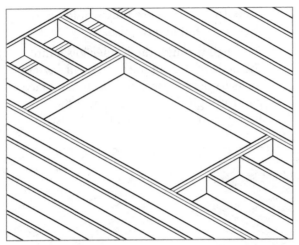

A completed opening in floor framing.

(Copyright: John Hannah)

This is the traditional way of making an opening. You can be less scrupulous about the sequence of positioning and nailing if you decide to use joist hangers for the header joists. You could put the two trimmer joists in place and then hoist up a double header joist and attach it to the sides of the trimmer joists with joist hangers that accommodate the thickness of two 2× material.

Once all the trimmer and header joists for a floor are installed, install the regular joists.

Final point: you may see on your floor framing plan what seems to be an extra joist running parallel with others but closer to one than 16". Likely, this is because a wall running parallel to the joists is to be built above, and the designer has called for an extra joist there to help support it. This joist should not normally be placed directly below the wall and it should not be too close to a regular joist. Rather it should be set far enough away from the regular joist so that ducting or pipes descending from inside the wall can then run between the joists.

Finger Tips

When you set one joist alongside another, as an inside header joist alongside the back one or an outside trimmer joist alongside an inside one, you may see that the crown of one rises higher than the crown of another. But you want the crowns to match, because each joist is meant to carry weight. If the difference is severe, try another piece of lumber. If the difference is slight, stand on the higher one until its top edge is flush or close to flush with the top edge of the lower one. Then toenail through the top of the higher one into the side of the lower on. This will bring a higher edge down to match the lower edge or hold the edges together if they are flush. Then do your face nailing through the side of one of the trimmers to firmly connect the two joists together.

Applying Subfloors

Now it's time to put on the subfloor. Normally, this is plywood but can also be a plywood equivalent, such as Oriented Strand Board (OSB); we'll use the term plywood to denote all panel subflooring.

Your designer, architect, or engineer has likely designated the type of subflooring to use and has made the design to accommodate this type's strengths. Each type has its own specifications with respect to span distance and nailing schedule. Do not substitute another type without checking with the designer and the building department. Follow the fastening and nailing schedule exactly.

Some plywood has squared edges; some has tongue-and-groove edges. In some instances, plywood with squared edges must have solid blocking under its edges which do not fall on a joist. Tongue-and-groove subflooring largely does not have to meet such a requirement because the panels lock together securely tongue into groove; thus edges are not likely to sag where unsupported from below.

Do some calculations with respect to your floor. No plywood panel should be less than 2' wide. If the dimensions of your floor are such that the last panels you put in place would be less than 2' wide, make the first one—and all subsequent ones in this first row—3' wide. Then the last row of panels will be more than 2' wide.

Setting the First Panel

To set the first panel, follow these steps:

1. Measure out 48¼" from the ends of the header joists, and mark the band joists there. Strike a chalk line across the top edges of the joists at this distance. It will serve as a guide for the edges of the first row of plywood panels. If the header joist is bowed out or in somehow, the 48¼ line will be a better guide for the panels than the header joist. (If you are trimming the panels to 3' as per the last paragraph in the previous section, then the chalk line should be 36¼" out from the header joist corners.)

   Even if your designer does not call for adhesive, it's a good idea to apply it to the joist edges before putting down the plywood. The reason is that there is likely to be shrinkage of the joists, which can loosen nails, which can lead to squeaks when you step on certain parts of the floor. Check with the manufacturer of the kind of plywood panels you are using to find out the recommended adhesive.

   The first plywood panel laid starts in a corner and runs lengthwise across the joists, ending on the middle of the edge of the sixth joist (not counting the band joist). Test it in this position to see that its end is going to fit properly to the sixth joist. If you are using tongue-and-groove

panels (and I assume that you will), have the tongue along the header joist, that is, facing outside the building. Have the entire tongue "inside the building," that is, not overhanging the outside of the band joist. Alternatively, you can use a circular saw to cut off all the tongues on this first row of panels.

Heads!

Carrying plywood panels can be tricky, especially on a windy day. Remember to lift with your legs and not with your back. Carry only one at a time. Remember that your vision is partly blocked in the direction of the panel, so move slowly and take care where you step. On a windy day, have another worker help you by taking one end of the panel.

2. Spread the adhesive far enough along joist edges to accommodate the first panel.

Apply adhesive to joist edges.

3. Set the first panel in place. Make sure it is square to the corner of the building and that its groove edge is running exactly along the chalk lines across the edges of the joists.

Drop the first panel into place.

4. Use the kind of nails noted in the nailing schedule. This might be 6d or 8d nails. Some plywood manufacturers call for ring-shank nails to assure a tighter grip. Nail the panel to the joists near the four corners, but not closer than 6" to the groove edge. The reason is that you often want some flexibility along the groove edge for when the panel with the tongue comes along to fit into it.

Make sure the panel is properly aligned; the end should extend half way across the joist edge.

Setting the Second and Subsequent Panels

To set the second and any subsequent panels, complete the following steps:

1. Spread adhesive in the location for the next panel, which will be end-to-end against the first. If these are not tongue-and-groove panels, leave a gap of $1/16$" between panels or as the manufacturer recommends. If they are tongue-and-groove panels, mate the tongue and the groove. It is better if the tongue is fitting into the groove, but this may not always be the case.

Setting the second panel.

It is better to fit a tongue into a groove because if the fit is difficult, you can go to the opposite end of the panel and "persuade" the panel to move properly into position. You can do this with a sledge hammer, but do not hammer directly against a groove. Instead, hold a length of 2×4 at least $1\frac{1}{2}$' long against the groove. At the same time, have a helper stand on the first, or nailed, panel to see where one panel or another is riding high; he can then step in those places while you hammer so that the tongue fits into the groove.

Finger Tips

If you are using tongue-and-groove panels, take special care in carrying and storing them. If the tongues are smashed or the grooves crushed, they are going to be especially difficult to mate when put into position on the joists.

If you have to press a groove around a tongue, you cannot use the 2×4 at the opposite end; it will flatten the tongue. But you can use a circular saw to cut a scrap piece of the plywood along a groove $1\frac{1}{2}$ to 2' long. You can use this instead of a 2×4, slipping the groove side over the tongue of the panel to be hammered and then hammering the side that has been cut with the circular saw.

2. Proceed down the joists until the whole first row of panels is laid. Go back and complete the nailing. This might be placing a nail every 6" along the edges and 10" along the interior portion of the panel. To make the nailing here easier—because your target is a joist edge you cannot see and that is only $1\frac{1}{2}$" wide—snap a chalk line along the plywood panel over the middle of the joist edges. You can do this by holding one end at the panel edge where you can see the joist (toward the interior of the building) and the other at the edge of the panel at the header joist— you can tell where the joists are from the face nails into them through the header joist.

3. After you have finished the first row, start the second row. Begin by cutting a panel exactly in half, that is, four feet long, so that its end will fall on the third joist (not counting the band joist). After spreading the adhesive, lay the cut edge along the band joist and the tongue end on the third joist. If you are using square-cut panels rather than tongue-and-groove ones, leave $\frac{1}{16}$" inch between the edges or as the manufacturer recommends. Nail the new panel down near the corners.

4. Follow the first panel in this row with a full 8' panel, and continue down to the far end of the building. Thus you are staggering the joints of the plywood panels.

Finger Tips

Do not leave any scraps of wood under a floor in a crawl space or outside the masonry foundation walls. Doing so only attracts termites.

The Least You Need to Know

◆ Use pressure-treated wood for sill plates on masonry foundations.

◆ Aligning the sill plates is critical for the proper layout of the floor and then the walls above the floor.

◆ The first interior joist is spaced differently than the remainder so that paneling ends fall properly on joist edges.

◆ Bridging and blocking between joists stabilize the floor and can serve as nailing surfaces for subfloor panels.

◆ Framing for openings such as stairwells requires doubled joists and headers.

◆ Gluing subfloor panels keeps a floor from squeaking.

In This Chapter

- ◆ The various parts of a framed wall
- ◆ Nailing the parts together
- ◆ Tilting a framed wall into place
- ◆ Making the wall plumb and straight
- ◆ Tying walls together at the corners
- ◆ Building nonbearing partition walls and connecting them to existing walls

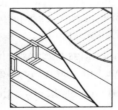

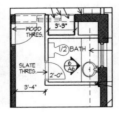

Chapter 12

Wall Framing

Many people consider the main work of carpenters to be building and putting up framed walls. Indeed, this is a good part of a framing carpenter's job. It is also one of the most satisfying, especially the tilting up of the wall and fastening it into place. This last job dramatically changes the way the jobsite looks and is visible evidence both of the framer's skill and of tangible progress.

Building walls requires exact adherence to construction principles. That is, a framer must build the proper *headers* to span window and door openings. In addition, a framer must measure precisely—to the sixteenth of an inch—to cut lumber precisely—to the sixteenth of an inch—and to make sure that what he erects is exactly square and exactly plumb.

He begins with a technique that is old beyond memory. He places the *sole plate* (the bottom horizontal 2×4 on which the wall is to rest) and the *top plate* (the top horizontal 2×4 that serves as part of the top of the wall) together and marks them identically. The effect is that when the sole plate and top plate are separated and the vertical studs placed in between, they align with paired marks and so will be perfectly vertical.

📖 **Framer's Lingo**

A **sole plate** is a horizontal 2×4 on which rest the vertical studs of a framed wall. A **top plate** is a horizontal 2×4 capping the studs at the top of a framed wall. A **header** is a heavy piece of framing running over the rough opening of a door or window that transfers the load from above to the left and right.

Tilting a wall up into place is a highlight of a carpenter's day. But it is short-lived because new duties follow. He must plumb and brace the wall and make sure that it is perfectly straight.

After the exterior walls are up, it's time to frame the interior walls. These are built just about the same as the exterior ones, except that nonbearing interior walls don't need to have headers as hefty as bearing walls. Nevertheless, you must take the same exactitude in laying out the walls, in cutting the lumber for the parts, and in making sure that they are plumb and straight.

Anatomy of a Framed Wall

A framed wall is a wonderful thing to build. It is big, so when it goes up, it really shows progress. It is a kind of carpenter's delight.

Framed walls everywhere are just about the same. No matter how many windows and doors, no matter the size of the windows, no matter how long the wall, they all generally follow the same terminology and rules. These rules generally apply both to exterior bearing walls, interior bearing walls, and interior partition (nonbearing) walls, except that some of the framing for the exterior and interior bearing walls must be stronger and beefier than the interior partition walls.

The walls are made of studs, that is, upright 2×4s. Some exterior walls are framed with 2×6s so that more insulation can be stuffed between them, but the same principles apply. In this book we will presume that the exterior walls will be 2×4s.

The studs rest on a horizontal 2×4 called the sole plate, also called the bottom plate. They rise to another horizontal 2×4 called the top plate. Generally, the studs are placed 16" apart, or 16" on center.

Because doors and windows are generally wider than 16", you must transfer the load that would otherwise flow down a stud in this location to either side by a heavy framing member called a header. The header runs clear across the *rough opening* of the door or window and carries the load to the left and right.

Rough openings for doors extend all the way to the subfloor, but rough openings for windows stop part way down the wall. The point at which they stop is placed a horizontal 2×4 called the *rough sill*.

📖 **Framer's Lingo**

A **rough opening** is an opening in a framed wall for a door or window. A **rough sill** is a horizontal 2×4 at the bottom of a rough opening for a window.

A shortened stud called a *jack stud* holds up the header. Some carpenters call it a *trimmer stud*, but in any event, it directly holds up the ends of the header. A jack stud marks the vertical limit of the rough opening for the door or window.

For stability, always place a jack stud beside a full-length stud, which is called a *king stud*. All rough openings have at least two king studs and two jack studs.

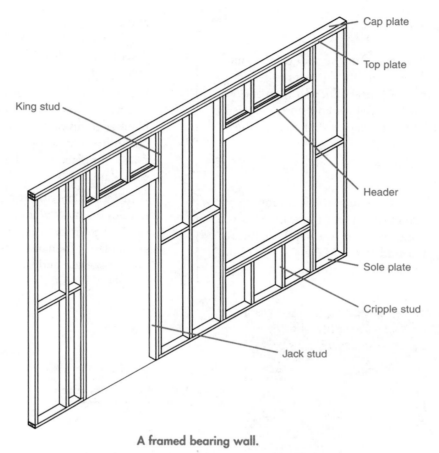

King stud

Cap plate

Top plate

Header

Sole plate

Cripple stud

Jack stud

A framed bearing wall.

(Copyright: John Hannah)

If there is room between the top of a header for a door or window rough opening and the bottom of the top plate, short studs, called *cripple studs*, are used here. Place these precisely where you would have placed ordinary studs had there been no rough opening. They are positioned this way so siding or wallboard nailed to full-length studs can be readily nailed to the cripple studs without doing extra measuring and so that if an edge comes over or under a rough opening, the edge will fall precisely along the middle of a cripple stud.

Cripple studs also run from the sole plate up to the rough sill defining the lower limit of the rough opening for a window. Again, place the cripple studs above the header and below the rough sill exactly as if they were full-length studs.

A header in a bearing wall is often made up of 2×8s or larger pieces. Architects or engineers make the calculations on the size of wood needed to carry the load and to satisfy the local building code. In a nonbearing wall, a header can often be a simple horizontal 2×4.

Framer's Lingo

A **jack stud** is a shortened stud at a rough opening supporting one end of a header (sometimes called a **trimmer stud**). A **king stud** is a full-length stud alongside and nailed to a jack stud. A **cripple stud** is a shortened stud placed over a header or below a rough sill.

Layout

Now is the time to layout the wall on the sub-floor. Nail all the studs and headers together while the parts are horizontal, and then tilt the whole up into place. Before you start, make sure that the subfloor edges are exactly where they are supposed to be.

Following are the steps for laying out a regular stud wall.

1. Use a broom to sweep the subfloor where you are going to lay out the wall. Measure in from one corner of the subfloor the width of a stud, $3\frac{1}{2}$". Make a mark. Go to the other end of the subfloor, and measure

and mark again. Snap a chalk line between these two marks. The chalk line will represent the inside edge of the wall you are laying out.

2. Cut a 2×4 to length for the sole plate. If you need two 2×4s, cut both. Lay the sole plate edge up on the house side of the chalk line. Cut a top plate of one or more 2×4s, and place it on the house side of the sole plate.

If the sole plate and top plate require more than one length of 2×4, make each so that the butt joint between 2×4s occurs at the same place. Toenail two pieces of sole plate together, and toenail two pieces of top plate together.

Lay the top and sole plates edge up on the house side of the chalk line.

If you need two 2×4s for a sole plate and top plate, make the joints at the same place.

3. Align the ends of the sole plate and top plate with the outside edges of the sub-floor. Toenail through the sole plate into the subfloor about every 3' to hold the sole plate in place.

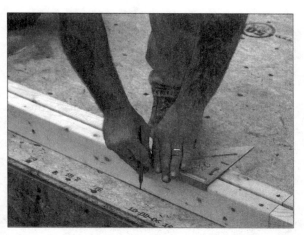

Mark for stud locations with a straight line across both studs. Place an X on the side of the line where the stud will go.

Toenail through the sole plate in several places, holding it in place to the subfloor.

4. Begin measuring from the same corner you did for the floor joists. This will place your studs over the floor joists below.

Mark for the first stud at the corner, as for the band joist. Mark for the second stud 15$\frac{1}{4}$" from the outside of the subfloor.

Mark for other studs to be 16" on center from this first one. Mark across both the sole plate and the top plate with a firm straight line; then draw an X on the side of the line where the stud will go.

5. If the wall is to have nothing but studs in it, the next step is to pick up the top plate and move it along the subfloor a distance equal to the studs that are going to go between the two plates. Then cut as many studs as you need to fit between the sole plate and top plate. Cut all the studs at one time. Check them for "crown," that is, a slight bulge running lengthwise. Place all the crowns down so that any bulges will be toward the inside of the house when the wall is erect. Walls tend to bulge out-ward, so if the crowns of studs are toward the inside of the house, the tendency to bulge out is counterbalanced. Set the studs into their positions on the subfloor. Nail through the sole and top plates into the ends of the studs.

Most often, however, a wall has at least one door or window opening and needs to be framed to accommodate these. So let's consider that aspect and deal with the studs there, too.

Framing a Door or a Window

If you have a framing plan for a wall, check it for the positions of the king studs and jack studs. If you don't, you can still determine the positions. The floor plan will either have the measurements from the corners to the edges of the openings, or more often, a measurement to the center of an opening. Note that the measurements on the plans may not be to the rough but rather to the finish openings, that is, with the windows or doors in place. In this event, you, the framer, must find out the thickness of the window or door framing that will fit into the rough opening and make calculations accordingly.

To frame a wall with a door or window opening, follow these steps:

1. Mark on the sole and top plates for the corner studs as for framing an all-stud wall. Then go back and measure from the corner to the position for the rough openings. If the sides of the rough openings are not marked on the plans, make a mark at the center line. Then measure from the center line forward and back half the width of the rough opening. Make marks there. These will be the inside edges of the jack studs.

   Then mark for king studs right alongside the jack studs. Some plans call for two jack studs or two king studs. If this is the case, mark for them.

   You can use your own markings for the studs. Generally, an X stands for a full-length stud, a J stands for a jack stud, a K stands for a king stud, and a C stands for a cripple stud. A C with a line through it stands for a center line, and, of course, no stud goes there.

Mark for the jack and king studs across both the sole plate and the top plate.

2. Pick up the top plate and move it a stud's length along the subfloor. Cut full-length studs to length and lay them in position between the sole plate and the top plate.

Cut the full-length studs and set them in place between the sole plate and top plate.

3. Nail through the plates into the ends of the full-length studs. Use two 16d nails into the ends of each stud. Where two 2×4s of a sole or top plate abut, have two studs support the joint.

Nail through the plates into the ends of the full-length studs.

4. Nail through the plates into the ends of the full-length studs.

5. Make the headers. Calculate the length of headers; it will be the same distance as between the insides of the king studs.

If you are using engineered lumber, as shown in Figure 12.9, two thicknesses together may be exactly the width of a 2×4, or 3½". This is convenient because the faces of the headers will align flush with the faces of the wall.

Often, however, you will be using dimensional lumber. Two thicknesses of 2×10, for example, make a header only 3" thick.

Usually what framers do is cut a piece of ½"thick plywood and place it between the two 2×10s, thus making the whole header the thickness of a 2×4.

After you have cut the pieces for the header, carefully align their ends and fasten them together. If the code calls for glue between the pieces, add glue to the adjoining faces in a wavy pattern. Face nail the pieces together using a nailing pattern prescribed by the code. Normally this would include 10d nails every 12" and two at each end.

If you are using engineered lumber for a header, you may not need plywood to make it as thick as a stud is wide.

If you are using solid dimensional lumber, use a filler of plywood or equivalent to make the two pieces as thick as a stud is wide.

A built-up header of solid dimensional lumber is as thick as a regular stud wall.

6. Put the header in place between two king studs. Cut jack studs to run from the sole plate to the bottom of the header.

Put the header in position, and then place two jack studs beneath it.

7. Nail through the king studs into the ends of the header. Nail the king studs and jack studs together by nailing through one into the other.

Nail through the king studs into the ends of the header.

8. Cut cripple studs to fit below window openings, and, if there is space, above headers. In these photographs, there is no extra space above the headers, and the plans have called for two jack studs on either side of a rough opening.

Cut cripple studs for use below window openings and above headers. Set them in place. Cut two extra cripple studs, one to be placed under each end of a window's rough sill.

9. Cut a rough sill for the rough window opening, and slip it into place. Set the cripple studs beneath it, including the ones at the ends. Nail through the rough sill into the ends of the cripple studs. Nail through the bottoms of the sole plate into the bottoms of the cripple studs. Nail through the end cripple studs into the jack studs.

Set the rough sill in place. Place cripple studs beneath it. Nail through the rough sill and sole plate into the cripple studs and through the end cripple studs into the jack studs.

10. At this point, some carpenters raise the wall. Others prefer to nail on sheathing while the wall is still horizontal, a sequence we will follow here. Nailing on the sheathing at this point has two advantages: 1) you won't be working against gravity as you would be nailing on sheathing when the wall is vertical; and 2) the sheathing strengthens the wall, acting as a brace and keeping the wall from shifting out of square left or right.

Before nailing on the sheathing, make sure the wall is truly square by measuring its diagonals. Measure diagonally from one outside point to the other, and then take the measurement of the other diagonal. If they are not equal, rack the wall until they are exactly equal. Toenail the top plate to the subfloor so the wall does not shift—or, if you are adding a short *cap plate*, as in these photos, add the cap plate, and toenail through it rather than the top plate.

Framer's Lingo

A **cap plate** is a 2×4 that goes on top of the top plate.

Blocking is made up of pieces of 2×4 nailed horizontally between studs as nailing surfaces for exterior sheathing and interior wallboard.

Before nailing on sheathing, check that the wall is perfectly square by measuring the diagonals. Rack the wall until the measures of the diagonals are equal.

11. A top plate receives a cap plate on top of it. This is a regular 2×4 running on top of the top plate. At corners, one cap plate falls short of the corner while an adjoining one laps onto the top plate of the adjoining wall. Doing this ties the walls together. Some framers choose to install the cap plates after the walls are erect. Some add the short, nonlapping cap plates now, as shown in these photos.

Add short cap plates now if you like. If you need two 2×4s, make the joint over a stud and no closer than 48" from any joint of the top plate below it.

Add short, nonlapping cap plates. Check the diagonals to make sure the wall is exactly square, and toenail through the cap plate into the subfloor to hold the wall while the sheathing is nailed on.

12. Add *blocking* for sheathing edges. Because sheathing comes in 4×8' sheets, some edges will be unsupported unless you add more wood to the walls. Supplying this support is called blocking. In a 2×4 wall, these short sections of 2×4s are nailed horizontally where sheathing edges are going to fall.

Carefully determine where sheathing edges are going to fall. Measure along the wall to these points, and nail in blocking so that the edges of the sheathing will fall along the centers of the blocking pieces.

Nail in blocking for sheathing so that sheathing edges fall along the centers of the blocking pieces.

13. Lay sheathing in place on the wall. At this point it doesn't matter if some covers window and door openings. Nail along the edges of the sheathing and along the interior of the sheathing into studs beneath.

Nail on sheathing.

14. Cut sheathing away from door and window openings as you go.

Cut sheathing away from window and door openings.

15. When you have nailed on all the sheathing and installed a shortened cap plate, the cap plate will look like the following figure.

When you have nailed the sheathing on over a shortened cap plate, a close-up of the top corner looks like this.

Raising a Wall

Raising a wall is a dramatic moment. Doing so takes a good portion of the whole framing crew and radically changes the way the jobsite looks.

The main job, of course, is hoisting and tilting up. A hazard is that if you tilt too far, the wall may topple off the subfloor in the direction you are pushing. Framers have different methods of preventing this. One is toenailing the vertically-standing sole plate to the subfloor as in the preceding step 3. Another is to nail vertical boards to the outside of the band joist below the wall. The boards should align with studs. The boards block any portion of the wall passing vertical away from the subfloor.

1. Remove toenails through the top plate or cap plate holding the wall square while the sheathing was nailed on.

2. Have two long 2×4s ready to act as braces once the wall is erect. Get several helpers to assist in tilting up the wall, one every several feet. Have everyone lift at the same time, lifting with the legs and not the back.

Have helpers all grasp the top plate of the wall and lift in unison.

3. Keep tilting the wall up. Slow the motion as the wall approaches vertical.

Keep tilting the wall up, slowing as the wall approaches vertical.

4. Have a couple of helpers hold the wall steady. Nail a 2×4 brace to the upper portion of the outside stud at one end. Have a helper hold a 4' level onto a stud near this end while you hold the lower end of the brace against the band joist running perpendicular to the wall. When the helper says the wall at this end is perfectly vertical, nail the bottom end of the brace against the band joist.

Do the same at the other end of the wall. Do not presume that because the wall is perfectly vertical at one end, it will be also at the other. Check it with a level and nail in the brace when this end is perfectly vertical.

When the wall is perfectly vertical at one end, nail a brace from the outside of one end stud to the band joist running perpendicular to it.

5. Look for the chalk line you made on the subfloor in step 1 of the layout. It should match perfectly with the inside edge of the sole plate. But sometimes the sole plate is too far inside or outside the chalk line. Shift the sole plate back or forward so that it aligns perfectly with the chalk line. Where it does, drive a nail into a joist below, not just into the subfloor. Sometimes you need a sledge hammer or a couple of strong helpers to assure that the sole plate is properly aligned.

The ends of the nails you toenailed through the sole plate in step 3 of layout will be exposed and sticking upward. Cut these off with nippers.

Add a brace every 10' along the wall. At each location, first nail down a piece of scrap 2×4, often called a *cleat*, making sure the nails go into a joist below the subfloor, not just into the subfloor alone. Then nail one end of a 2×4 brace to the upper portion of a wall stud. If you have not applied sheathing, do not let the end of the brace protrude beyond the outside face of the wall.

Check each portion of the wall for plumb, and then add a brace at that location to hold the wall steady and perfectly vertical.

Framer's Lingo

A **cleat** is a short stout piece of wood used to support another or to which another is nailed for stability.

Have a helper with a level check the portion of the wall that is being braced, then nail the low end of the brace to the scrap wood nailed to the subfloor and joist below.

Continue in this manner every 10' along the wall.

6. Check that the top of the wall is straight. Some framers do this by climbing a long ladder and eying down one edge of the top plate or cap plate. Another way to do it is to nail temporary 2×4 blocks to the outside corners of the top plate, run a taut line between the blocks, and then guide a 2×4 scrap by hand along the top plate. If a gap shows up between the line and the outside of the scrap 2×4 as you move it along, the wall is bowed in and has to come out in that section. If the 2×4 scrap presses the string outward, the wall is bowed outward there and has to come in.

Defects of bowing in or out should have been taken care of when you checked the wall for plumb and braced in these locations. You may have to start all over again, checking that the sole plate is perfectly aligned with the chalk line on the subfloor, that the ends are perfectly vertical, and that the intermediate braces hold their sections perfectly vertical.

A shortened cap plate nailed on top of a top plate looks like this. The cap plate of the adjoining wall will lap onto the top plate of this first wall, fastening the two walls together.

Fire Blocking

Your building code may call for *fire blocking* (sometimes called fire stops) in the walls. In the event of a fire, the blocking stops flames from shooting from low inside a wall all the way up to the bottom of the top plate. It cuts such flames short and helps to prevent fire spreading from one story of a building to one above it. In platform framing, fire blocking is often not required unless the walls are 10' or more high.

Framer's Lingo

Fire blocking is horizontal framing pieces in a framed wall nailed in place to cut short heat and flame rising inside a wall in case of fire.

Blocking consists of framing pieces, 2×4s in a 2×4 wall, 2×6s in a 2×6 wall, nailed horizontally between vertical framing members.

Fire blocking may align one with another on opposite sides of vertical studs. Arranged in this way, the blocking also serves as nailing blocking for edges of sheathing or wallboard.

If the blocking is not to serve as nailing blocking for sheathing or wallboard, then it can be unaligned on opposite sides of vertical studs. It is easier to install if unaligned, because the nailing can be face nailing through the faces of studs into the ends of the blocking. If the blocking is aligned, at least half of the nailing has to be toenailing.

A technique for rapid fire unaligned blocking mimics the method for installing blocking between floor joists:

1. Snap a chalk line at the height wanted for the blocking.

2. Nail in the blocking, alternating blocking edges one above and the next below the chalk line.

To install unaligned fire blocking, strike a chalk line at the height for the blocking. Nail through the vertical studs into the ends of the blocking. Alternate the heights of the blocking so all nailing can be face nailing and not toenailing.

The result of unaligned fire blocking looks like this.

Dealing With Corners

Some quick reflection of wall framing will tell you that when two such walls as framed above meet, there will be a problem on the inside of the corner: on one there will be nothing into which to nail wallboard. Framers have two ways of dealing with this problem.

One way to deal with the problem is to use two extra studs—or more often one extra stud and blocking to take the place of the third stud—into the wall that needs a nailing surface.

The other way is to nail a stud on edge along the wall that needs a nailing surface.

You can nail these studs, or studs and blocking, in place before you raise a wall to the vertical position or after you raise and brace the wall. But if a wall has been sheathed already, then the on-edge stud method needs to have its on-edge stud nailed in place before the sheathing goes on.

First, let's look at the blocking and stud method:

1. Erect a second exterior wall to meet the first. Brace it and plumb it as you did the first wall. Set a cap plate on the second wall to lap onto the top plate of the first wall. Nail through the cap plate of the second wall to fasten into the top plate of the first wall, tying the two walls together.

2. Face nail blocks—about 10" long—to the top, bottom, and middle portion of the end stud on the wall that has no interior nailing surface. You may use a full-length stud, but of course, this is more expensive.

After you nail the blocks in place, face nail a full-length stud to the blocks.

A block corner arrangement looks like this from the outside.

A block corner arrangement looks like this from the inside.

The alternate, or on-edge, method goes like this:

1. On the inside of the corner, set a stud edgewise behind the end stud of the adjoining wall, creating a nailing surface for wallboard or paneling.

2. Face nail through the outside of this on-edge stud into the end stud of the adjoining wall. Toenail through it into the end stud of its own wall (the stud on the same sole plate). Toenail this on-edge stud into the sole and top plates.

An on-edge stud corner arrangement looks like this from the inside.

An on-edge stud corner looks like this from the outside.

Interior Walls

You build interior walls the same way as exterior walls. If they are bearing walls, you build them in exactly the same way. If they are nonbearing walls, also called partition walls, their headers do not have to be as hefty.

All interior walls must tie into the exterior walls they meet and have nailing surfaces at the corners for wallboard or paneling.

1. Layout and nail together interior walls in the same fashion as exterior walls. If the walls are bearing walls, use the size of headers determined by architects, engineers, or experts in your building department.

    If the walls are to be nonbearing walls, you can use horizontal 2×4s as headers.

Finger Tips

If you are thinking of using horizontal 2×4s for partition wall headers, take note that most interior doors, or interior windows, require nailing surfaces for the finished wood trim—door casing or window casing—that is to be put around them. If you only use a single horizontal 2×4 as a header, you will have nothing to nail the upper portion of the trim to. Think about the dimension of the door trim, and add nailing surfaces as appropriate. In addition, using a beefier header, indeed, jack studs also, makes for a more solid wall, one that does not shudder when a door slams.

Build interior walls with rough opening framing according to approved plans. Here a nonbearing wall header is a simple 2×4.

2. Layout and erect the longest interior wall first, then the next longest and so on to the shortest. Determining position from your plans, snap a chalk line on the subfloor at the position of one edge of the interior wall. Mark an X on the side of the line over which you will lay the sole plate.

3. Cut a sole plate for the interior wall, and set it on edge alongside the chalk line. Cut a top plate for the interior wall, and set it alongside the sole plate. Mark the sole plate and the top plate for the studs and cripple studs just as with an exterior wall.

4. Shift the top plate, and assemble the interior wall as you did the exterior walls. Make rough openings as determined by the approved plans.

   When the wall is assembled, check that the diagonals are equal, which means the wall is square. If the diagonals start out as unequal, after you shift the wall to make the diagonals equal, nail on a diagonal brace to keep the wall from shifting back out of square.

A temporary brace on an interior wall.

5. Once the interior wall is tilted into place (step 6) you will have to nail the interior wall end stud to the exterior wall. Framers have a couple of ways of doing this. One is to have a stud on edge at the inside face of the exterior wall and two regular studs on either side. Another is to have two regular studs on either side of the position of the interior wall and blocking in between.

An exterior wall is ready for a partition wall to be set up against it. Two regular studs flank an on-edge stud (parallel with the sole and top plates).

Interior walls may meet exterior walls with mere blocking between studs. This affords less nailing surface for wallboard.

6. Tilt the wall into position. While helpers steady the wall, check that the sole plate is aligned with the chalk line. Then nail through it to the subfloor, and preferably through the subfloor into joists below.

7. Check the interior wall for plumb. When it is plumb, mark the position of the top plate of the interior wall against the top plate of the exterior wall. If the cap plate is in place on the exterior wall and not cut away to accommodate a tie-in cap plate from the interior wall, cut out a $3^1/_2$" space for a tie-in cap plate from the interior wall.

Make a $3^1/_2$" opening in the cap plate of the exterior wall to accommodate a tie-in cap plate from the interior wall.

8. Set a cap plate onto the interior wall long enough to fit all the way across the top plate of the exterior wall. Hammer it in place.

9. Check that the interior wall's end stud against the exterior wall is not bowed left to right but perfectly plumb. When it is, nail through the end stud into the stud or blocking that helps form the corner there. If the wall is slightly bowed, toenail through the point of the worst part of the bow into the stud or blocking first to correct the bow. Then complete the rest of the nailing.

Framing at the Ceiling

It can happen that once the ceiling joists are put in (see Chapter 13), the cap plate or a corner of an interior wall does not align with ceiling joists. In this case, you need to add some blocking to give the cap plate stability and wallboard something to be nailed to.

Where a top plate runs between joists—here between the lower edges of engineered joists—nail blocking into place to stabilize the top plate and add nailing surfaces.

Where a corner is left with nothing to nail against above, add blocking.

Where a corner falls between joists, add blocking.

Bathroom Framing

Bathrooms generally require some special framing because of supply pipes and large waste pipes that feed into and away from them. Check your plans carefully, or consult a bathroom designer to make sure that what you are framing is going to work for the fixtures you intend to use. Where the large drain pipes are to go is often called a *wet wall*. Sometimes these are made of 2×6s to accommodate the large diameter waste pipes.

Even in 2×4 walls, you will need extra blocking to act as support for sinks or vanities or for pipes.

Here two supply pipes and one waste pipe emerge from a wall for a sink. Blocking has been placed at the proper height to support the sink. The plumber or the framer has nailed on steel plates to protect the pipes against nails or drilling after the finish walls have been installed.

Pay attention to special framing needs for the likes of bathtubs and whirlpool tubs.

Blocking has been installed to stabilize a supply pipe to a toilet tank.

Where a whirlpool tub is to be installed, you need special framing. Generally, the manufacturer of the tub supplies a drawing for this framing.

The Least You Need to Know

◆ Exterior walls are mainly vertical studs but very often also door and window openings that require headers at the top and jack, king, and cripple studs for support.

◆ The easiest way to lay out an exterior wall is from a framing plan that shows all the proper headers, jack studs, and so on.

◆ Layout a wall by marking the sole plate and top plate together, showing position of studs.. Precision in marking the location of all studs is critical to success.

◆ Tie together walls at the corners in part by lapping a cap plate from one onto the top plate of the other.

◆ Frame interior walls much like exterior walls, but nonbearing interior walls can have less hefty headers.

◆ Some building codes may require fire blocking in framed walls.

In This Chapter

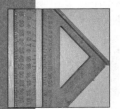

Chapter 13

Ceiling Joists and Roof Framing

Once you get the walls up, you tie them together with joists. These are called ceiling joists to persons below. If they create a floor above, they are floor joists to anyone above them.

Then the next big job to look forward to is making a roof. There are exceptions, but we'll presume here that the rafters will rest on the same cap plates as the ceiling joists.

Cutting rafters requires the use of a framing square. It helps you figure out the length of the rafters and the cuts at the top and bottom. Once you plan and cut one rafter, you can use it as a template to cut all the others.

Much roof framing today is done with trusses, assemblies of 2×4s that do not require the fancy measuring and cutting as for rafters. Ordered from a factory, they are delivered ready-made. Unfortunately, they do not offer as much attic space as regular rafters, and they are somewhat awkward to put into place. But because they are so prevalent and so handy in so many situations, we conclude this chapter with a brief section on erecting trusses on a one-story building.

Installing Ceiling Joists

Setting up ceiling joists is a lot like setting up joists for the first floor. In fact, the ceiling joists of one floor are often the floor joists for the living space above. But often there is no living space above, and the joists have no double designation, so they are ceiling joists.

The same rules apply to ceiling joists as to floor joists. They must meet local code for span and size; the greater the span, the "deeper" the joist has to be.

You may have to trim the top outside corners of the ceiling joists to accommodate the slope of the roof. Doing so is not difficult, but the method is best understood after understanding how to cut rafters. See the section "Trimming Ceiling Joists to Accommodate the Slope of the Roof," which follows the section on cutting rafters.

When you set ceiling joists into place, you will be working from a ladder, generally a sturdy step ladder. Before working on ladders, review all of the safety precautions about them written in Chapter 5. Make sure your helper knows all the precautions as well.

To make and install the ceiling joists that cap the walls made in the preceding chapter, follow these steps:

1. Set up any beam that ceiling joists are meant to rest on or connect to.

Hoist a beam into place.

2. Place a beam and check it for level.

Check the beam for proper position.

3. Secure the beam to its support walls and posts.

Secure the beam to its supports.

4. Consult your framing plan to see where the ceiling joists are meant to go and where the openings are for stairs, chimneys, and so forth. Mark the locations of ceiling joists on the cap plates of the stud walls.

5. Cut ceiling joists to length, keeping in mind that a band joist is going to go across the ends of the ceiling joists and itself rest on the cap plate.

6. Hoist joists into position. Some will rest on cap plates.

Position joists on a cap plate.

7. Toenail the joists to the cap plate.

Toenail the ceiling joists to the marks you have made
on the cap plate.

8. Where ceiling joists are meant to have
their tops flush with a beam rather than
rest on top of the beam, set them temporarily in place by suspending their top
edges flush with the top edges of the
beam. You can do this by driving a nail
firmly into the edge of a joist (here an
engineered lumber joist) then bending the
nail down flat over the end of the joist.
The nail holds the joist top flush with the
top of the beam. It is then easier to attach
the joist hanger and be assured that the
top of the joist is flush with the top of the
beam. Trying to hold the joists flush while
also trying to hammer in the joist hanger
often leads to a joist top edge too high
or too low with respect to the top of the
beam.

Suspend a joist with a bent nail so that its top is flush
with the top of the beam.

The joists will look like this suspended by the nails before the joist hangers are nailed on.

9. Attach the joists to the beam with joist hangers.

Attach the joists to the beam with joist hangers.

10. At a cap plate, install a band joist by nailing through the outside of the band joist into the ends of the ceiling joists.

Install the band joist by face nailing through it into the ends of the ceiling joists.

Where possible, place ceiling joists over studs.

Where possible, place ceiling joists over studs in the wall below.

Be aware of what might be positioned between ceiling joists and adjust their spacing accordingly.

Think ahead to what you might have to position between ceiling joists. Here an air conditioning register is set between two ceiling joists.

Roof Framing

You have two ways of framing for a roof. One is to order trusses of the proper breadth and slope for the roof you have in mind. I discuss setting up trusses in the following section.

The other way is to cut rafters out of solid dimensional lumber, as carpenters have been doing for centuries and which is still an excellent method.

But this cutting does require some study, some familiarity with terms, and some work with a framing square. It all looks a bit bizarre at first, but when you see the logic of it, the method makes good sense. Another welcome part of the process is this: once you cut one rafter that you

test and see is proper in every respect, all you have to do to make the others is trace the lines of the first on similar dimensional lumber and then make the cuts to make rafter clones.

To this point in the framing of a house, most of the work has been in right angles. Every thing has been plumb or level, and all the cuts right angles. With rafters that all changes. The rafters are sloping pieces of dimensional lumber.

In one respect, rafters are like joists. The greater the distance they have to span, the "deeper" they have to be. Although you have to consult a professional architect, engineer, or your building department, in general here is what different rafter dimensional lumber can span if the spacing is 16" on center: 2×4s can span 5'4"; 2×6s can span 8'4"; 2×8s can span 11'; and 2×10s can span 13'11". These are only approximations, however, because a certain amount depends on the grade of the wood and how steep the roof will be.

Which brings us back to angles. Rafters slope or as some would say, they have *pitch*. Another way of saying this is that for every foot they project horizontally they rise a certain amount as well.

The horizontal distance a rafter spans is called the *total run*. The vertical distance the rafter covers is called the *total rise*. If a rafter covers 10 horizontal feet and descends 5 feet from its highest point to the wall that bears up its lower end, then its total run is 10 feet and its total rise is 5 feet.

Also note here the terms *unit run* and *unit rise*. The unit run is always 12". The unit rise is the number of inches of rise per unit run. If the total run is 10' and the total rise is 5', the unit run is 12" and the unit rise is 6".

The unit rise and unit run is often placed on a blueprint of a roof and shows up as two perpendicular lines, one representing the unit run and one, the unit rise. The lengths in inches of unit run and unit rise are marked next to the perpendicular lines.

Framer's Lingo

Pitch is the slope of the roof, usually referred to in unit of rise per unit of run. **Total run** is the span in horizontal feet of a rafter. **Total rise** is the vertical distance a rafter rises over the distance of its total run. **Unit run** is 12" of run. **Unit rise** is the number of inches of rise in a unit (12") of run.

We can express this pitch in another way, by giving the rise in inches for every 12 inches of run. In the example above, the rise is 6" for every 12" of run. This is often noted as a slope of 6 in 12. This is a steep roof, a slope of 45°.

We also need to make another very important point about rafters and their rise and run. The run is not generally measured as you might think to the absolute end of the rafter. Instead it is measured to the outside of the wall—this is called the *building line*—that supports it on its lower end. If the rafter extends beyond this point, as it nearly always does, this extra length is not counted in its official total run (nor in its span). Instead, this distance is added on later to calculate the full length of the rafter. The portion of a rafter that extends beyond the outside of the wall that supports its lower end is often called the *tail*.

Nor is the run on the other end completely logical at first glance. At their upper ends, rafters attach to a framing member called a *ridge beam*, or ridge for short. For calculation purposes the run measures to the center of the thickness of the ridge beam. And for calculation purposes, the rise measures to the center of the height of the ridge beam.

You should be familiar with several other rafter terms as well. The *ridge cut* is the cut of the rafter to fit against the ridge. The *bird's mouth cut* is the cut at the lower end of the rafter to set it on the cap plate of a wall. The *overhang cut* is the cut at the end of the rafter tail, generally perpendicular to the ground.

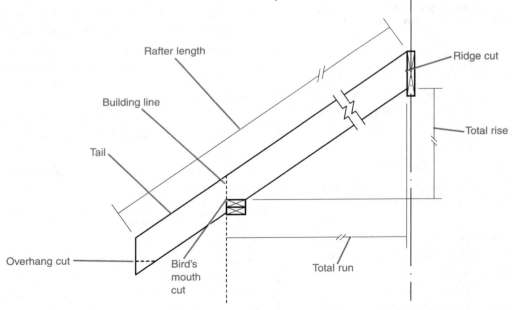

Rafters have certain terms and concepts with which you should be familiar.

(Copyright: John Hannah)

Framer's Lingo

The **tail** is the portion of a rafter extending beyond the lower supporting wall.

The **ridge beam** (or ridge) is the piece of lumber at the top of the roof to which the upper ends of the rafters are nailed. A **ridge cut** is the vertical cut at the top end of a rafter to fit it against the ridge. A **bird's mouth cut** is the two-sided cut near the lower end of a rafter so that it fits to the top of the wall on which it rests. A **building line** is the vertical line of the outside of the house wall supporting the lower end of the rafter, and is also a line drawn on a rafter to represent that line. An **overhang cut** is the cut at the lower end of a rafter, generally parallel to the house wall.

Finger Tips

When you set out to buy lumber for rafters, you'll want to know how long they need to be (which is not the same as total run). If you have drawn plans (blueprints) of the job, you may be able to estimate the length of rafters by measuring on the plans and converting from the scale of the drawing. But here is another way by using a framing square.

Lay a framing square on a work table. On the outside of the narrow arm of the framing square, find the rise in inches. Let's say the rise is 8". On the outside of the wide arm of the framing square, find the run in inches. Let's say the run is 12". Measure roughly between the 8" mark on the narrow arm to the 12" mark on the wider arm. Convert inches to feet. This distance (almost 14½') is roughly how long the rafter has to be between the ridge and the plate of the wall that will support it. You have to add on extra for the amount of overhang you want the rafter to have.

Getting to Know a Framing Square

In order to make the proper cuts for a rafter, you have to use a framing square, sometimes called a steel square. Generations of carpenters have used this tool to do just this sort of work.

A framing square consists of two perpendicular arms. The wider and longer one is called the *body*, or sometimes the *blade*. The shorter and thinner one is called the *tongue*. The body is 24" long and the tongue is 18" long.

Both the body and tongue are marked in inches on their outside and inside edges. In between are tables that help carpenters mathematically calculate rafter lengths, but we are going to use what we call the *step-off method*, so we can ignore these tables.

Using a framing square often calls for shifting it along the edge of a dimensional piece of lumber and aligning the unit rise and unit run measurements again and again with the lumber edge. To make this task easier, some framers apply tape at the measurements. Also devices called framing square guides screw tight to the framing square tongue and body edges. These allow the framer to quickly shift and align the framing square to the measurements he wants.

Buy a framing square that comes with instructions. These will explain the important components and how to use the framing square for marking and cutting both rafters and stair stringers. It will also have information on the tables, information you generally will not need until you get into advanced framing.

Framer's Lingo

The **body**, or **blade**, is the wider and longer of the two arms of a framing square. The **tongue** is the thinner and shorter of the two arms of a framing square. The **step-off method** is a way of using a framing square to physically mark off the lengths and cuts of a rafter or stair stringer.

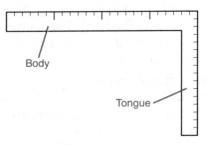

A framing square.

(Copyright: John Hannah)

Stepping Off a Rafter

A rafter has two vital cuts and one not quite so vital. These are the ridge cut, the bird's mouth cut, and the overhang cut. The first two cuts must be exactly at the correct angle and exactly at the correct location. If the overhang cut is a little off (it won't be if you follow these instructions properly), it can just be duplicated on all the other rafters.

1. Lay a piece of lumber stock across two saw horses. Determine which edge is the "crown" edge. This is the edge that should face upward after the rafter is cut. Position yourself on the opposite side of the rafter.

2. Position the framing square near the left end of the rafter and along its top edge. Put the tongue on the left and the body on the right; make the outsides of these two arms close to you. Position the tongue so that the unit rise in inches (here 8) as measured on the outside of the tongue

touches the top edge of the rafter. Position the body so that the 12" mark (the unit run) on the outside (the near side to you) of the body touches the top edge of the rafter. Draw a line along the outside of the tongue from the upper edge of the rafter to the end of the tongue. In my illustrations, the unit rise and unit run are marked at 8" and 12" on the outside of the tongue and body with tape.

Position the framing square to make the ridge cut line.

3. Mark a line down the tongue of the framing square from the top edge to the bottom of the tongue. This is the beginning of the mark for the ridge cut. With a straight edge—one edge of the framing square will do—extend the line you began all the way down to the lower edge of the rafter. This is the ridge cut.

Extend the ridge cut mark to the lower edge of the rafter.

4. Mark the "inches" portion of the run. Let's say your total run (that is, the horizontal distance for the rafter between the center of the ridge and the outside of the cap plate to the wall that will support it) is 7' 3". The "inches" portion is 3", and we take care of that first. Place the framing square along the top edge again as in step 2. Hold it so that the unit rise (8) touches the upper edge of the rafter and the unit run (12) touches the upper edge of the rafter. Use the outside of the framing square for these marks, that is, the sides close to you. Make a mark along the body at the distance for the "inches" portion of the run (here 3").

Shift the framing square along the rafter to mark for the first full foot of run. Shift it so the tongue touches the "inches" mark made in step 4. With the unit rise and unit run marks on the rafter edge, mark where the unit rise, the 12" mark on the body, crosses the upper edge of the rafter.

Mark for the inches portion of the run, here 3".

5. Shift the framing square to the right. Shift it so that the outside of the tongue touches the "inches" portion mark that you just made. Check that the unit rise shown on the outside of the tongue and the unit run shown on the outside of the body touch the upper edge of the rafter. Make a mark at the upper edge of the rafter where the body crosses the upper edge of the rafter (this will be at the 12" mark on the body). If you like, you can trace all the way around the framing square in its position on the rafter, but the main point is the mark at 12" along the body.

6. Shift the framing square again, this time so that unit rise mark on the tongue aligns at the upper edge of the rafter with the 12" mark made in step 5. Make a mark again at the unit run (12") mark where it crosses the upper edge of the rafter. This lays off the second full foot of run.

Mark the second foot of run.

7. Continue in this fashion down the rafter marking as many feet of run as the rafter is meant to span.

Mark for as many feet of full run as there are in the total run of the rafter.

8. Mark the outside of the wall. After all of the full foot marks have been made, shift the framing square one more time. Align the tongue with the last unit run mark made. Make sure that the unit rise and unit run on the outside of the tongue and body are aligned in the proper fashion with the upper edge of the rafter. Draw a line down the outside of the tongue as you did to begin the ridge cut line in step 3. Shift the framing square to extend this line to the bottom edge of the rafter as you did for the ridge cut line in step 4. This line, sometimes called the building line, conforms to the outside of the wall on which the rafter will rest. It also is the vertical cut line for the bird's mouth.

Extend the last mark across the rafter. This represents the outside of the wall on which the rafter will rest.

9. Measure down the building line from the top edge of the rafter to the bottom edge. Mark down from the top edge $2/3$ of this distance.

Measuring from the top, make a mark $2/3$ of the way down the building line.

10. Make the line for the horizontal cut for the bird's mouth. To do this, flip the framing square around so that the inside edges face you. Position the inside of the tongue along the building line. Shift the intersection of the tongue and body up and down along this line until the distance from the intersection to the lower edge of the rafter (the edge nearest you) equals the width of the cap plate on which the rafter is going to rest. If the wall is a 2×4 wall, this will be $3\frac{1}{2}$"; if a 2×6 wall, this will be $5\frac{1}{2}$".

When the framing square is thus positioned, draw a line along the inside edge of the framing square from the tongue-body intersection along the inside of the body to the lower edge of the rafter. This line should not be any higher up the rafter than the $2/3$ mark along the building line you made in step 9. This is to prevent too much rafter material being removed from the rafter and thus compromising some of its strength.

Mark from the building line to the lower edge of the rafter a line as long as the cap plate on which it is to rest is wide, $3^1/_2$ inches for a 2×4 cap plate. This line should not be more than $1/_3$ of the way up the building line from the lower edge of the rafter.

👆 **Finger Tips**

It may be that for a low slope the bird's mouth cut is low on the building line and does not remove much rafter material, which is fine. It may be that with very steep slopes, the bird's mouth is higher on the building line, but it should go no higher than $1/_3$ up the building line. This may mean that the horizontal part of the bird's mouth is less long than the cap plate is wide, and this is acceptable.

11. Mark for the overhang. Reverse the framing square again and set it up as in step 2. Place the outside of the tongue along the marked building line. Check that the unit rise and unit run align with the upper edge of the rafter. Mark for the length of overhang. If this is to be less than 12", mark the distance along the outside of the body; then mark a line through this mark parallel to the marked building line. If the distance is to be more than 12", mark the distance off in the same manner you marked off the total run distance of the rafter from the ridge cut line to the building line. At the last mark, draw a line across the rafter parallel to the building line.

Shift the framing square back in imitation of its position in step 2. Mark off the distance from the building line to the desired position of the overhang cut.

12. Now cut the rafter. Cut along the ridge line and along the overhang line. Cut along both the vertical and horizontal lines marking the bird's mouth.

✋ **Finger Tips**

The method described for cutting rafters did not account for the fact that the total run is really a distance from the outside of the wall at the lower end of the rafter to the *center* of the ridge. If the ridge is 2× material, the rafter should receive a new ridge cut parallel to the first but ¾" further down the rafter. Some carpenters prefer not to make this cut right away but rather wait to see how the rafter fits and make adjustments afterwards.

Trimming Ceiling Joists to Accommodate the Slope of the Roof

The ceiling joists rest on the same cap plate that the rafters do. Accordingly, their upper outside edges are likely to stick up above the upper edges of the rafters unless the ceiling joist upper edges are trimmed to the slant of the upper edges of the rafters. Here is the way to do that:

1. At the bird's mouth of the master rafter, measure up the building line (the plumb line of the bird's mouth cut) from the top of the bird's mouth to the top edge of the rafter. This is the vertical distance the rafter edge will be above the cap plate at the building line.

2. Mark the distance determined in step 1 on the end of a ceiling joist beginning at the bottom of the joist and measuring up. Make a mark on the end of the ceiling joist at this point.

3. Set a framing square on the ceiling joist, outside of the tongue and body away from you. If the end of the ceiling joist is on your right, have the tongue on your left and the body on your right. Position the tongue so that its mark for the unit rise is on the upper edge of the ceiling joist.

Position the body so that the 12" mark is on the upper edge. Shift the outside of the body until it touches the mark at the end of the ceiling joist made in step 2. Draw a line along the outside of the body from the end of the ceiling joist to the top edge of the ceiling joist. Above that line is the waste to be cut away so that the end of the ceiling joist matches the slope of the rafters.

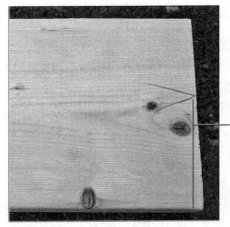

Vertical distance: the rafter edge will be above the cap plate at the building line (Distance A).

Ceiling joists often have to be trimmed to meet the slope of the rafters.

Unit rise   Unit run

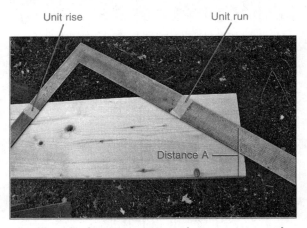

Distance A

Holding the framing square to the proper rise and run, shift the body until its outside edge touches the mark representing the height of the rafter above the cap plate at the outside of the cap plate. Draw a line along the outside edge of the framing square. Above this line is wood to be removed from the ceiling joist.

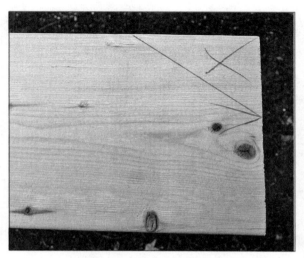

Cut away the material from the marked line to the ceiling joist corner. Now it will fit properly with the rafter beside it.

Putting Up a Ridge Beam— Method One

There are two methods of putting up a ridge beam to which rafters at their upper ends are attached. The first puts up the ridge and several rafters simultaneously; the other puts the ridge up on braces and then fastens rafters to it.

Following are the steps for putting up a ridge and several rafters simultaneously:

1. Choose a ridge that has at least as much depth as the ridge cut of a rafter is long; this gives full contact to the rafter end against the ridge.

2. Layout the ridge along the top plate. If the ridge is to extend beyond the wall that runs perpendicular to the one that will support the rafters, allow for this extra length. Lay the ridge on top of the ceiling joists resting on top of the cap plate that will support the rafters. Mark the ridge for the positions of the rafters. Normally, the rafters at their lower ends meet side by side with a ceiling joist. Mark the ridge accordingly so that the rafters descend to meet the ceiling joists.

Normally ceiling joists and rafters meet side by side at a cap plate.

3. Cut three more rafters, using the first as a template.

4. If there is no flooring on top of the ceiling joists in the area you are going to work, put some temporary flooring down now. A rafter that rests on the cap plate of the wall perpendicular to the ridge is often called a *rake rafter*. Nail through the ridge into the end of a rake rafter. Similarly attach a rafter at the other end of the ridge. You may need some scaffolding or sturdy ladders for the next steps; get some ready.

Framer's Lingo

The **rake rafter** is a rafter that rests on the wall perpendicular to the ridge.

Finger Tips

If you need more than one ridge piece to extend as far as the rafters are required, two ridge pieces should join at a rafter. Cut the first ridge piece to end half way across a rafter and the second one to begin at that same rafter.

5. Have one person at the lower edge of each rafter and at least one for raising the ridge. Raise the ridge, and hold it while the two others check the position of the rafters at the cap plate. If the rafter cuts look good and all is fitting, toenail the rafters to the cap plate and face nail through them into the ceiling joists. Have the two framers who did the nailing then set the other two rafters against the ridge and cap plate on the other side of the ridge. Nail these rafters to the cap plate and ridge. Normally the rafters on the second side would align with the rafters on the first side. Toenail them to the ridge, and nail through the ridge alongside the first rafters into the ends of the second pair of rafters.

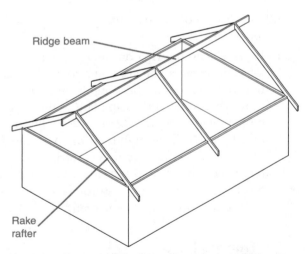

Raise the ridge with a rafter at each end. If the cuts look good, add a pair of rafters on the other side.

(Copyright: John Hannah)

Putting Up a Ridge Beam— Method Two

The other method of putting up a ridge beam involves braces. It does not require that you have four rafters cut and ready to go. Therefore you can test your master rafter before cutting other ones.

To put up a ridge and rafters by first supporting the ridge with a brace, proceed as follows:

1. The height of the ridge must be exact because you have cut the rafter to meet it at just an exact height. Therefore, the brace that is to temporarily hold the ridge in place has to be cut to a precise length. Calculate the length of the brace as follows: the total rise; plus the length of the vertical portion (plumb line) of the bird's mouth cut from the top of the cap plate to the upper edge of the rafter; minus the depth of a ceiling joist; minus the thickness of subflooring on top of the ceiling joists; minus the depth of the ridge beam itself.

2. Make braces of the proper length to support the ridge beam. Toenail them to the underside of the ridge, and support the joint with scraps of 2×4s face nailed to each, making a scab joint. Or make the braces longer than they need to be and face nail them to the ridge beam while the bottom of the ridge beam is positioned to a line on the braces marking the proper height for the bottom of the ridge beam.

3. Erect the ridge over a center line on the subflooring over the ceiling joists. Secure each brace holding up the ridge with two braces of its own, the two new braces being perpendicular to one another.

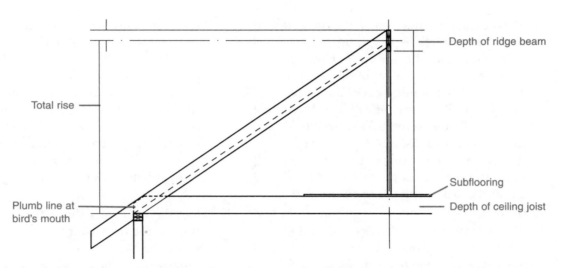

To calculate a brace to support the ridge to the proper height, figure on these measurements.

(Copyright: John Hannah)

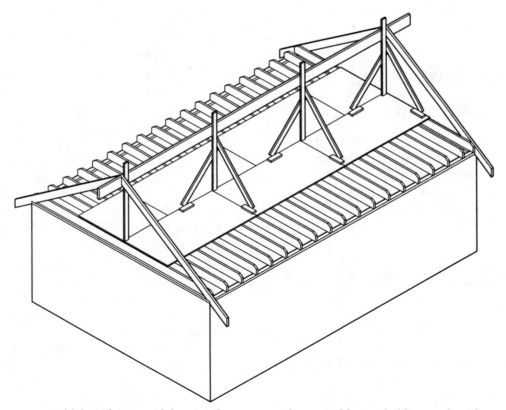

Hold the ridge up with bracing that supports the vertical braces holding up the ridge.

(Copyright: John Hannah)

4. Try the master rafter against the ridge. If all the cutting was perfect, if the ridge is at the proper height, and if you have not yet trimmed the ridge cut of the rafter to accommodate the thickness of the ridge, then the bird's mouth cut will be shifted at the bird's mouth toward the outside of the building by a distance equal to half the thickness of the ridge beam. If this is so, trim the ridge cut of the rafter by a distance equal to half the thickness of the ridge beam.

5. Test the rafter again. If it fits against the ridge and the cap plate as it should, use this rafter to be the template for all the others.

6. Cut the rafters, and set them up in pairs, first at the ends of the ridge and then filling in between.

Plumb the Rafters and Install Gable Studs

Now you have to make sure the assemblage of rafters and ridge is not tilted one way or the other, that is, shifted out of plumb. When you have done that, brace it in place. Then build what is called the *gable end* by erecting *gable studs* between the cap plate and the last rafter.

Framer's Lingo

The **gable end** is the house wall under the rake rafters. The **gable studs** are studs that are the framing for the gable end.

To make sure the rafters are plumb and to finish the gable wall, follow these steps.

1. Make sure that the rafters are plumb. Up at the ridge, hold the string of a plumb bob to the outside of a rake rafter. Hold the string so that the bob of the plumb hangs just above the cap plate of the wall below. Shift the ridge back and forth until the bob points to the outside edge of the cap plate. Hold the ridge steady at this point and run long 2×4s as temporary diagonal braces across the underside of the rafters. Run such temporary diagonal braces at both ends of the building and on both sides of the ridge.

2. Hold the string of a plumb bob under the center of the ridge over the cap plate of the wall below. The bob will point to the center point of the cap plate. Mark this as the center line of the cap plate. Measure left and right half the distance between studs (generally 8" so that the studs will be 16" apart). Mark for studs to be 16" on center left and right down toward the ends of the cap plate.

3. Hold a 2×4 to a mark on the cap plate where a stud is meant to go. It will not cover the last 1½" of the cap plate because it will meet the rake rafter at its upper end. Notch the gable stud to slide all the way across the cap plate and be perfectly vertical. Have a helper hold a level to the 2×4 to make sure it is plumb left and right. Make two pencil lines across the edge of the stud, one at the top of the rake rafter and one at the bottom.

4. Make a bevel cut across the stud at the upper mark. Cut away all the wood between this cut and the lower pencil line but only to a depth of 1½", the thickness of the rake rafter. Now the stud should fit all the way across the cap plate at its bottom, and at its top allow the rake rafter into the stud's notch. The top cut of the stud should align with the slope of the upper edge of the rake rafter.

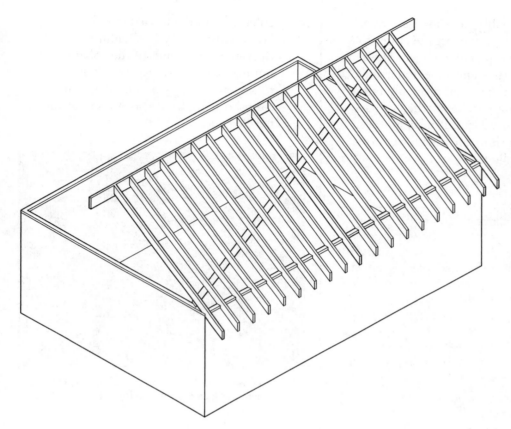

When the rafters are plumb, hold them that way with temporary 2×4 braces running diagonally at each corner on the underside of the rafters.

(Copyright: John Hannah)

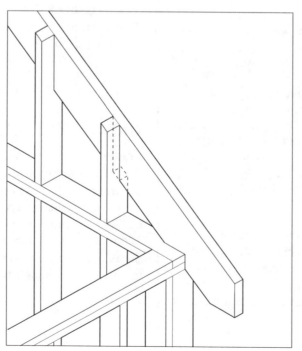

Cut gable studs to fit around the rake rafter and to match its upper edge slope.

(Copyright: John Hannah)

5. Cut all of the gable studs in this way, each being shorter than the last the closer to the end of the cap plate you get. The center gable stud runs up to the underside of the ridge beam, does not meet any rafter, and does not have to be notched or have its upper end bevel-cut. It may, however, have to be cut short for a gable vent (see sidebar that follows).

👆 **Finger Tips**

Two complications can occur at the gable. First, there is the temptation to use the gable studs to push up the rake rafters they help to support. But this only gives the rake rafters a crown not mimicked by the other rafters of the roof, so resist this temptation.

The other is that many gable ends call for a vent of some sort, either a passive vent—a louvered opening that allows air to circulate—or an opening for a venting fan, which forces air circulation when the fan is turned on.

Generally, these vent openings are just under the ridge. If your plans call for a vent opening, check the framing plans, which should specify the size of the opening. If a vent opening is called for, do not install a full-length center gable stud under the ridge. Instead, nail parallel 2×4 sills running horizontally from the longest gable stud on one side of the ridge to its counterpart on the other side, defining the top and bottom limits of the gable vent opening. Then add a cripple stud below the lower of these 2×4s and a cripple stud above the upper 2×4. You may have to add two vertical 2×4s running between the upper and lower gable vent space sills to define the left and right limits of the opening.

---

6. Some designs call for framing members called *collar ties*, which are pieces of dimensional lumber connecting opposing pairs of rafters and help stabilize the roof structure. If your designer has called for

collar ties, find out what size they should be. Install them by face nailing them to the rafters. The ends of the collar ties do not necessarily have to extend all the way to the upper edges of the rafters but can stop short and have a square rather than a beveled end.

Where a designer has called for collar ties, cut and nail them in place against the faces of the rafters.

📖 **Framer's Lingo**

A **collar tie** is a framing member connecting a pair of rafters, each on an opposing side of the ridge beam. Collar ties stabilize the roof structure.

Gable Overhang

In many instances, a house has a *gable overhang* that matches the overhang at the eaves. A pair of rafters meet at the end of the ridge beam to form the overhang. The rafters are supported by what are called *outriggers*. These are pieces of 2×6 that run from the pair of rafters just inside the rake rafters, across notches in the rake rafters to the overhang rafters. Here is how you do this:

1. Roughly divide the length of a rake rafter above the cap plate into four parts. Mark the division between the parts; there will be three marks. At each of these marks, cut a notch for the outriggers. These would be $1^1/_2$" deep and $5^1/_2$" long. Cut outriggers from 2×6 material to run from the face of the next-to-the-last rafters across the rake rafters to the inside faces of the overhang rafters.

2. Set the outriggers into their notches in the rake rafters. Nail through the rafters next to the rake rafters into the ends of the 2×6 outrigger pieces. Nail through the outriggers into the notches of the rake rafters.

3. Using scaffolding, nail overhang rafters to end of the ridge and to the ends of the outriggers.

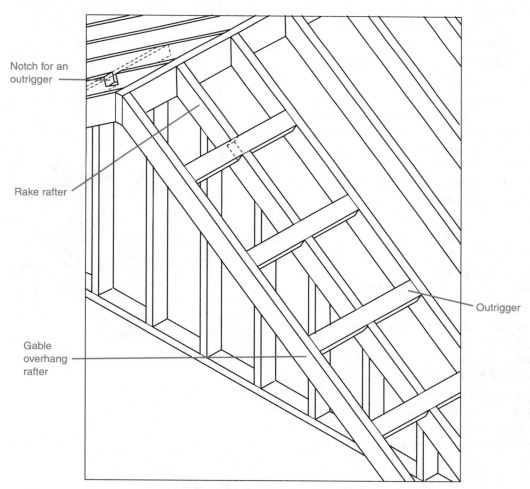

Notch for an outrigger

Rake rafter

Gable overhang rafter

Outrigger

Support gable overhang rafters with outriggers.

(Copyright: John Hannah)

Eaves

Finishing off the rafter tails at the *eaves* is normally considered a finishing job and not a framing one. But it is appropriate here to discuss how this is normally done. The construction at the eaves is sometimes called the *cornice*.

Your designer may have his or her own ideas about how the rafter tails should be treated. If so, this person should be able to provide you with detailed drawings on the construction.

Rafters can end in several ways. They can be untrimmed, which means the end slants back toward the house. They can end in a plumb cut, or they can end with a plumb cut near the top and a horizontal cut as the bottom.

Here we consider the notion of the rafter ending in a plumb cut.

For a simple treatment called *open eaves*, you simply nail a board, called a *fascia*, across the ends of the rafters and leave everything else exposed. If this is to be the treatment, then blocking needs to be nailed between the rafters at the cap plate to keep wind and weather out of the area under the rafters.

Another treatment is called *boxed eaves*. Here you nail a fascia to the ends of the rafters and then a piece of sheathing on the underside of the rafters running from the fascia back to the house wall. This piece of sheathing is often called a *soffit*.

A more sophisticated boxed eaves makes the soffit horizontal. Pieces of 2×4 called *lookouts* are nailed to a *lookout ledger*, which is a straight board running horizontally on the house wall. The lookouts run horizontally to the ends of the rafters. The soffit is nailed to the underside of these lookouts. Soffits often require ventilation screening in them, preventing condensation in the area between rafter insulation and the underside of the roof sheathing.

Framer's Lingo

Eaves are the construction where the rafter overhangs the wall of the house. **Cornices** are the constructions at the eaves. **Open eaves** are eaves with no more than a fascia nailed to the ends of the rafters. **Fascia** is a board nailed to the end of rafters. **Boxed eaves** are eaves with a fascia and a soffit, closing off the weather to the underside of the rafter tails. A **soffit** is a piece of sheathing running from the ends of rafters back to the wall of the house. A **lookout** consists of 2×4 pieces running from a lookout ledger to the ends of the rafters. A **lookout ledger** consists of a horizontal board nailed to the house wall to support lookouts.

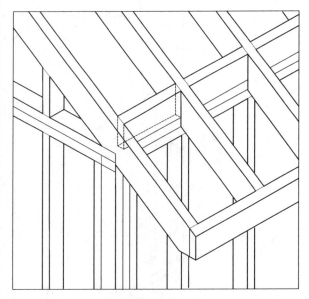

Open eaves.

(Copyright: John Hannah)

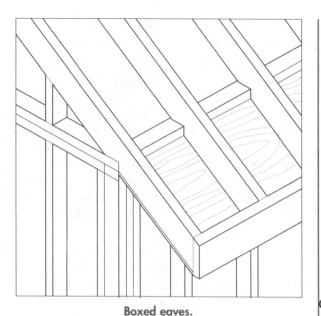

Boxed eaves.

(Copyright: John Hannah)

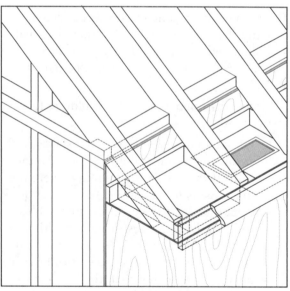

Boxed eaves with a horizontal soffit.

(Copyright: John Hannah)

Sheathing

Sheathing a roof is much like sheathing a floor. Begin at the lowest part of the roof. Check the plans to see how the eaves are to be built and how far the sheathing should overhang the end of the rafter and a possible fascia board.

Check with the manufacturer about the proper amount of gap between panel ends and panel long edges. If you are using OSB panels, check if one side is rough and one side smooth. If one is smooth, place the smooth side down; the rough side will give a better grip to your shoes on the roof.

Heads!

Working on roofs is dangerous. Consider having professionals install the sheathing and roofing materials for you. If you want to do the sheathing yourself, work from firm scaffolding to put up the lowest panels of sheathing. Then nail 2×4 cleats parallel to the sheathing as you work your way to the ridge. You can also use harnesses when working on a roof. These envelope your torso and connect to a cable you fasten to the roof so that if you slip, you won't fall to the ground.

To sheath a roof, proceed as follows:

1. Choose the proper sheathing for the job. Make sure it is rated for the spacing between your rafters and for its work as roof sheathing.

2. Think ahead. Because you will start at the bottom of the rafters and work toward the ridge, you will have to trim the last panels to fit at the top. Panels at the top should not be less than 16" wide. If this would be the case, trim the bottom panels so that the top ones will be wider than 16".

3. Begin at the bottom of the rafters working on firm scaffolding. Install the first panel flush with the end of the outermost rafter and falling along the center line of a rafter 8' away. Always install the panels perpendicular to the rafters.

4. Trim the last panel in the lowest course. Begin the next course with a half panel so that the ends of panels are staggered.

5. At the ridge, trim the panels for the top course. Save the trimmed pieces for using on the other side of the roof.

Sheath the roof with roof sheathing panels. Work up toward the ridge. Stagger the joints of the panels.

Using Trusses

You can avoid the precision of cutting rafters by framing a roof with trusses instead. Trusses are made of 2×4 material laid flat in factories. The 2× pieces are joined with metal fasteners called truss plates or gussets. A horizontal bottom chord spans the distance from outer wall to outer wall. Two top chords form the slope of the roof and 2×4 pieces called webbing make an engineered supporting configuration (often in a W shape) between the bottom chord and the top chords.

But there is a trade-off. When you use trusses, you generally lose storage space in an attic because the trusses require components running between the top and bottom chords. You also make it more difficult to create dormers.

In addition, putting up trusses is tricky. If you are building a garage or shed or some other one-story structure, you are lucky; you could probably put the trusses up with a few helpers. If the structure is higher, you likely will have to have a crane to hoist the trusses to the top cap plate. Moreover, stabilizing the trusses is vital. For a one-story building you can do this with long 2×4 braces running from stakes in the ground. For higher buildings, braces have to run from subflooring.

Trusses are custom-ordered. You give the dimensions of the building, the height you want the truss to go, the length the overhang should be, the kind of cut at the end of the overhang, and so on. Trusses are normally delivered bundled and should be kept as dry and out of the weather as possible.

Often the end or gable truss is assembled differently than the others. Rather than diagonal webbing, end trusses will likely have vertical 2×4 material so that sheathing can be nailed to them.

To erect trusses on a one-story building, follow these steps:

1. Have two long 2×4 braces and stakes ready at the end of the building. Along the cap plate at the end of the building where the first truss is to go, nail a 2×2 $1\frac{1}{2}$ inch back from the outside edge of the plate. This will help hold the first truss in position. In addition, nail two 2×4s to the end wall below so that the 2×4s rise vertically above the cap plate higher than the location of the top chords of the trusses; these will act as temporary stops to brace the first truss.

2. You might want to sheath the first truss while it is still on the ground. Doing so will save some trouble later, although a sheathed truss will be heavier than an unsheathed one, making the hoisting more difficult.

3. Working with trusses is awkward because they are large, but they do not weigh much. Carry the first truss upside down into the building. Hoist one end so that its top chord rests on the cap plate of a wall to which it will be perpendicular, that is, a side wall.

4. Slide the truss out until you can hoist the other side up and set the opposite top chord on the opposite wall's cap plate. You will have to be working from steady scaffolding for this work.

5. With a person at each end inside the building on scaffolding, have a third person use a 2×4 to push the peak of the truss upright. The top chords on the cap plates will rotate and the bottom chord will end up on the cap plates.

6. Shift the truss over to the end wall cap plate. Set it between the upright 2×4 braces you have nailed to the outside of the end wall and the 2×2 nailer 1½" back from the outside edge of the cap plate. Align the truss left and right; then nail through the vertical 2×4 braces into the top chords of the truss and through the bottom chord of the truss into the 2×2 nailer.

7. Check the first truss for plumb. When it is plumb, nail the braces running from stakes in the ground to the top chords.

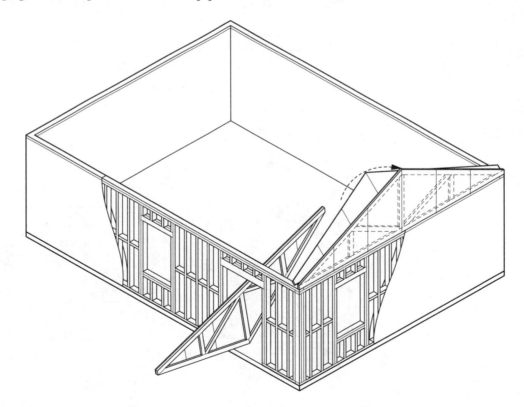

Bring in the end truss upside down, setting its top chords on the cap plates. Then use a long 2x4 to rotate it upright.

(Copyright: John Hannah)

Stabilize the second truss with a 2×4 running from the first truss.

(Copyright: John Hannah)

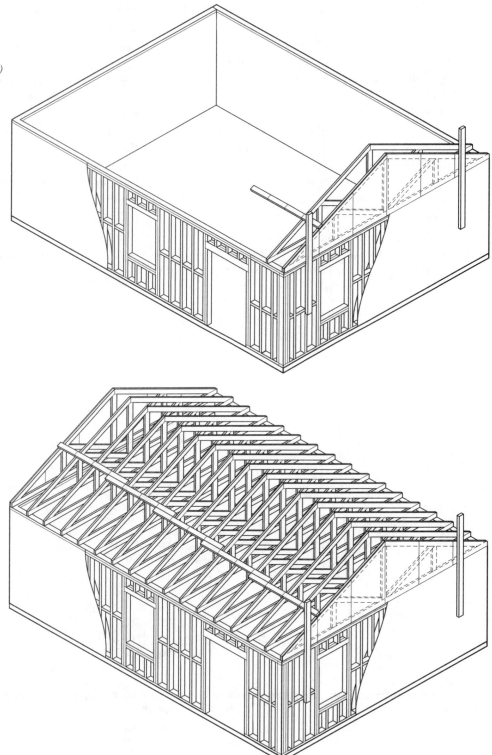

Bring up, nail, and brace more trusses. Brace each one with 2×4 temporary braces running from trusses preceding it.

(Copyright: John Hannah)

8. Bring in the next truss upside down. Set it up to the plates upside down as with the first, and then rotate it into position. Set the bottom chord to the proper position on the cap plates of the side walls—this would generally be over studs below—and toenail the bottom chord to the cap plates. At a point more than 4' up from a side wall, nail an 8' 2×4 to one of the top chords of the first truss and to the adjacent top chord of the second truss, thus stabilizing the second truss; make sure that the spacing is proper before doing the nailing. Make a similar brace on the top chords of the opposite side of the peak.

9. Bring up subsequent trusses. Toenail each to its proper position on the cap plates. Brace each with the 8' 2×4 temporary brace running across the top chords. Add new temporary braces as needed, lapping braces one truss space as you go along.

10. At the far end, put up the last truss before the three that would precede it so you can rotate it up more easily. Bring in the last three upright. Nail and brace each into position.

11. Check the whole assembly for plumb again, and adjust the outside braces as needed. Start nailing on roof sheathing at the lower ends of the trusses. When a whole bottom course is nailed on, remove the temporary 2×4 braces nailed to the top chords and put on the second course of sheathing. Proceed in this manner up to the ridge.

12. The truss manufacturer or your designer may call for internal bracing for the trusses. These may run horizontally along the tops of the bottom chords or from low on the inside of a top chord to high on the inside of the top chord of another several trusses away, fastening to any top chords it passes.

The Least You Need to Know

◆ Ceiling joists tie together opposing walls.

◆ Roof framing with rafters requires work with a framing square.

◆ Cutting rafters is very exacting and even a slight error results in a poor fit.

◆ Some roofs have a gable overhang where rafters extend beyond the end wall of the house.

◆ Rafters are usually enclosed at the eaves with fascia boards (at rafter ends) and soffit boards (below the rafters).

◆ Trusses are useful for some roofing situations, but they offer less attic space than rafters and are awkward to put into place.

◆ Working on a roof is dangerous. Either have professionals do this for you or work with extreme caution. Use temporary cleats nailed to sheathing as you work up toward the ridge or fall-prevention tethers that hold you to the roof should you slip.

In This Chapter

- ◆ Vocabulary of stair building
- ◆ Building a small stair
- ◆ Headroom and landing clearance
- ◆ Cutting a stair carriage

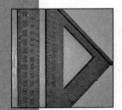
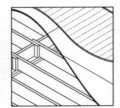

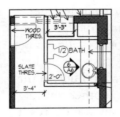

Chapter 14

Stairs

Stair building is somewhat like rafter cutting; we get back to the rise and run idea again. And, not surprisingly, with rise and run we use the framing square again.

Stairs have a special quality; a relationship exists between how far you step upward and how far you step forward. The higher you step up, the less you move forward comfortably. And if you were to move comfortably forward, you would step up less high. Think of a steep stair as compared to a shallow stair. A steep stair comes close to being ladder-like; you gain in height, but you don't move forward that much. A shallow stair comes close to being a ramp; you move ahead quite a bit, but each step is shallow.

Ancient peoples understood this as well as we do, and their stairs show the same respect to a ratio between the amount of stepping upward and the amount of stepping forward as ours do.

As you might have suspected, the term for the amount of height you gain in a single step is called the *unit rise*. And the term for the amount forward you progress in one step is called the unit run. We can express the ratio between the unit rise and the unit run in a comfortable stair in this way: in a comfortable stair the sum of the unit rise and the unit run should equal between 17" and 18". If you step up 9", you are most comfortable stepping forward 8 to 9". If you step forward 11", you are most comfortable stepping upward only 6 or 7". The steeper the stair, the less unit run. The shallower the stair, the more unit run.

In a stair, the unit rise should generally fall between 6 and 9". Beginning with this measure, determine how many steps the stair is to have, and then determine the precise measurements of the unit rise and unit run.

First, let's introduce a bit more vocabulary. The total run of a stair is the sum of all the units run, and the total rise of the stair is the sum of all the units rise. A *tread* is what you put your foot on. Its measurement back to front is a unit run, plus any extra it has for the *nose* or nosing, the rounded portion that hangs over the tread below. The portion that rises from the level of one tread to that of the next one above is called a *riser*. In a crude stair, the treads rest on cleats, which are attached to a side piece called a *stringer*. In a crude stair there are no risers. In more sophisticated stairs there are risers, and the stringer becomes a *carriage*. These are like stringers but have been cut so that the treads rest on the horizontal portions of the carriages, and the risers are fastened to the vertical parts.

Framer's Lingo

Unit run is the distance forward in one unit of the stair. **Unit rise** is the distance up in one unit of the stair. **Total run** is the sum in a stair of all the units run. **Total rise** is the sum in a stair of all the units rise; it is equal to the distance measured from the finish floor at the top to the finish floor at the bottom.

Tread is the piece of a stair on which your foot steps. A **riser** is a vertical piece between treads. A **nose** is a portion of a tread that extends out over a riser. A **stringer** is a piece of dimensional lumber used in a crude stair, and a **carriage** is a piece of stringer material that has been cut for horizontal and vertical portions on which and to which treads and risers are fastened.

Let's begin with baby steps here, then get progressively sophisticated. I'll begin by showing you how to build a small stair, say one of three treads.

Next, I'll explain how to make a full-length stair you might want to use on a framing job, then move on to building a more sophisticated stair.

Even a small crude stair requires precise measurements and cutting. Small mistakes lead to tilted stairs or stringers you must discard. Calculate with precision. Measure twice and cut once.

In addition, be sure your stair conforms to the local code. Even short stairs sometimes are required to have railings. Some wide stairs need a carriage in the middle to support the treads. When in doubt, call the local building department.

Finger Tips

Note that in regular stair building, there is one less tread than the number of risers. This is because the last "tread" is where your foot falls on the upper floor (if you are climbing the stair) or on the ground floor (if you are descending the stair). This "tread" is not part of the stringer or carriage, but it enters into the calculations.

Note also that the first riser rises from the ground floor to the first tread. It corresponds to the first unit rise.

In addition, note that the unit run does not include the nose of the tread. Thus the extra distance of the nose does not enter into our calculations. This becomes important when you are thinking about tread material. If you are using treads with nosing on them, do not trim these to be as wide as a unit run. They have to be as wide as a unit run *plus* however much nosing is meant to project beyond the riser below, usually about an inch.

Building a Short Flight of Steps

Let me show you how to build a short flight of stairs, one of three treads. I want to set the treads onto cleats that are face nailed to the stringers, not onto a cut carriage. For this example, I am saying the total rise of the stair is 26". If you were building such a stair, for example, to descend from a deck to a patio, this would be the distance between the top of the flooring of the deck and the level of the patio.

To make a small stair of the type just described, follow these steps.

1. Divide the total rise by 7". The 7" represents an average rise for one stair. The result of dividing 7 into 20 is 3.7.

2. After dividing the total rise by 7, round the result off to a whole number. You can round up or down; rounding up gives one more stair in your flight of stairs than rounding down.

3. Let's round off 3.7 to 4. This means we will have four steps. But note that the fourth step (going up) is really the level of the deck itself. Our little flight of steps will have three treads.

4. Divide the total rise (26") by the number of steps, 4. This gives us the unit rise, here 6.5. This is the rise for each step.

5. Now we need to calculate the unit run. Remember that the unit rise plus the unit run should equal 17 or 18 or some figure in between. We subtract 6.5 from 17.5, and the unit run is 11.

6. Because the unit run is going to be 11" and we are going to have four steps, the total run will be 44".

7. Prepare a long 2×12 material for cutting into stringers. Set it on top of two saw horses.

8. Place a piece of tape on the wide arm—the body—of a framing square at the dimension for a unit run, in our example 11". Place a tape on the narrow arm—the tongue—of the framing square to represent a unit rise (in our example, 6.5"). Use the outside scales of the body and tongue for each measurement.

9. Place the framing square on the 2×12 so the body is on the left, the tongue on the right, and the inside scales toward you. Place the unit run tape at one corner of the 2×12, and place the other tape on the near edge. Mark around the outside of the framing square.

Unit run tape   Unit rise tape

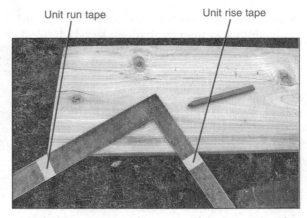

With the unit run on the corner of the stringer and the unit rise on the same edge, mark around the outside scale of the framing square. This marks the lower portion of the stringer.

10. Shift the framing square along the edge of the 2×12 until the unit run tape touches the end of the unit rise mark and the unit rise tape is on the edge of the 2×12. Mark around the 2×12 again.

Shift the framing square along the edge of the stringer until the unit run tape touches the end of the unit rise mark made in step 9. Check that the unit run mark is on the stringer edge. Mark around the framing square again.

11. Continue up for as many rises as you will have; in our example, four triangular marks are required for the stairway of four rises and three treads.

12. Return the framing square to the first unit run mark, the one made in step 9. Extend the first unit run mark to the backside of the stringer.

Return the framing to the first unit run mark. Extend this line to the far side of the stringer.

13. Return the framing square to the last unit rise mark, the one made in step 11. Extend the last rise mark to the backside of the stringer.

Extend the last unit rise mark to the far edge of the stringer.

You should have 2×12 marked as shown in the following figure.

The 2×12 board now looks like this. The stringer's bottom part is here showing on the left and the upper part on the right.

14. Saw along the extended marks made in steps 12 and 13. At the bottom of the stringer, saw along the first unit run mark, the one made in step 9. You now have a stringer looking like that in the following figure.

Cut along the two extended marks and along the first unit run mark. The stringer will look like this.

15. Make the second stringer the mirror image of the first.

16. Measure down from each run or tread line to account for the thickness of the boards you are using for treads. Let's use 1" stock, so the thickness is going to be 1". Draw a line in those places.

17. Nail or screw cleats to the stringers so that their top edges align with the lines drawn in step 15.

Attach cleats for the treads. The top of the cleats should be below the unit run lines a distance equal to the thickness of the treads.

18. Cut treads as long as the stair is meant to be wide. While a helper steadies the stringers, attach the treads to the cleats on the stringers.

The little stair will now look like this. Figures 9, 10, and 11 show other views.

A second tread view showing the insides of both stringers.

A third view showing the stringer meeting an upper header.

A fourth view showing the upper and lower ends of the stringer from the outside.

Attach the stringers to headers at the top of stairs with framing connectors.

Landing Clearance and Headroom

Building a full stair follows the same principles but uses more units rise and units run and longer stringers. You also have to deal with the elements of *landing clearance* and *headroom*. Landing clearance is the horizontal distance required by building code at the top and the bottom of a stair in order to enter and exit the stair easily. Headroom is the minimum distance required by building codes from the top of a tread to any joist or header above it.

If you are working with a stair opening already framed, you know you have to start against one of the headers. But the way you construct the stairs can increase or decrease the landing distance and can increase or decrease the headroom.

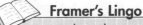

Framer's Lingo

Landing clearance is a horizontal distance needed at both the top and the bottom of a stair to enter and exit the stair comfortably. A minimum landing clearance is the width of the stairway. **Headroom** is a vertical distance between a tread on the stairway and the bottom of the stairway header above it.

First, let's look at the landing clearance. The landing clearance must be no less than the width of the stairs. Before you cut a stringer, make sure the total run will leave enough space for a proper landing clearance.

Use a plumb bob to find a point directly under the header of the stairwell opening against which the upper end of the stringer of the stair is to be attached. Mark this point on the lower floor.

Measure in the direction that the stair will take, the total run as you have calculated it plus the width of the stair. If in marking off this distance you run into a wall or other barrier, you'll have to make some adjustments.

You could reduce the unit run, thus reducing the total run. This would make each tread less wide. There is a limit of how narrow they can be, however, around 9". Or you could reduce the number of treads. If you calculated for, let's say, 15 treads, you can recalculate with 14 treads. This will make the stair a little steeper but will also decrease the total run.

You can get a rough idea of the headroom by running a string from the top of the stairwell header where the stair is to begin slanting down to a point beneath the opposite header, a point marking the total run on the lower floor. Then measure up from the string to the header above. This distance should be more than what your local code calls for in headroom, often 6' 8". Even this is pretty short for a person a few inches over 6' tall.

If you want more headroom, reduce the unit run, or eliminate a tread or two, thus reducing the total run. This will shorten the stair and make it steeper, but it will offer increased headroom. If these tactics don't work, you'll have to lengthen the stairwell opening.

Making a Full-Length Stair

Creating a full-length stair is like making the short stair earlier in this chapter but creating longer stringers. Really all you do is step off more marks with the framing square. Here is how to make a full-length stair:

1. Calculate the total run, unit run, total rise, and unit rise for the stair. Calculate the total rise by measuring from the top of the finish flooring at the top of the stair to the top of the finish flooring at the bottom. If the finish flooring is not on yet—and it usually isn't while the house is still being framed—find out what the thickness of the finish flooring is going to be on the upper and lower floors, and enter these into your calculations.

2. Lay out the cuts for the first stringer in the manner as for a short stair earlier in this chapter. Make the cuts at the top and the bottom of the stringer. Duplicate for the second stringer.

3. Add cleats along the lines for the units run. Nail tread material down to the cleats.

4. Attach the upper part of the stringers to the header at the top of the stairwell. If the stair is descending along a wall, nail through the stringer into the exposed studs. The best support is for the stair to descend between two stud walls because then both stringers can be supported.

A full-length stringer stair.

Making a Carriage Stair

The difference between a stringer stair with cleats and a carriage stair is cutting out the stringer along lines for the units rise and units run. Of course, this makes a more attractive stairway. Here is how to make a carriage stair:

1. Lay out a stringer, and mark off the units rise and units run. Take into account the thicknesses of the finish flooring on the upper and lower floors.

2. Make the cut at the top to fit against the header. The bottom cut is going to be different, however, from the stringers cut in the preceding sections. For those stairs the tops of treads were aligned with the unit run marks. For a carriage, however,

the treads are placed on top of the unit run cuts. Accordingly, the carriage must be dropped by the thickness of a tread. Mark a line parallel to the bottom line on the 2×12 representing the thickness of a tread. Saw the 2×12 along this line. Note, however, that this presumes the carriage is going to rest on the finish floor. If it is going to rest on a subfloor and have finish floor built up around it, then make a further adjustment before you make the bottom cut.

Cut along the units rise and units run lines, creating a saw-toothed piece of 2×12 called the carriage. Create a second carriage.

A full-length cut carriage looks like this.

3. Fasten the carriages to the upper header with framing connectors. Nail the carriages to the floor at the bottom. Nail through the carriages into any stud walls alongside.

4. Nail on the first riser, the one that will rise from the floor to the level of the bottom of the first tread (or, if the finish flooring is not yet installed on this level, leave this riser off for the time being. Nail in the second riser against the carriage. Snug the first tread against the first riser, and nail it to the carriage. Work your way up the stair by nailing risers and treads as you go.

Cut the rise and run lines to make a carriage.

The Least You Need to Know

◆ Like rafters, stairs deal in total run, total rise, and units of rise and run.

◆ Comfortable stairs respect an age-old formula between how much you step up compared to how much you step forward.

◆ Crude stairs can be built with stringers and cleats, but with no risers, which are the vertical pieces often rising between treads.

◆ More sophisticated stairs use the same principles as cruder ones, but the treads rest on their supporting members rather than cleats.

In This Chapter

- ◆ The framing of walls inside existing homes
- ◆ Closets, pocket doors, and sliding doors
- ◆ Old warped studs, joists, and rafters
- ◆ Building a knee wall under the slope of a roof
- ◆ Making an opening in a bearing wall
- ◆ Porch framing

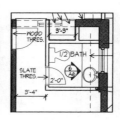

Chapter 15

Framing in Existing Buildings

Of course, plenty of framing is done in existing homes because people like to remodel. They make new closets or divide one larger room into two smaller ones. They might even want to remove a wall and place a supporting beam in its place.

Framing in existing homes follows the same principles as framing in new construction. If the wall is to be a bearing wall, it must have the proper headers. If the wall is to be a nonbearing or partition wall, you don't have to pay as much attention to the width of headers.

Putting up a wall in an existing house is made somewhat more difficult because of limited space. This means you may have to build the wall piece by piece and not tilt it up as in new construction.

Another problem with working in an existing home is that the studs or joists might have sagged or bowed with age. Trying to tie a new wall to old ones and old ceilings can be difficult unless you can make the old structure true again. In this chapter, I give you a couple of ways of doing that.

I also tell you how a convenient door called a pocket door is made for use in a home. A pocket door recedes into the wall. Thus it does not swing into a room or hall and is good where space is tight, as for a bathroom or closet. And I tell you how to make knee walls, short walls under the slopes of rafters. These make storage space on their far sides while giving better shape to living space on their "habitable" side.

Removing walls is somewhat more problematic. If an architect or structural engineer is confident that the wall is not a bearing wall, then you can remove it without the need for anything to take its place. But if the wall is a bearing wall, then a beam must take its place. A homeowner with helpers can reasonably erect a beam up to 8' long. But he has to erect temporary supporting walls on both sides of the wall—or portion of it—he is removing and leave the temporary support walls in place until the new beam takes over the work of supporting the weight the old wall carried.

Building Standard Walls

Building walls inside existing homes is in some respects like building them in new construction but in some respects different. The main similarity is that a framed wall in new work and a framed wall inside an existing home follow the same framing principles.

The main difference is that in an existing house, you have limited space to work with. For example, you can't tilt a wall up into place unless you build it shorter than it needs to be and fill in above the top plate (cap plates are generally unnecessary). But even then you are not likely to have the room to build a wall on the floor; it's simply too bulky.

The alternative is to build the wall piece by piece. Doing so requires marking precisely where the wall is going to go, putting in the sole plate and the top plate, and then nailing the studs and headers in between. Making sure the top plate and the sole plate align perfectly is essential.

Another problem with building a wall in an existing room is the existing ceiling and floor. You have to decide whether to remove portions of them or leave them in place. Often, the decision lies with the material. If the present flooring is carpet, you must cut out at least a strip of it to make way for the sole plate. If it is ceramic

tile, then you must remove a strip of the tile. If the flooring is resilient tile or wooden flooring, then you can put the sole plate over it.

At the ceiling, the problem is more one of fastening the top plate than of the kind of material. Likely the ceiling is made of plaster or wallboard, so fastening the top plate securely to the joists above is difficult because the position of the joist bottoms is hard to find with plaster or wallboard covering them.

It is not impossible, however. With a tool called a stud finder, you can detect the joists. Stud finders either locate the joists by means of radio waves finding the mass of wood or by means of magnets that swing smartly toward painted-over nails holding plaster lath strips or wallboard to the joists.

If the top plate is going to run perpendicular to the ceiling joists, you can nail directly through the ceiling material into the joist bottoms. I don't recommend this, however, if the ceiling is made of plaster; the pounding of the nailing could crack or loosen the plaster. Carefully drilling through the plaster and then using screws is a way around this. Another idea is to remove a strip of plaster to allow the top plate to fit directly against the bottom edges of the joists.

If the top plate is to run parallel to the ceiling joists, then you are lucky if you want the top plate to run directly under one of those joists. You can nail or screw directly up through the top plate into the bottom of that one joist. If, however, the top plate has to run parallel to the joists and yet not directly under one of them, you need to add blocking between a pair of joists for the top plate to fasten to. This requires removing all the ceiling material between two joists. That done, toenail blocking between the joists. While you are removing ceiling material between joists, remove it half way across the width of each joist bottom. That gives backing for new wallboard to go up for patching the ceiling hole.

The place where the new wall is to meet an old wall is treated much like the top plate. If you can fasten the end stud of the new wall to a stud in the old wall, so much the better. However, if the new stud is not going to be in a position to meet an old wall stud, then you have to remove wall material between studs so you can place blocking for the new walls's end stud between the studs of the old wall. Follow these steps to achieve your goal:

1. Determine the location for your new wall. Use a sturdy ladder, and determine the location of the top plate on the ceiling. Near where the new wall is going to meet an existing wall, hold a plumb bob's string to the ceiling so the plumb bob hangs just above the floor. Ask a helper to mark the floor at this spot. Repeat at the other end of the location for the new wall. Snap a chalk line between the two marks on the floor and between the two points where you held the plumb bob's string at the ceiling. Snap a chalk line along any old wall the new wall is going to meet; it will be between the chalk line on the floor and the chalk line on the ceiling.

2. Check that the chalk lines conform to where you want the wall to be. Determine where the ceiling joists and studs in the old wall are. If the top plate is going to run perpendicular to the ceiling joists, fine. If the new wall is going to run parallel to the ceiling joists, consider shifting the wall to run directly under one of the joists. If you cannot make such a shift, you must add blocking between joists. In similar fashion, determine where the studs are in the old wall. If the new wall is going to run between studs, you have to remove wall material to add blocking between studs.

Finger Tips

When you build a new wall in an existing room, you are likely to run up against baseboard that is nailed along the bottom of the existing wall. You will need to remove a section of this baseboard at the location of the new wall. So after you have determined the exact location for the new wall, mark the baseboard vertically where you plan to remove it.

A good tool for doing this removal is a reciprocating saw, which you can rent. Make a hole in the wall above the baseboard in order to get the saw blade above it. Check carefully below this hole to make sure there are no hidden pipes or electrical cables. If the path is clear, saw down through the baseboard to the floor—you may have to finish with a keyhole saw or an old chisel. If you cannot use a reciprocating saw for the whole job, use a keyhole saw.

If there is crown molding at the top of the existing wall, you will have to remove a portion of it as you did the baseboard. Use the same techniques but at the top of the wall. Be very careful because you are going to be working from a ladder. Here a keyhole saw may be a better choice than a reciprocating saw because if the blade of a reciprocating saw binds on something, it can buck in your hands and throw you off the ladder.

3. If you want to shift the location of the wall, rub out the old chalk lines and snap new ones. Remove ceiling material and wall material if you have to. Toenail in blocking between joists and between studs.

4. Lay out a top plate and sole plate in the same fashion as for making a new wall described in Chapter 12. Place the top plate and sole plate together, and mark both for the vertical studs. Mark for the studs to be 16"on center.

Add blocking between studs to which a perpendicular wall can attach. (This shows new work and a stubby wall that is really nothing more than framing for a door opening, but the blocking principle holds for work in an existing building.)

5. Fasten the top plate to the joists or blocking or to the one joist if it is to run beneath a single joist.

   Hold the string of a plumb bob against one edge of the top plate to make sure that the chalk line on the floor is in the proper position. If it is not, rub it out, and make a new chalk line.

   Place a sole plate along the chalk line of the floor, and nail it down. Hold the string of a plumb bob to a stud mark on the top plate for checking how it aligns with its corresponding mark on the sole plate to see if either plate has shifted during the nailing. If there has been a shift, make compensation for it when you nail up the studs.

6. Cut studs to fit between the top plate and sole plate. Measure for each one individually because in an existing house the distance between the ceiling and the floor at any two points may be different.

   Toenail each stud in place along its mark. Nail through end studs into studs in the old wall or into blocking you have put between studs of the old wall.

7. If you are making walls with a corner, you may need blocking for the top plate at the corner.

Add blocking between joists if a top plate is going to run between joists. (This shows new work, but the blocking would be the same for an existing ceiling.)

Where there is a corner in new walls, add blocking above the top plate for the corner to fasten to.

Finger Tips

Another method of putting up such a wall is more like putting up a wall in new construction. Obviously you can't build the entire wall and tilt it up as you would in new work; the ceiling would block your attempt. What some framers do if they have the room is this: attach the sole plate to the floor. Attach the studs to the top plate while all the pieces are lying on the floor by face nailing through the top plate into the ends of the studs. After you have fastened all the studs to the top plate, lift the wall into place, and fasten the top plate to the joists. Then shift the bottoms of the studs into place at the sole plate, and toenail them into place.

You can really only put up a wall this way if you have room to do the layout next to where the wall is going to go. In addition, you run the risk of cutting the studs either slightly too long or slightly too short if the ceiling or the floor undulates.

Framing a Closet

If you want to frame something like a closet or small room, proceed in the same manner as described in the first section of this chapter as you are just making more walls and adding a door opening.

Sketch out the closet on the floor; then make the appropriate chalk lines on the ceiling and along the old walls where the new ones will meet them.

Remove any ceiling, floor, and wall material to make way for blocking or good fastening. Remember to build the walls piece by piece as described in the previous section.

When it comes time to make a door, do regular door framing, though you're not going to need substantial headers above the door's rough opening. Sometimes the code allows a simple 2×4 nailed horizontally, sometimes two 2×4s on edge. Whatever the header, begin by putting up the king studs first. Follow these with the jack studs. Place the header on top of the jack studs, and then the cripple studs on top of the header.

The door opening in a newly framed wall, as long as it is not a bearing wall and local codes permit, can have a 2×4 as a header.

Framing for a Pocket or Sliding Door

In some instances you will want to—or have to—install a *pocket* or *sliding door*. This door does not swing out into a room but rather retracts into the wall. One can come in very handy where a regular door can't swing all the way open owing to a fixture, appliance, or piece of furniture. They are often seen as doors to small bathrooms.

Framer's Lingo

A **pocket** or **sliding door** is a door that slides horizontally into a wall cavity rather than swinging into a room.

You can install a pocket or sliding door in new construction or in existing homes where you are willing to build a new wall as in the previous section.

Manufacturers of pocket doors furnish their own hardware and requirements for framing the wall, so you have to buy the door and then follow the instructions. A lumber yard or store where you would order the door may have a set of instructions or specifications on hand for you to look at so you can decide if the door is going to work in the situation you have in mind for it before you buy it.

Normally, the metal hardware for the door fits into a 2×4 wall. Most important is the metal track at the top. The door slides along this track, which is attached to a 2×4 header. Metal vertical supports descend from the track to the sole plate. Sometimes these metal vertical supports are covered by strips of narrower wood such as 1×3s. At the rough opening, the track is covered with wood also. The covering acts as a nailer for finish door trim once the wallboard has gone up.

Pocket door framing requires fastening the metal hardware to 2×4 framing and often covering parts of it with narrower pieces of wood.

Another view of pocket door hardware and framing.

Correcting Old Studs, Joists, and Rafters

When you work in older homes, you are likely to run across studs, joists, and rafters that have warped over time. The wallboard, plaster, or flooring that covers them may actually mask the framing members deficiencies, or the wavy nature of the walls, ceilings or floors has simply been ignored or not noticed. But if you take off the wall covering—either because it is past its useful life or you want to do some reframing—the warps and bows of these framing members become obvious and possibly difficult to deal with. This is especially true for walls when wallboard or thin paneling is to go back up. In older homes where lathing was placed over studs and plaster placed over the lathing, plasterers could spread the plaster to various thicknesses, creating a smooth wall. But you can't do that with wallboard, which comes in sheets of uniform thickness and shows all hills and valleys once you nail it to the studs.

If you remove wall or ceiling covering and find warped or bowed framing members behind, you can deal with them a couple of ways. We'll work with walls first.

One way to deal with bowed studs in an old wall is to find a 2×4 that is almost as long as the wall and is straight to the eye. Place the 2×4 along the wall, and see where you can rock it back and forth along the studs. This should reveal where the "high" spots are. If the spot seems to be unique, you can trim it back with a hand or power planer (once you remove all the nails) so that it lines up with the other studs. Or you can "build out" the other studs to meet the high spot or high spots of the warped studs. You can use whatever framing material works for the distance required—2×2s, 2×3s, 2×4s—nailed to the sides of the old studs so that the new framing members protrude past the faces of the old

framing members. Alternatively, you can rip cut 2× material to nail to the edges of old studs or joists, ripping them so that they protrude to make the wall or ceiling even.

Add new framing pieces to the sides or edges of the old framing pieces so that the faces of the new framing pieces protrude further into the room than the faces of the old pieces. Here 2× material has been ripped and then nailed to the edges of old studs.

Using a long straight stud to help correct the bulges and valleys of an old wall is tricky because the wall is in two dimensions and the straight stud only detects bulges in one dimension. So another and more precise way of dealing with an erratic wall is as follows:

1. On the ceiling in front of the wall, measure out 2" from the wall at each end, and snap a chalk line between these points. Tack nails along this line in front of every stud in the wall. It's best if you can nail into ceiling joists.

2. Hang a plumb bob from one of the nails. If the nail is not nailed into a ceiling joist, it may not support the plumb bob. In this case, have a helper on a ladder hold the string of the plumb bob to the position of the nail. Measure several distances from the taut hanging string to the stud in the wall, and take notes of the distances as you move the plumb bob from stud to stud. The point where the distance from the plumb bob's line to a stud is the shortest is the point where the wall protrudes furthest into the room, that is, the wall's "high point."

3. With 2×2s, 2×3s, or 2×4s nailed to the sides of the old studs—or 2× material rip-cut and nailed to the edges of the old studs—build out to the high point, taking care that you check each new framing member with a 4' level as you put it up to make sure it is perfectly plumb.

You can also use *furring strips* and *shims* in the place of rip-cut 2× material. Furring strips are thin, rough pieces of wood about $1\frac{1}{2}$" wide, which you can tack to the edges of the studs. Shims are then slipped between the furring strips and the edges of the old studs or joists and used to shift the furring strips out as much as needed to make a smooth wall or ceiling.

Framer's Lingo

A **furring strip** is a thin piece of wood about $1\frac{1}{2}$" wide often used to make a new and elevated edge for a stud, joist, or rafter. A **shim** is a thin piece of wood, often wedge-shaped, placed under a larger piece to alter the position of the larger piece.

Working out the bows in joists and rafters follows the same principles as working out bows in studs.

Knee Walls

The top floor of a house is sometimes poorly used. Although a good deal of space is available, people avoid it because they soon bump their heads walking toward the rafter ends—the slope of the ceiling ultimately makes an area where you cannot stand up.

A good solution is to make knee walls. These walls don't gain any space but make what is available more attractive and useful.

The way to frame knee walls is to make walls that begin at the rafters and drop vertically to the floor. On the higher ceiling side of the wall, you have workable space in which you can stand up. The knee wall disguises the area where only crawling is possible. This blocking technique alone creates a more welcoming area because you are no longer aware of the diminishing space on the other side of the wall. At the same time, you can build small doors or hatches into the knee wall and use the space behind it for storage.

Typically knee walls are 4' to 5' high, especially where the habitable portion is meant to be a bedroom. But they can be shorter in order to make the habitable room larger. Book shelves might be built against them if the room is meant to be an office, or, if a children's room, chests of toys placed against them.

To make a knee wall, proceed as follows:

1. Determine where you want the knee wall. The higher you make it, the more area you lose on the "habitable" side. The shorter you make it, the more room is left on the "habitable" side but the less room left for storage—and the more stooped you have to be when pushing items into the storage area.

2. Snap a chalk line along the underside of the rafters to mark where you want the front of the knee wall to go. Hold a plumb bob's string to a mark on one of the rafters

so that the plumb bob hangs just above the floor. Mark where the plumb bob points. This will be the front of the bottom of the knee wall. Do this marking in several other places along the floor, and snap a chalk line along the floor along these marks. Nail a sole plate to the floor to be the bottom of the knee wall.

3. Tack a stud between the sole plate and the edge of a rafter. Use a T-bevel to duplicate the angle that the rafter makes with the stud. This is the angle that the top plate is going to have to make.

A knee wall top plate has to be rip-cut to the proper angle.

4. The top plate has to have a rip cut along it to match the angle that the rafters make with the temporary stud.

You can have your lumber yard do the rip cut of the top plate for you for a small charge, of course. If you do it yourself, clamp the 2×4 that will become the top plate very securely to a work bench. Unplug your circular saw, and shift the angle of the base plate until it approximates the angle of the cut. Make the angle perfect by holding the T-bevel set to the

proper angle against the base plate and the blade. Tighten the base plate thumb screw. Cut the top plate with the circular saw base plate set to the proper angle. If the top plate is very long, occasionally unclamp it from the work bench and move it so that wherever you are cutting with the circular saw, the top plate gets good support from the work bench; you don't want to be cutting so far from the work bench that the 2×4 moves about.

5. Fasten the top plate to the undersides of the rafters. Use a plumb bob to make sure that the sole plate is in the proper position directly underneath the top plate.

6. Cut studs to the proper length and angle to fit against the top plate. Face nail through the top of the studs into the top plate, and toenail the bottoms of the studs into the sole plate.

A view of another knee wall.

Knee walls can be fairly short. They can also turn corners where they meet framing for a shed dormer.

Framing for a short knee wall.

Finger Tips

You can forego a top plate for a knee wall by nailing studs cut to the proper angle directly to the underside of the rafters. The problem with this approach is that when you come to apply the wallboard, the piece attaching to the rafters is unsupported between rafters, and the piece attaching to the studs is unsupported between the studs. This is not a terrible situation if the wallboard at this location is not going to get a lot of stress (it might in a child's room). You can, however, put blocking either between the top of the studs, between the joists at the top of the studs, or in both locations. This will give the wallboard pieces a firmer backing along the line where they meet.

Building a Temporary Support Wall

Maybe you want to remove a wall in your home. This may not be much of a problem, other than being messy, if the wall is a nonbearing one. But if the wall is an interior bearing wall, then another structure has to take over the weight it bears toward the ground. This would be a beam, really a very long header that transfers weight along itself to strong vertical framing members that then transfer the load again toward the ground. The beam must go in place below the ceiling, so it will be visible even after the work is done. Though it is made of wood, you can cover it with wallboard and blend it in with the walls and ceiling. But in essence what you will be doing is removing a wall or a portion of it and replacing the removed portion with a visible arch, dropping the headroom there.

Note that the beam has to be supported by posts at either end that in turn deliver weight directly to a beam or bearing wall below. A post supporting a beam should not rest on a section of unblocked sole plate in a location between joists. If it does, use blocking between the joists so the post delivers weight directly to the beam holding up the joists. If the post ends above an exterior bearing wall, solid blocking and then solid 2×4s or another post should carry its weight directly down to the foundation wall.

Remember you will have some cosmetic work to do afterward. You will have to patch wall areas where the section of wall you are removing used to end. Normally you can do this with strips of wallboard. You will also have to deal with the flooring where the old wall was. The wall being removed has a sole plate resting on the subfloor. When you take up the sole plate, you will have a strip 3 1/2" wide of no finish flooring. One solution is to put in new wall-to-wall carpeting over all the old flooring in the two rooms now joined under the arch-beam. Another is simply to patch in some finish flooring level with the flooring on either side. It will be distinctive, but it can also be excused as a purposeful reminder that once a wall stood in this location.

A homeowner can reasonably install a wooden beam that is no more than 8' long. A beam longer than this should probably be made of steel and requires more sophisticated effort. For general span distances of beams and how to install a beam, read on.

Finger Tips

Although it is tempting to remove a wall, there is often more to a wall than meets the eye. Most walls have wiring in them to serve receptacles. Some have pipes, and some have heating or air conditioning ducts. An electrician can take care of the wires. Heating and air conditioning ducts can usually be cut back to floor level and a grating put on them there. But pipes can be more problematic. If a bathroom or kitchen is above or below the wall you want to replace with a beam, there may be pipes running in it. Pipes can be rerouted, but it generally is a good deal of trouble and quite expensive.

Because removing part of a bearing wall involves the integrity of the structure of your home, have an architect or building engineer advise you. Take your plan to your local building office for approval.

In any event, if you remove part of a bearing wall, you will have to build temporary supporting walls to hold the weight of the structure above until you can get the new beam installed.

Building a temporary support wall is much like building a newly framed wall in an existing room (See Building Standard Walls at the beginning of this chapter). The difference is that you build the temporary wall shorter than the distance from floor to ceiling and then use shims between the top plate and the ceiling.

Build temporary walls adjacent to any section of wall you intend to remove and replace with a beam. Build a temporary wall on either side of this area to hold up the weight now carried by the wall you are going to remove.

If the temporary walls are going to block your ability to bring in big materials, build the beam—or bring in the lumber for it—before erecting the temporary walls. Keep the beam or the beam materials between the temporary walls while you do the work of removing the old wall.

To remove a wall or part of a wall, follow these steps:

1. Find out where the joists, which will be running perpendicular to the bearing wall, are in the ceiling. Mark the joist locations with pencil.

2. On one side of the wall section you are intending to remove, build a temporary support wall. Make the wall a couple of inches shorter than the distance between the ceiling and the floor. In addition, there is no need to make the wall fit snugly against the wall that the bearing wall meets; it can go up two inches shy of this surface so you will not scratch it. Assemble and nail the temporary wall on the floor. Nail through the sole plate and top plate into the ends of the studs. Nail a 2×4 across the assembled wall from one corner of the sole plate to the opposite corner of the top plate to act as a brace. Nail the brace to each stud that it crosses.

3. Tilt the temporary wall into place about 30 inches away from the wall that you plan to remove. Place shims above the top plate at the locations of the ceiling joists. At every joist location, press in a shim from either direction. Tap in the shims until they are snug against the ceiling surface. Erect a temporary wall on both sides of the section of bearing wall you are removing.

Here a temporary support wall, shims at the top, supports joists from which all wallboard has been removed.

4. Remove the portion of the bearing wall that you are replacing with the beam. First, turn off all electrical circuits to wiring that may be in the wall; then use a stud finder to locate the studs in the wall. Put down drop cloths; wear dust masks or respirators; wear old clothes, hat, and gloves; and open windows. Use a key hole saw to cut wallboard away from the studs. Take care; if your saw hits something, stop and try to figure out what it is; you don't want to cut into cables or pipes. Cart the wallboard out for disposal. If the wall is made of plaster, you can use a circular saw to cut through the plaster along the sides of the studs. Set a carbide-tipped blade to just the depth of the plaster and the lath that holds the plaster in place.

5. Have an electrician come in to deal with the electrical cables and a heating and cooling technician to deal with any ducting in the wall.

6. Saw through the studs about half way up their lengths. Use your hands and arms to pry the lower part of the studs off the sole plate and the upper parts away from the top plate. If you are removing an entire wall, the stud that connects the wall being removed to the adjoining wall is nailed to studs or to blocking in the adjoining wall. Use a pry bar to edge it away from the framing members it is connected to by beginning at the bottom of the stud. As you work the pry bar toward the ceiling, eventually, you should be able to use your hands and arms to pull the stud away from the framing members of the wall.

7. Remove the old sole plate by cutting through it in two places about a foot apart near its middle. Pry up the foot-long piece. If you are removing an entire wall, pry up one of the longer pieces beginning at the one-foot gap. When you get this piece high enough, you should be able to pull it up with your arms and back—keep your back straight. Pry up the piece leading in the other direction. If you are removing a portion of a wall, cut through the sole plate where the portion ends.

8. Remove the top and cap plate in the same fashion. Cut through them in a couple of places. Using a pry bar, pry the top plate and cap plate down together. Eventually, you will be able to get a grip on it. The cap plate will be nailed to the top plate of the adjoining wall, but you should be able to wrench it free. Remove the top plate and cap plate going in the other direction as well. Now you have revealed the bottoms of the joists running perpendicular overhead. If you are removing a portion of a wall and not the whole wall, cut through the cap plate and top plate where the wall portion ends.

9. If you are removing a whole wall, remove any blocking or nailer studs in the adjoining wall used to make the joint with the old bearing wall. You will have to cut back to adjoining studs on either side in order to do this, but this will create space you will need in any case to properly set the post and beam.

Adding a Beam to Replace a Section of Bearing Wall

To build and install a beam that replaces a wall or wall section, follow these steps:

1. Build a beam that is up to 8' long to carry the weight formerly carried by the removed wall. Make the beam 7" longer than the removed wall so that it will project 3½" into each wall space. Make the beam of two pieces of 2× material specified by your building department with a piece of ½-inch-thick plywood in between (See Framing a Door or Window in Chapter 12).

   As a general guide line, the following pieces of dimensional lumber, doubled with a ½" piece of plywood between can span the following distances: 2×6s can span 3½'; 2×8s can span 5'; 2×10s can span 6½'; and 2×12s can span 8'.

2. Set the beam on edge. Cut a notch at the upper part of one end that is 3½" long and 3" deep. In this way, the beam will fit up against the underside of the joists in the ceiling while the notch accounts for the top plate and cap plate of the adjoining wall. Repeat at the other end.

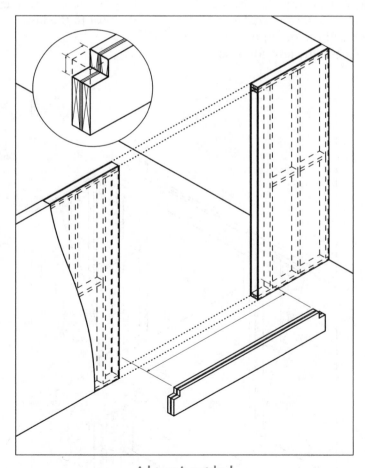

A beam is notched.

(Copyright: John Hannah)

Notch the upper side of the beam to accommodate the top plate and cap plate of the walls to which the beam will fit. Pictured is a situation in which the beam spans walls in line with the beam's length.

3. Shift the beam into the groove where the old sole plate was, notches facing up. The ends will be resting on the sole plates of the adjoining walls. At one end, measure the exact distance between the bottom of the notch and the underside of the top plate above. Cut a 4×4 post to exactly this distance. Repeat at the other end.

4. With helpers, lift the beam into position against the joists above and so that the notches fit up against the top plate of the adjoining walls. Have someone wedge in a post under each end the beam; the fit should be snug. Check the post for absolute plumb.

5. Toenail the bottom of each 4×4 post to its sole plate. Toenail each 4×4 top to the underside of its beam end.

6. Where a beam meets a wall perpendicular to it, nail a 1×4 at least 1' long running up the upper portion of a post side and onto the face of the end of the beam above. This helps tie the post and the beam together and also gives some nailing surface to wallboard that will go up to patch the wall. This 1×4 will be totally inside the adjoining wall and out of sight when the wall is patched. Nail a 1×4 nailer of this sort on each side of the beam.

Where a beam meets a wall in line with its length, use flat framing connectors to tie the post to the beam.

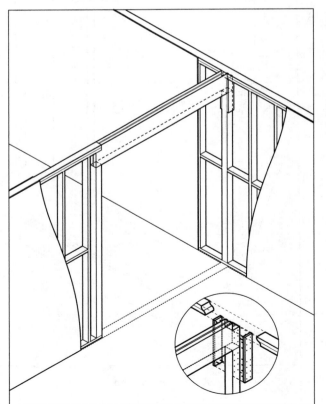

Raise the beam and set 4×4 posts under it. In a perpendicular wall, nail 1×4s to the post and the beam ends to tie them together (inset). In an in-line wall, use framing connectors.

(Copyright: John Hannah)

7. Remove the temporary walls. Patch the walls with wallboard, and cover the beam with wallboard unless it is decorative wood you would like seen. Patch the floor.

Porch Framing

Perhaps you want to add a shed roof porch to your house. You can do this by attaching a rafter ledger to the house wall and a joist ledger somewhat below it. Then run rafters and joists out to a beam supported by posts running down to either a deck or patio or concrete footings that are set firmly into the ground.

First attach a ledger to the house by stripping away the exterior siding in the location it is to go; any sheathing material remains. Then bolt the ledger either to wall studs or to a rim joist inside the house wall. Usually $3/8"$ lag bolts long enough to penetrate well into the studs or band joist are used to fasten the ledger in place.

Once a rafter and joist ledger are in place, erect a beam on posts at the outer limit of the porch. Then run rafters from the rafter ledger to the beam and joists from the joist ledger to the beam. Fasten these in place where they meet at the beam. Then put roof sheathing on top of the rafters and roofing material on top of the sheathing.

To create a shed roof porch on the side of a house, proceed with these steps:

1. Attach a rafter ledger to the outside of the house wall with $3/8"$ lag bolts and washers.

A rafter ledger at the top portion of this illustration is bolted over wall sheathing. The lag bolts are set 16" on center in wall studs.

2. Attach a joist ledger below the rafter ledger.

A joist ledger is attached below the rafter ledger. Lag bolts—with washers—are fastened through old sheathing into framing members inside the wall.

3. Erect a beam at the outer edge of the porch. The rafters and ceiling joists come together at the beam. Secure the rafters to the beam with framing connectors; face nail the ceiling joists to the ends of the rafters and toenail to the beam.

4. Secure the ceiling joists to the joist ledger with joists hangers.

The rafters and ceiling joists for a porch come together at the beam on the porch outer edge.

The ceiling joists are connected to the joist ledger with joist hangers. The rafters attach with good toenailing.

The Least You Need to Know

◆ Framing inside an existing home follows the same principles as framing for a new home.

◆ You can frame for closets or subdivide large rooms.

◆ Build knee walls in attic spaces to better utilize available space.

◆ You can remove partition walls as you like.

◆ You can remove portions of bearing walls if you build temporary walls to support the weight carried by the removed bearing wall portions until you install a new supporting beam.

◆ You can build a porch with rafters, joists, beams and posts, attaching the rafters and joists to ledgers fastened to the house wall.

In This Part

"So tell me again why you absolutely must have a gable dormer?"

Special Framing

Now you know how the basic floors, walls, and roofs go up in a new home and how new walls are built in old homes. In Part 4, I go off in new directions and show you how to handle some special situations.

I start first with bay windows. These, of course, you can frame into new homes. But you can also frame them as an addition to an existing home; owners like to open a wall and make a nice sunny breakfast nook out of one or otherwise to improve and expand a room. I also describe dormers, which can be built onto a new roof being erected or as an addition to existing attic space. I discuss both the shed dormer and gable dormer types. I also tell you how to do framing in a basement, often done to convert an unfinished basement into usable and enjoyable living space. And last, I describe three built-in projects using the framing skills you learned earlier. These are a built-in cabinet, built-in bookcases, and a built-in bench whose top is partly a lid so you can use the space below for storage.

In This Chapter

◆ Planning for a bay window

◆ Cantilevering a floor for a bay window

◆ Building the walls and roof for a bay window

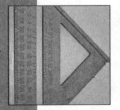
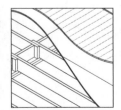

Chapter 16

A Bay Window

Bay windows have always been popular. They can make a breakfast nook or a window seat for reading and brighten an otherwise dark area with lots of extra light.

But they do take some consideration and planning, whether being built new into a new home or set into an old home as a remodeling project.

Of course, you must pay attention to codes. Because a bay window extends a house beyond its normal wall, that takes the window closer to the property line, and most communities have a regulation about how close to a property line any portion of a home may go. So check before you commit yourself to such an extension as a bay window.

Fortunately, most bay window areas do not need foundations. They can be built on floor joists that tie back to the main floor joists of the home. The bay window floor joists then are partly supported by the house foundation wall. Because the bay window joists extend beyond the foundation wall and are unsupported at their ends, they are called *cantilevered*. There is a limit to how far bay window joists can be cantilevered. So check with an architect or structural engineer, especially if you intend to remove a section of an existing house wall and build a bay window as an extension to an existing home.

You might also make note that because a bay window adds a bit to the living space of a house, this extra space is going to require heating and cooling, so your utility bills will go up a bit. And because glass, even double- and triple-pane glass, is not as good an insulator as that stuffed between studs in a regular wall, the new space will be more expensive to heat and cool than if the extension had no glass at all.

A bay window generally has a front wall parallel to the main wall of the house. It then has two *angled walls*, each running from the bay window front wall back toward the house. In the main example of a bay window here, the angled walls do not intersect with the main house wall but rather with side walls, each projecting perpendicular to the main house wall.

Framer's Lingo

Cantilevered is said (yes, "said") of a framing member supported at one end and near its middle but not supported at the other end. An **angled wall** is a wall connecting at a greater-than-right-angle to the front wall of a bay window. Sometimes it meets the main wall of a house and sometimes side walls that run back to the main wall of the house.

Building the Floor Framing

Bay window joists will either run parallel or perpendicular to the joists of the main house. If they are perpendicular to the joists of the main home, they normally are joined to them several joist-spacings back from the foundation wall. They then run out over the sill plate on the foundation wall and terminate as far out as the bay window is to go.

To make the floor framing for a cantilevered bay window, follow these steps:

1. If you are joining the bay flooring joists to a perpendicular regular floor joist, reinforce this regular floor joist. Set a companion floor joist beside it, and face nail these together for strength. This reinforcing joist can go on the house-side or bay-side of the regular flooring joist.

   Also double joist the cantilevered joists left and right of the bay window floor. And check that the distance from the main house wall to the ends of the joists is the same for every joist.

Connect bay floor joists to the main floor joists inside the foundation of the house. Run them out over the sill of the foundation to project as far from the house as the bay window is to extend. Note the doubled joists left and right. Here the joists are engineered joists. Solid wood joists would follow the same principles.

Where bay floor joists meet the regular flooring joist, reinforce the regular joist with a second joist. Attach it on either the house-side or the bay-side of the regular joist. Face nail through the one into the other, making a strong framing member almost like a beam.

If the bay window joists are to be parallel to the regular house floor joists, they are then merely extensions of the regular house flooring joists or add-on extensions. In new construction, don't build the band joist in the vicinity of the bay window. Instead, extend the regular floor joists out as far as they need to go to support the bay window floor. An alternative is to add onto the regular floor joists. To do this, face nail new joists material of the same depth as the regular floor joists onto the regular floor joists, but extend them out over the foundation wall to create the shape of the bay window floor. The extension joists should lap the regular floor joists by a distance equal to twice the extension width of the bay window.

If you are putting the bay window into an existing house, you must cut away the band joist where the bay window will go. Then nail extension joists to the regular floor joists as in the paragraph above.

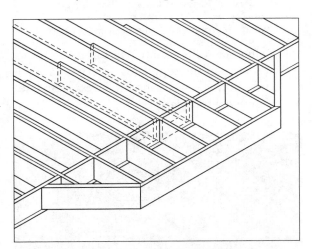

Where bay window joists will run parallel to regular floor joists, they can be face nailed as extensions onto the regular floor joists.

(Copyright: John Hannah)

2. Cover the ends of the bay window joists with band joists. From the ends of the band joist covering the ends of the bay window floor joists, run pieces of band joist back to the wall of the house at an angle. This gives the bay window its particular shape.

Check that the distance from the main house wall to the outside of the bay window front band joist is the same all along the band joist's length. If it is not, make corrections now.

3. Nail plywood down as a subfloor, following the angled shape of the bay window at its left and right corners.

Building the Walls

The walls of a bay window are like regular walls but follow the angle of the floor.

To build the walls for a bay window, proceed as follows.

1. Begin by cutting the sole plate for the front of the bay window. Cut its ends at the proper angle to fit to the floor. One way you can do this is to use a sliding T-bevel. Hold it to the angle of the floor where it angles from the front wall toward the main wall of the house. Lock the sliding T-bevel to that angle. Transfer that angle to a 2×4 to serve as the sole plate. Do this for both ends of the sill plate. Cut the sole plate, and then trace its length and angles for the top plate.

2. Cut a top plate to match the sole plate, and then set the sole plate and top plate together as for making a wall in the section "Layout" of Chapter 12. Mark the sole and top plate for studs. Also mark them for headers, king studs, and jack studs.

3. Lay out the sole plate and top plate on the bay window floor. Cut the headers, king studs, jack studs, and cripple studs. Nail through the sole and top plates into the ends of the studs to assemble the wall. Add the headers for the window openings and the jack and cripple studs.

Erect the front wall of the bay window.

4. Cut the sole and top plates for the side walls, taking care with the angles where these plates will meet the plates of the angled walls.

Assemble all the components for each side wall, including any needed headers, king studs, jack studs, and so on. Erect each side wall, and brace it when it is plumb.

Assemble and erect the side walls.

5. Cut the sole and top plates for the angled walls, again taking care with the angles where these plates will meet the plates of the front and side walls.

Assemble all the components for each angled wall, and erect each angled wall between the front wall and side walls.

This illustration shows the sole plate for one of the angled walls just before it is erected in place between the front wall and one of the side walls.

After the walls are up, nail cap plates to the tops of the top plates. Every intersection between walls should have a cap plate lapping a top plate.

Nail cap plates onto the top plates.

Where walls come together, you will have a gap between studs that may cause problems for the persons putting up dry wall. The solution is to rip cut a stud to fit into this location.

Rip cut a stud to fit into the space where the front meets a side wall.

Adding a Ledger for Roof Rafters

Bay windows normally receive a shallow sloping roof. The rafters run from a ledger fastened to the main wall of the house out to the top of the bay window front wall.

To make the ledger to which the rafters will attach at the house, follow these steps:

1. Measure for a ledger board that will be attached to the main wall of the house. It should be as long as the bay window and as wide as whatever the length of the rafter ridge cut is going to be.

2. Cut the ledger and attach it to the house.

Attach the ledger to the house.

Check that the distance between the ledger and the top of the cap plate of the bay window front wall is the same all the way along the length of the cap plate of the front wall. Otherwise you will have to cut rafters to different lengths.

If the distance between the ledger and the cap plate of the bay window front wall is equal all along the length of the cap plate, sheath the outer walls of the bay window. The sheathing will help stabilize the walls, holding them in proper place for the rafters.

Make sure all the measurements are correct, and then sheathe the bay window walls.

The underside of the bay window will now look like this. The joists are cantilevered, and the wall sheathing is nailed on.

Finger Tips

Bay windows can enliven any area of a house. They can be especially welcome by letting in sunshine where otherwise there would be very little. Choose an eastern exposure if the bay window will also serve as a breakfast nook.

A southern exposure would be good if the glass of the bay window were also to bring in some solar energy. This may be particularly welcome in the wintertime. But take note, if you live in a hot southern climate, you might not want a lot of glass passing in sunshine and heat. If you want to let in sunshine and heat from a southern exposure, keep the view clear. If you want to block sunshine and heat, plant trees or tall shrubs outside the window that will interfere with summer sun.

A western exposure is nice because you receive the glow of sunsets. But again, in the hot climates you might want to forego a western exposure because generally a hot day is still pretty hot even as the sun descends toward the horizon.

A northern exposure gets the least sunshine of all. This may be welcome in hot climates. But even in cold climates, a northern exposure can let in winter light to a section of the house that otherwise would receive too little, and if a pleasant view is to be had there—of a tree, bird house, backyard—then this is the place for a bay window to be.

Adding the Rafters

Normally, bay windows receive short shallow roofs, enough to shed snow and rain but not so steep as to draw much attention to itself.

To make the rafters for a bay window, proceed as follows:

1. Cut rafters as described in Chapter 13. Here the rise of the rafters is from the top of the cap plate of the front wall to half way up the width of the ledger. The run

is the horizontal distance from the outside of the cap plate to half way through the thickness of the ledger.

Mark the first rafter as described in Chapter 13, and make allowance for the overhang or tail of the rafter, here 12". Make the ridge, bird's mouth, and tail cuts. Either make the adjustment cut for the thickness of the ledger now, or wait until you have tested the first rafter in position.

Measure and mark the first rafter.

2. Hold the rafter up to the ledger and to the cap plate. Check that the rafter cut at the upper end touches the ledger all along the cut's length. Check that the bird's mouth cut aligns with the cap plate. If you have made a plumb cut for the end of the rafter, check that the cut is plumb when you hold the rafter in position.

Cut the first rafter and test it in place.

3. When the fit of the rafter is good, copy the lines of it onto rafter stock for the next rafters. Toenail the upper end of the first rafter to the ledger.

When the cuts look good, toenail the house end of rafters to the ledger.

4. Add more rafters, spacing them at 16" or 24" as your designer or plans call for.

Add more rafters.

5. As the rafters go into place, check across them with a 4' level to make sure they align across their top edges. If some are too high, remove them from their locations, and cut down slightly on their bird's

mouth cuts. Test them again before toe-nailing them to the cap plate.

Toenailing the rafters usually suffices in these applications, but check your building codes. You may have to use framing connectors.

6. Add nailers to the rafters if you want a level ceiling in the bay window. Here the framers have face nailed 2×4s to the lower section of the rafters so that when the wallboard is nailed up, the ceiling will be level.

Here is a look at the underside of the rafters at the ledger end. The nailer 2×4s are nailed to the lower section of the rafters.

Other Configurations

Now, you can make bay windows in many ways, so let's look at a few examples of alternatives.

Bay windows can show a tremendous amount of glass. The one pictured in the following figure is one doing just that. This bay window has a western exposure, which will help to keep the house naturally lighted later in the day. The ledger for the rafters is set in front of the main beam supporting the wall above. This ledger rests on the ends of the bay window walls to the left and right. Screening keeps the weather out during construction.

This bay window is going to have floor-to-ceiling glass and allow in a great deal of light.

Bay windows can occasionally call for complex rafter cuts. The rafters in the next illustration are called hip rafters because they meet the ledger not perfectly perpendicular but at an angle.

Cutting these kinds of rafters is beyond the scope of this book. To learn how to make these kinds of cuts on rafters, consult a text book on house carpentry.

Some complex rafter cutting is sometimes needed for bay windows.

Finger Tips

You can buy bay windows in a kit. Manufacturers make bay windows, and a shallower variety called bow windows, that are installed in openings cut into exterior walls. Generally, these bay window kits do not need floor joists because they are mere projections from the house exterior wall. They allow in light and create space for such items as indoor plants or collectibles without the floor framing and rafter work of larger framed bay windows.

The Least You Need to Know

◆ Bay windows let in lots of light and make more living space, but they also create more space to heat and cool.

◆ Most bay window floors are cantilevered, that is, the joists do not require a foundation but are suspended beyond the foundation wall.

◆ Bay window walls meet at odd angles and require ripped 2×4s for nailing surfaces at corner intersections.

◆ Bay windows require rafters running from a ledger board on the house to the cap plate of the outermost wall.

In This Chapter

- ◆ Working on a slanted roof
- ◆ The building of a shed dormer
- ◆ The construction of a gable dormer

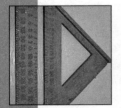
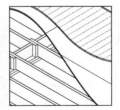

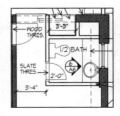

Chapter 17

Shed and Gable Dormers

Dormers have always been a nice option for extra living space in a home. Dormers are areas under the roof, or to be more precise, areas that project out and away from the main roof to have smaller roofs of their own. They offer extra space to what would otherwise be cramped and dark areas.

A *shed dormer* is a wide expanse of living space. Its roof is a *shed roof*, which is a single plane of identical sloping rafters. The rafters slope to a wall at their lower end, a wall that rises near the front edge of the roof. Normally the wall holds large windows so that a good deal of light can reach inside. Triangular side walls rise along the roof back to the upper reaches of the rafters.

Shed dormers offer greater living space than their smaller cousins, the *gable dormers*. With a shed dormer you can convert what would otherwise be a slanted and cramped attic into a bedroom, bathroom, hobby room, or what you will. Shed dormers can run almost all the way across a roof. But the end walls of a shed dormer cannot align over the main roof rake rafters.

If you are building a shed dormer into a new home, then its roof and walls are part of the blueprint plans. Everything should be noted on paper, and if there are framing details, so much the better.

You can also build a dormer onto an existing home if the roof is made of conventional rafters. If the roof is made of trusses, the job is not impossible but only more trouble.

If you are thinking of cutting through the roof to make a shed or a gable dormer, check right away with your local building department, zoning department, or neighborhood association to make sure that it is an acceptable addition. Then consult a structural engineer to make sure it can be done in your home.

If you are creating a shed dormer in a house that already exists, in essence what you are doing is changing a good portion of the roof to accommodate three new walls. The work requires doubling up the rafters upon which the side walls will rest. To begin the job, you have to cut through the main roof at the place where the lower part of the front wall is to rise. You do not have to remove the larger part of roof that will have to come out until most of the shed dormer construction is complete. This will help keep the weather out of the attic while you are doing the work.

A gable dormer is smaller than a shed dormer. It is narrower and has a small *gable roof* on top, rafters running left and right down from a small ridge beam. Gable dormers give visual interest to the exterior of a home. They also bring daylight into the attic space. But because they are smaller than shed dormers, their functions are more limited. Wide ones have taken in narrow beds or even made small bathrooms. But more ordinarily, dormers are places for window seats, desks, or tables.

Framer's Lingo

A **shed dormer** is a space projecting out from the main roof of a home that has a shed roof, two triangular side walls, and a front wall resting just above or nearly so the main exterior wall of the house. A **shed roof** is a single plane roof. All rafters begin along a ridge, run parallel to one another, and are cut identically. A **gable dormer** is a space projecting out from the main roof of a house and that has a gable roof. A **gable roof** is a roof with a ridge and rafters running down opposite sides of the ridge to side walls.

Working On a Roof

When you build a dormer onto an existing home, you will be working outside on a slanted roof. This is hazardous work, so do not attempt it unless you are in good physical condition, sure of your balance, and have the proper safety equipment.

There are a number of ways of working safely on a roof. One is to use a *harness and lanyard*. A harness straps around your torso. It is hooked to a lanyard that in turn is fastened to something on the roof that will hold fast if you fall. If you do fall, the lanyard and harness will keep you from reaching the edge of the roof.

Also several kinds of equipment give you a comfortable place to step, sit, or work. One kind is an adjustable *roof bracket*, which adjusts to the slope of the roof. A pair, set wide apart, can hold a 2×10 level, and from the 2×10 you can kneel, sit, or stand.

Another piece of equipment for maneuvering and working on a roof is called a *ladder hook*, which fastens to the upper rungs of an extension ladder and hooks over the roof ridge. This fastens the ladder to one side of the roof and allows you to move up and down it as you work.

Framer's Lingo

A **harness and lanyard** is a device for preventing falls from a roof. The harness straps around the torso, and the lanyard connects to the harness and something firmly attached to the roof. A **roof bracket** is an adjustable bracket that attaches temporarily to a roof. A pair of roof brackets can hold a 2×10 to form a platform from which to work on a roof. A **ladder hook** is a device that fastens to the upper rungs of an extension ladder and hooks over the ridge of a roof. It holds the ladder to the roof so a worker can move safely and sit safely on a roof.

A Shed Dormer

A shed dormer is a large expanse across the main roof of the house, which has a slanting roof of its own and two triangular side walls. The front wall is normally one with a lot of window space.

A shed dormer.

A shed dormer has side walls that rise on slanting rafters of the main roof. These rafters have to be doubled in order to carry the weight of the shed dormer side walls.

An interior view of a shed dormer.

Note that the shed dormer in the above figure has doubled rafters left and right. Short side walls rise from these rafters. Both rafters and ceiling beams run to a top plate of the shed dormer's front wall.

Knee walls project left and right under the regular rafters of the main roof.

The front wall of the shed dormer is built like any exterior wall. It has the proper header for windows required of an exterior wall, with the proper king and jack studs. Beneath the windows are the proper rough sill and cripple studs.

Here you can see the doubled rafters on the right side of the shed dormer. The blocking between this and the next rafter on the right serves as nailing support for the roof sheathing.

Here is a view of the doubled rafters of another shed dormer being built into a new home.

Building a Shed Dormer into an Existing Home

Building a shed dormer into an existing home is a big job that requires working from scaffolding and working on the roof and should only be undertaken by experienced persons. It also exposes the attic to rain and weather, so it is best to work in a season of little rain and storms.

As mentioned, involve a licensed architect or structural engineer to assess the structural elements of the work and to assure that the new dormer is not going to weaken the integrity of the house in any way. Then you must take all the plans to the local building department for approval. Inspections need to be made by the local building department at appropriate times during the construction.

Following are the steps for building a shed dormer into an existing roof:

1. To begin the work of creating a shed dormer within an existing roof, double the rafters on which the side walls are going to rest. Do this by getting lumber of equal dimension to the rafters in place, duplicating the cuts at the upper and lower ends of the rafters—a sliding T-bevel can be used for this work—and then face nailing the doubling raters to the rafters already in place.

2. Drill up through the roof sheathing just inside the doubled rafters at the upper and lower extremities of the planned shed dormer. Up on the roof, snap chalk lines between these four drilled holes to show the general positions of the upper portions of the shed dormer roof, the two side walls, and the front wall.

3. Cut away about 2' of the old roof above the cap plate of the house wall. Make the cuts between the two chalk lines marking the side walls for the shed dormer and above the chalk line marking the lower extremity. Make the long horizontal upper cut first; then saw down from this along one of the side wall marks toward the house wall. You want this second cut to end above the outside of the cap plate of the house wall. It may take a bit of probing to find this point. Proceed slowly. Stop the circular saw often. You may want a helper inside the house using a flashlight to tell you how close to the cap plate outside edge you are. Remove the 2' of the old roof (both shingles and sheathing) above the cap plate and uphill from the cap plate.

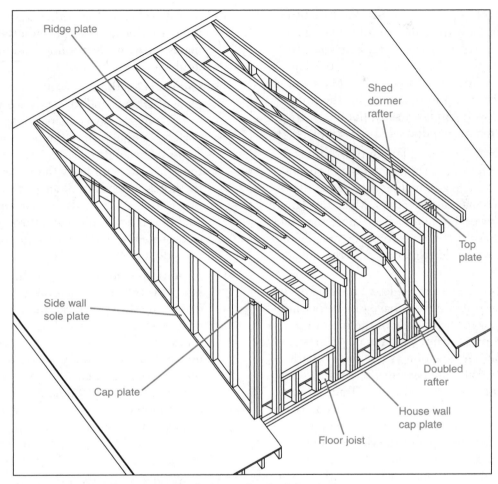

Ridge plate

Shed dormer rafter

Top plate

Side wall sole plate

Cap plate

Doubled rafter

House wall cap plate

Floor joist

The framing of a shed dormer.

(Copyright: John Hannah)

4. To the left and right of the opening you have made, pry up shingles—but not sheathing—above the doubled rafters. Make a space large enough for corner posts for the shed dormer. These should be two 2×4s with 2×4 blocking between as described in section "Dealing with Corners" of Chapter 12. You do not have to pry up shingles where the side wall sole plates are going to lie; you can fasten them through the shingles into the doubled rafters.

5. Assemble the corner posts. Cut the bottoms of the posts to match the slope of the roof. Cut the tops so the tops will be at the proper height for the front wall, taking care to allow for the top plate and cap plate. Set the slanted end of a corner post on the sheathing over one of the doubled rafters, and toenail it in place. Plumb it in both directions, and then run a brace to it from further up the roof. The brace can connect at the shingles to a scrap of foot-long scrap of 2×4 nailed into the shingles and sheathing below. Repeat for the other post at the other end of the opening for the shed dormer.

6. Nail a top plate to the tops of the corner posts. Construct the front wall piece by piece. Erect the studs and king studs first. Their bottom ends will rest on the cap plate of the main house wall. Then nail up the headers and jack studs for the rough window openings. Lastly, put in the rough sills for the windows and the cripple studs.

7. At the ridge, nail a length of $1/2$"-thick plywood to the roof shingles and sheathing to serve as a nailing surface for the upper ends of the rafters. Make this length of plywood (you may need more than one piece) so that it runs from the outside of one pair of doubled rafters to the outside of the other pair.

8. To determine the angles of the cuts of the shed dormer rafters, have one helper hold a rafter to the outside of the top of the top plate of the front wall in a position that imitates its position as if a bird's mouth cut had already been made. Set the other end on the plywood nailer. Trace around the top plate onto the rafter; this marks it for the bird's mouth cut. At the upper end, transfer the angle of the slope of the roof to the upper end of the rafter. Cut the rafter and test to see how it fits to the upper nailer and to the top plate.

9. When the rafter is well fitted, use it as a template to cut as many others as you need. Toenail the upper ends of the rafters to the nailer near the ridge. Toenail the lower ends to the top plate or use framing connectors.

10. Make sole plates for the side walls. These will be 2×4s running between the rafter nailer near the ridge to the lower ends of the corner posts of the front wall. The ends of the sole plate will need angled cuts, one to fit under the upper end of the outside rafter and the other to fit against the corner posts. Nail through the sole plates, through the roofing, and into the doubled rafters below.

11. Cut studs for the side walls. Mark the sole plate of an end wall for studs every 16". At the first mark, have a helper hold a stud perfectly plumb. Mark the bottom of the stud for the angle cut it needs to fit against the sole plate, and mark the upper part for the notch it needs to fit against the end rafter. Toenail through the bottom of the stud into the sole plate and through the rafter into the stud at its notch. Make all the side wall studs in this way.

12. Remove the old roof shingles and sheathing between the doubled rafters, the upper end of the shed dormer rafters, and the opening created in step 3. Do this by removing this material between the existing roof rafters. Note: you do not have to remove roof material all the way up to the bottom of the plywood nailer. You only have to remove enough to allow for collar beams to run level from the top plate of the front wall back to rafters on both sides of the house ridge (see the next step).

13. Run collar beams level from the top plate of the shed dormer front wall to rafters on the both sides of the house ridge. Nail the far side of the ceiling joists to rafters on that side of the ridge. Nail ceiling joists to each rafter on the shed dormer side of the house ridge; these collar beams serve to support these rafters, soon to be cut away. The collar beams also solidly tie the shed dormer front wall back to the main roof structure of the house. The collar beams can also be set higher than the top plate, as shown in the drawing, giving greater headroom, so long as the design meets code.

14. Sheath the shed dormer walls and roof, and install the windows.

15. Remove the sections of the old rafters within the shed dormer area. These will be sections running between the bottom of the front wall of the shed dormer at the rafter low end and the collar beams at the upper end.

A Gable Dormer

A gable dormer creates less inside room than a shed dormer but lets in good sunlight and can make pleasant space out of a living area in the attic. It can shelter a narrow bed, a window seat, a reading chair, or a desk. In addition, dormers add classical interest to the outside of a house. Generally, a house looks better with a series of gable dormers than without. Thus a gable dormer or series of gable dormers increases the value of the home.

Gable dormers can be built as a new house rises or added to an older home as a home improvement project. The roof should be made of regular rafters, however, and not trusses.

A gable dormer normally has a roof pitch that equals the roof pitch of the main roof.

Like its shed dormer cousin, a gable dormer's weight rests in part on rafters that should be doubled. Side walls then rise from the sloping doubled rafters to top plates. From the top plates rise short rafters to a ridge beam.

A gable dormer.

In new work, the side walls of a gable dormer rise from the top of double rafters.

The top plate of the side walls is the resting place for the small gable rafters that will rise to the gable ridge.

If you are thinking of building a gable dormer in an existing home, you'll be glad to know it is less of a project than a shed dormer. It requires less professional assistance. In fact, in simple applications, you can make drawings on graph paper and submit them to your building department for approval. You will have to work on the roof and remove sections of existing rafters, but the project is manageable, especially if you work in a season of little rain and fair temperatures.

To make a gable dormer, the attic height to begin with should be 9'. This will allow for a gable dormer ceiling of 7' off the attic floor and 2' beneath the main roof ridge.

Generally, a gable dormer extends across at least three rafter spacings or 4'. This is the type I'll show here.

Building a gable dormer requires making upper and lower headers between the doubled rafters. These headers, made of dimensional lumber, are the same dimension as the existing rafters and fastened in vertical position with joist hangers wide enough to accommodate them.

To build a gable dormer into an existing roof, follow this sequence:

1. Double the rafters on which the side walls of the gable dormer are to rest as I described in the section on building a shed dormer, step 1.

2. On the underside of the rafters, mark where the dormer is to go. Draw vertical lines where you are to cut the main roof rafters. Allow for the thickness the top and bottom headers, each of which will be 3" thick.

3. Drill holes up through the roof to mark the locations of the upslope side of where the top header will be and the downslope side of where the bottom header will be.

4. Up on the roof, snap chalk lines between the holes drilled in step 3. Remove the shingles in this area. Remove shingles left and right for sole plates and for dormer wall sheathing and siding, plus a few inches for comfort.

5. On the roof determine where the ridge beam of the gable dormer is going to intersect the roof. Snap chalk lines down from this point to the top corners of where you have cleared shingles. Clear shingles away in this triangular area, but do not remove the roof sheathing here.

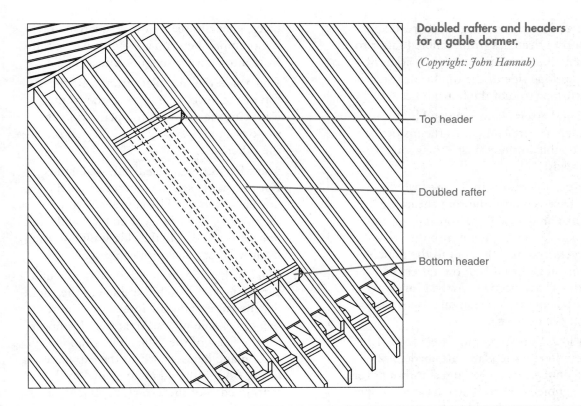

Doubled rafters and headers for a gable dormer.

(Copyright: John Hannah)

Top header

Doubled rafter

Bottom header

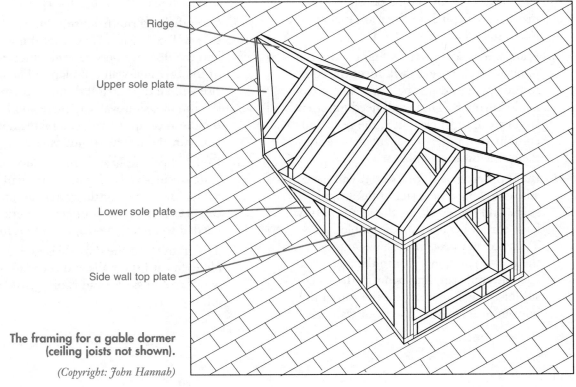

Ridge

Upper sole plate

Lower sole plate

Side wall top plate

The framing for a gable dormer (ceiling joists not shown).

(Copyright: John Hannah)

6. Cut away the sheathing in the rectangular area that stretches from doubled rafter to doubled rafter and from the position of the upslope side of the top header and the downslope side of the bottom header.

7. Cut and assemble the top and bottom headers for attachment to the insides of the doubled rafters. Have their joist hangers ready.

8. Cut out the rafters in the area where you have removed the roof sheathing. Immediately install the top and bottom headers by setting them into the joist hangers and nailing them to the doubled rafters plus the ends of the rafters whose sections have been cut away. Now you have a supported rectangular opening for the gable dormer.

9. Cut lower sole plates for the side walls. These lower sole plates are made of 2×4s long enough to run on the sheathing over the doubled rafters. The cuts at the upper and lower ends should be beveled cuts matching the pitch of the roof, making the lower sole plate ends vertical.

10. Make upper sole plates running from the point where the ridge will meet the roof to the upper ends of the lower sole plates made in step 8. These will need miter cuts so they can meet cleanly at the peak and combination miter-bevel cuts where they meet the lower sole plates.

11. Build the front wall of 2×4s. It will have a header, king studs, jack studs, cripple studs, and rough sill for the window. It will have corner posts made of doubled 2×4s. These corner posts must have miter cuts at the bottom so they fit onto the sole plates. Cripple studs running beneath the rough sill for the window rest on the top of the bottom header. After the front wall is in place, check to see that it is square and rising plumb. Then run a 2×4 brace across it from a top corner to a bottom corner.

12. Run a side wall top plate from near the top of the lower sole plate to the front wall. Cut the side wall top plate to fit the slope of the lower sole plate. Repeat on the other side.

13. Mark for, cut, and install side-wall studs. For this work, see the section on shed dormers, step 11. The cuts at the top of these studs, however, will be level and will not be notched. Tie the side walls and the front wall together with cap plates.

14. Make a ridge beam of a 2×6. Make a miter cut at one end match the slope of the roof. Set the cut end on the intersection of the two upper sole plates. Make a 2×4 support for the front of the ridge. The support will rest on and be toenailed to the cap plate of the front wall and be toenailed to the bottom edge of the 2×6 ridge so that the upper edge of the 2×6 ridge is level.

15. Cut rafters to run from the ridge to both side-wall cap plates. The total run will be half the distance between the outer edges of the two side-wall cap plates. The total rise will be the vertical distance between the top of a side-wall cap plate and half the distance up the ridge. Create an overhang for the rafters or not as you please.

16. Run 2×4 ceiling beams from side-wall cap plate to side-wall cap plate. Face nail them to the lower ends of the rafters and to the cap plates. Bevel their upper corners as needed to match the slope of the rafters.

17. The framing of the dormer is now complete. Sheath the walls and roof; install the window; add siding and roofing; and your job is done.

The Least You Need to Know

- ◆ Shed dormers have a flat sloping roof, and gable dormers have gable roofs.
- ◆ Both types of dormers add light and living space to an otherwise inhospitable and dim attic.

- ◆ Building dormers requires work on roofs, which is hazardous.
- ◆ Dormers require doubling the rafters on which the side walls rest.

In This Chapter

- ◆ Dealing with water or moisture
- ◆ Framing walls
- ◆ Dealing with cables and pipes
- ◆ Dealing with beams and ducts
- ◆ Handling sagged joists

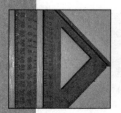
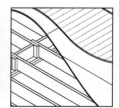

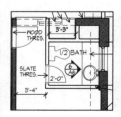

Basement Framing

An unfinished basement is a very tempting target for additional living space. A recreation room, television room, hobby area, or even a spare bedroom have all been built successfully into unfinished basements.

The first step is to assure that your basement will not have water, moisture, or mildew problems. Consult a basement waterproofing professional before hammering together framing walls in your basement, or you may regret some of your work.

If the joists in your basement have sagged over the years, there are ways to realign them, though the process can take months. If the sagging is severe, secure the assistance of a structural engineer.

When you are confident the new living space will not be hampered with dampness and that the ceiling joists will anchor a flat ceiling, then do the framing for the walls. The framing proceeds much like framing walls inside a house discussed in Chapter 15. But basements do in some respects require special treatment.

Making New Living Space in the Basement

Many people who want new living spaces in their homes look first to their basements. This makes a good deal of sense, as long as the basement is not plagued by flooding, periodic moisture, or mildew. All of these problems can be solved—at a cost—and then making a recreation room, study, or spare bedroom is a real possibility. But there is not much point in putting new framing into a basement that is troubled with humidity and water problems.

If your basement gets standing water during heavy rains, you need professional help. The problem can be solved on the outside of the foundation or handled on the inside. Outside the procedure is to dig dirt away from the foundation down to its bottom, install gravel there, and then also drain tile, which carries water away from the foundation. For good measure, professionals generally treat the exposed walls with asphalt or other water repellant treatment, then replace the earth that was removed.

But excavation on the outside is costly and often not practical owing to decks and patios. So a solution is often sought inside, and this takes the form of what is sometimes called a "French drain." Around the perimeter of the basement professionals cut through the basement floor, dig down a foot or so, and lay in gravel and drain tile. They also dig out an area in one corner for a container about as big as a large garbage can. Then they cover the drain tile and gravel with concrete.

When water saturates the ground around and under the foundation, it finds its way to the drain tile before being able to penetrate the floor or walls. The drain tile directs water to the container, which holds a sump pump powered by an electrical cord plugged into a nearby receptacle. When water rises to a certain level in the container, the sump pump turns on and pumps the water up through a discharge pipe that carries the water away from the house (to the yard, street, or storm sewer).

If the problem is less severe than occasional flooding, then some simpler measures may suffice. These include treating the walls and floor with waterproofing materials. If the basement suffers no more than trouble with mildew, then the solution may be a dehumidifier or two. These turn on and off automatically to lower the humidity in the air, and mold will not grow in dry air. Dehumidifiers need access to electrical receptacles and a place to discharge the water it removes from the air.

Framing the Walls

Framing walls in the basement is much like framing the walls in an existing home. Most likely, these are going to be partition, or non-bearing, walls. This gives you more freedom in choosing where you put the walls and what materials you use for the walls, including headers in the walls for over doors.

Partition walls in the basement are really the bones for division of space. Accordingly, they can be made out of 2×3s rather than 2×4s because all they will be supporting is wallboard. Using 2×3s saves precious space, which in a basement is at a premium. Using 2×3s also saves money because they are less costly than 2×4s.

There are a couple of circumstances when you would not want to use 2×3s, however. If you are framing for a bathroom, you may want a wall of 2×4s or even 2×6s. You will need the greater thickness for the supply and drain pipes. You may also need wider walls if they are to contain heating or air conditioning ducts.

> ☞ **Finger Tips**
>
> To get some idea of what you are planning in the basement, lay down 2×3s or 2×4s as sole plates in the approximate position they are to go or snap chalk lines there, and walk around in the new spaces you've created. This will give you a feeling for what the new basement spaces will be like. For a more realistic trial, set up poles and string lines over which you can hang sheets to approximate the walls. After you see what the spaces are going to be like, you may want to do some adjusting.

When framing in a basement, use pressure-treated wood for the sole plates because the concrete will always contain some moisture. In like manner, many framers do not like to have the framing members of their walls touch the foundation itself, but keep the studs a fraction of an inch away.

To begin framing for a basement, make a detailed plan, and apply for the appropriate permits from your local building department.

To frame walls in a basement, beginning with walls along the foundation walls, proceed as follows:

1. To build a wall along an exterior wall running perpendicular to joists, measure out along the underside of the joists the thickness of the framing material, 2×3s or 2×4s, plus ¹/₂". Mark several joists in this way, and snap a chalk line that connects the marks.

2. Use a plumb bob from several places on the chalk line crossing the joists to points on the basement floor. Snap another chalk line connecting these points on the floor to mark the location of the sole plate.

3. Use a pressure-treated piece of wood for the sole plate. Place it edge up on the basement floor, and align it with a regular piece of wood of the same dimension that will serve as the top plate.

4. Mark both the top plate and the sole plate at the same time for the wall studs.

5. Cut the studs to fit between the sole plate and the top plate.

6. Fasten the sole plate to the basement floor. You can do this in one of two ways. One is to use a hammer drill to drill holes for the kinds of anchors described in Chapter 3. The other is to rent a nailing gun from a tool rental store that is capable of propelling a nail through a sole plate and into concrete. Ask for instructions in their use.

7. With the top plate and the studs lying on the basement floor, face nail through the top plate into the ends of the studs at the locations the studs are meant to go.

8. With a helper or two, hoist the top plate and its attached studs into place. Align the top plate with the chalk line across the joists. Nail through the top plate into two joists to hold the top plate in place.

9. Shift a bottom of one of the studs to its mark on the sole plate. Check it for plumb. If it is not plumb, either the top plate or sole plate is out of position; so adjust as needed. Check that the stud is slightly removed from the surface of the foundation wall.

Check that the stud does not touch the foundation wall.

10. If the stud is not touching the foundation wall and is plumb, nail through the top plate into all the joists. Toenail the bottoms of the studs to their marks.

You may have gaps between the top of the top plate and the bottom of some of the joists because the joists have settled to different degrees. If this is the case, slip shims into the gaps, and hammer them in tight. Cut off any portion of a shim that projects out to either side of the top plate.

If the joists are sagged appreciably, consider shoring them up as described in the final section of this chapter.

Erect a frame wall along a foundation wall.

11. To raise a wall along a foundation wall that runs parallel to joists, nail blocking from the band joist to the joist just to the inside of it. The blocking will serve as a nailing surface for the top plate of the framed wall. Erect the wall as for a wall running perpendicular to the joists.

A wall running parallel to joists requires blocking between two joists for the top plate.

12. Where corners are needed along foundation walls, provide for nailing surfaces for the wallboard for attaching to both walls.

Provide nailing surface for wallboard to be put up on both walls. For corner details, see Chapter 12.

13. For corners where a wall intersects a wall alongside the foundation wall, provide nailing surfaces with extra studs in the wall being met. For corner details, see Chapter 12.

Where one wall abuts another, use extra studs in the abutted wall to provide nailing surface for wallboard.

14. Make as many framed walls as needed to make the spaces you want in the basement.

Frame as many walls as you believe convenient.

15. Where walls are to be run parallel to joists, add blocking between the joists to which to nail the top plates of the walls.

For walls running parallel to joist, add blocking to which to attach the top plate.

16. Frame around windows and doors as needed. You don't need strong headers for partition walls, but think ahead about how you will fasten the trim after you have attached the wallboard.

Frame around windows and doors as needed. Nonbearing walls do not need beefy headers.

17. Add blocking as needed to stiffen walls or to meet code.

Add blocking as called for by code or designer.

Dealing With Cables and Pipes

Once the wall framing is done, electricians, plumbers, and duct men come in to install their cables, pipes, and ducts. Generally, they can bore holes and make notches as they see fit in nonbearing top plates. But their cables and pipes should be protected with metal plates nailed to the edges of the plates. These stop any nail from harming the cables or pipes once the wallboard is put into place and the location of the cables and pipes are hidden from view. Where cables and pipes pass through studs and joists, the edges of the studs and joists that will be covered over with wallboard should be similarly protected.

To assure that plumbers and electricians can work effectively and finish their work within code requirements, proceed as follows:

1. Be aware that pipes and cables can be routed through framing members.

Plumbers and electricians will install their pipes and cables.

2. If the electricians and plumbers have not done so, tack metal plates to locations on studs, joists, and plates where cables or pipes pass through them.

Make sure metal plates are tacked to studs, joists, and plates where cables and pipes pass through them.

Dealing With Ducts and Beams

Probably your idea of finished living space in the basement does not involve looking at a steel or wooden beam or at the shiny metal of ducts meant to route warmed or cooled air. Remedy this by making nailing surfaces that allow you to attach wallboard around these structures. Framing around beams or ducts is often called *boxing*. The framing around a duct is often called a *chase*.

If the beam is wood, you have no problem nailing wallboard to it. But steel is a different matter.

Framer's Lingo

To **box** is to frame around an obstruction such as a beam, giving nailing surface to wallboard that then disguises the obstruction. A **chase** is a framing enclosure boxing around an obstruction such as a beam or duct.

The general theory of boxing around beams or ducts is to provide adequate nailing surface for the wallboard while surrendering as little living space as possible.

Dealing With a Steel Beam

If the steel beam was put in place with a wooden top plate on it, you can use this plate as the upper nailer. You can attach a lower nailer with bolts if the steel beam has been predrilled. If it has not, you can order it predrilled or have a professional drill bolt holes for you.

If there is a wooden top plate on top of the steel beam, this can serve as the top nailer. A bottom nailer can be held with bolts.

Another method is to nail a framing member—a 2×2 or 2×3—on either side of the steel beam to the underside of joists. These framing members become the supports that hold up the entire chase. Other short vertical pieces of 2×2s, 2×3s, or 2×4s are toenailed up into these horizontal framing members and then longer horizontal pieces are nailed up into the shorter vertical pieces. The vertical pieces are set at 16" intervals so that wallboard edges fall upon them.

Construct a chase by nailing upper pieces to the undersides of joists, then nailing vertical pieces to them and bottom pieces to the vertical pieces.

Toenailing is a skill much called upon when boxing and building chases.

The boxing does not have to go below the steel beam. It can stop flush with the bottom in order not to take more headroom from the space below the beam.

Make the framing descend no farther than the lower edge of the beam, thus saving headroom.

Dealing With Ducts

The strategy for building a chase is much the same. This is a good place to use up all the scraps of 2×4 or other material you have created cutting plates and studs for the walls.

A pipe and duct chase are suspended from the ceiling. Because the space taken up by the duct and pipe together was so large to begin with, 2x4s were used here to make the chase without adding much percentage to the area of the ceiling taken up.

Detail of a pipe chase.

Because the framing members of chases generally serve as nailing surfaces, they can be notched or trimmed to accommodate the elements around them.

If a framing member is serving merely as a nailer, it can be notched to accommodate other construction members.

Dealing With Sagging Joists

If you suspect that the joists of the basement ceiling have sagged in places and would make a finished wallboard ceiling look waved or bowed downward, you may be able to raise the sagged joists enough to make a ceiling more presentable. You can do this with 4x4s or a house jack. If the sagging is severe or if the sagging is more toward the exterior walls than between the exterior walls, consult a structural engineer for guidance.

To shore up sagging basement ceiling joists, follow these steps:

1. Use a taut string to determine if the bottoms of joists have sagged. This might be near stairwells or under particularly heavy items such as bathtubs or pianos.

2. You can solve small sags by building a support wall under the sags and forcing in shims. Place a 2x8 on the floor under the sagging joists, and cut a 4x4 top plate to fit under the sagging joists. Toenail 4x4s to this every 3' to act as studs. Cut them so that when attached to the 4x4 top plate, the top plate will just rest under the worst of the sags.

3. Raise the top plate and 4x4 studs together and fit them under the sagging joists. Check each of the 4x4 studs for plumb; then toe nail them to the 2x8 sole plate.

4. Hammer in shims between the bottom of the sagging joists and the 4x4 top plate until they are snug. Each day try to hammer them in a little more, raising the joists bottoms about $1/16$" a day.

   You can also do this work with a rented or purchased house jack, which can replace some of the 4x4 studs. Once the jack is up and snug beneath the 4x4 top plate, tighten the screw so that the top plate rises $1/16$" a day.

5. Once you have taken the sag out of the joists, you can leave the 4x4s in place and the house jack also if you have bought it and don't care to replace it with a 4x4. Merely cut away the excess of the sole plate and cover everything over with wallboard. If the support wall is not in a location where you want a wall, build your partition walls tight against the underside of the raised joists, and remove the support wall.

The Least You Need to Know

◆ Before framing in a basement, take care of water and dampness problems and of sagging overhead joists.

◆ Use pressure-treated wood for the sole plates of all basement framing.

◆ Hold studs a small distance off the inside of masonry walls.

◆ Frame around steel beams, ducts, and pipes so that wallboard can fit around them and put them out of sight.

In This Chapter

- ◆ Building a recessed wall cabinet
- ◆ Building a corner floor-to-ceiling bookcase
- ◆ Building an alcove bench with lid

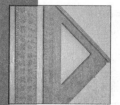

Chapter 19

Built-Ins

As an added benefit, you can use some of your framing skills to make built-in structures in your home. These built-in structures can add beauty, give you more storage space, and increase the value of your home.

In this chapter, I give you three built-in projects: a recessed cabinet; a floor-to-ceiling bookcase; and an alcove bench with a lid. None of these requires more than cutting 2× material, 1× material, and plywood and fastening them in simple ways. Once you get these built-ins painted, they will look as if they were always there, ready and useful in your daily life around the house.

Built-In Cabinets

One of the easiest built-ins is a cabinet. One can be recessed in a wall as a medicine cabinet in a bathroom. In fact, some people like to make their own medicine cabinets and use cabinet doors from old chests.

The simplest kind of cabinet built-in is one placed between two studs. You remove wall material between two studs, hammer in a top sill and bottom sill, and you already have the frame. Then you can slide in a metal cabinet, such as a medicine cabinet made to be recessed, or build your own.

If you want to have a wider built-in cabinet (and some manufacturers make metal ones to fit in spaces $30^1/_2$" long—the distance between two studs 32" on center with one removed between them—then you have to remove any studs in the way. This is not particularly difficult, unless the wall is a bearing wall (see Chapter 15). If you remove a portion of a stud in a bearing wall, you must replace it with headers at top and bottom to carry the weight from above.

Before you begin removing any wall section, always stop to determine if there are pipes, ducts, or electrical wiring behind. A stud finder may help you here. You can also do some detective work: if a toilet, tub, or sink is directly above, there may be plumbing pipes in the wall. The same works with duct registers. Wires are harder to predict, and they may have been run low or high on the wall.

To make a recessed cabinet between studs in a nonbearing wall, proceed as follows:

1. Use a stud finder to locate the position of studs in the wall; very likely they will be 16" on center or 24" on center.

2. Draw lines on the wall to define the outline of the recessed cabinet, and remove the wall's surface material from within the lines. Wear a dust mask or respirator for this work. If the wall material is wallboard, a utility knife and hammer can do the job. If the wall material is plaster, score along the outline lines as best you can with a utility knife. Then use a carbide-tipped blade in a circular saw set for a depth no greater than the thickness of the plaster plus the wooden lathe that anchors it. Wear eye protection.

3. Measure between the studs at the top and bottom of the opening in the wall. Cut 2×4 material to fit snugly between the studs at these locations. These will act as a top and bottom sill.

4. Set the top sill into position. Check it for level. Toenail it in place. It will be easier to toenail if you predrill holes for the nails first. If you find nailing in this confined space too difficult, use screws.

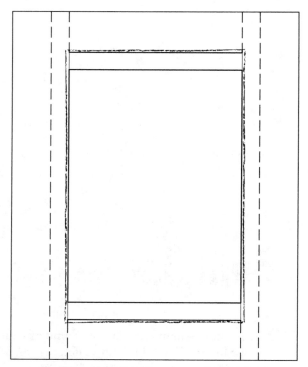

Make a frame for the cabinet by installing top and bottom sills between vertical studs in a wall.

(Copyright: John Hannah)

5. Now you can do what you want. If you have a metal medicine cabinet the size of this opening, you can slip it in. Its side flanges cover the ragged edges of the opening and you screw through holes in the cabinet sides to hold it in place. Alternatively, you can glue a thin plywood panel to the back of the opening and glue, nail, or screw attractive 1×4 wood pieces to the top and bottom sills and the vertical studs. These pieces can be sanded smooth and stained or painted an attractive color. You can attach a door for the cabinet by hinging it to one of the side pieces. If you would like shelves, you can screw thin pieces of wood to the sides of the opening and then cut shelving material to rest on top.

Floor-to-Ceiling Book Shelves

Another fairly easy project to make are floor-to-ceiling book shelves in the corner of a room. The shelves use the side of one wall for support, and you can make the shelves as wide as you want using 1×8, 1×10, or 1×12 material.

The shelves have more of a built-in appearance if at the bottom baseboard skirts along them as it does around the rest of the room. This requires removing the existing baseboard where the new shelves are going to go and then refastening the pieces to the shelves after you have built them or buying equivalent pieces from the lumber yard and using them.

As described here these shelves will not have a back. The painted wall serves as one. If you want a more solid backing for the shelves, cut plywood and attach it to the backs of the vertical supports.

To make this kind of project, proceed as follows:

1. Let's say you want shelves that are about 9" wide. Along the wall that will act as a side support for the shelves, measure out into the room along the top of the existing baseboard the width of a 1×10, which is 9$^{1}/_{4}$" wide. Cut down vertically through the baseboard at this point and remove the short piece running from the cut back to the corner.

2. Measure along the wall that will be the backside of the shelves a distance equal to how wide you want the shelves to be. Again, mark the baseboard at this distance. Cut down vertically through the baseboard. Remove this piece.

3. If there is crown molding at the ceiling, mark, cut, and remove pieces corresponding to the pieces of removed baseboard at the floor. Save these pieces of crown molding for installing at the top of the shelves or for taking to the lumber yard to buy equivalent pieces.

4. Cut or have your lumber yard cut two vertical 1×10s to act as the sides of the shelves. One goes up against the wall at the corner so that its bottom fits where the first piece of baseboard was removed. Fasten this 1×10 to the wall by screwing it into studs behind the wallboard at the corner and to the sole plate and top plates at the bottom and top of the wall.

5. Erect the other 1×10 by first attaching cleats to the ceiling and floor just to the inside of where you want this side of the shelving to go. The bottom cleat you can nail or screw to the floor. The top cleat you can fasten to a joist covered by the wallboard or simply well anchor it to the wallboard with two anchors sold for just this purpose of securing objects to wallboard alone. Then fit the 1×10 to the outside of these cleats and screw it to them. Now you have two vertical 1×10s.

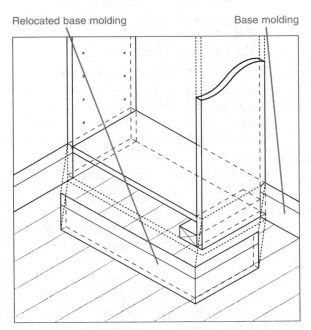

Relocated base molding   Base molding

The lower view of a built-in floor-to-ceiling bookcase.

(Copyright: John Hannah)

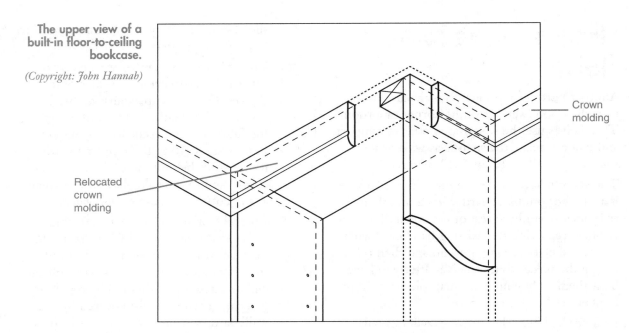

The upper view of a built-in floor-to-ceiling bookcase.

(Copyright: John Hannah)

Crown molding

Relocated crown molding

6. Fasten the first piece of baseboard removed to the outside of the second 1×10. Fasten the second piece of baseboard removed across the front of the two 1×10s—or use new pieces of baseboard. To make their meeting look good, give each piece of baseboard a 45° bevel cut before screwing them to the bottoms of the 1×10s.

7. If you removed crown molding, reinstall the two pieces at the top—or new pieces—just as you did the baseboard pieces at the bottom. Now you have two vertical 1×10s, one anchored to a wall and the other to two cleats at ceiling and floor, and each tied in more firmly and attractively to the ceiling and floor with crown and base molding.

8. Now you can add shelving as you wish. The shelves can fit onto cleats you screw to the insides of the 1×10s. Or you can support them with pegs sold for this purpose and set into small holes drilled into the insides of the 1×10s. Or use hardware made for adjustable shelving. Make the lowest shelf level with the top of the baseboard.

Finger Tips

You can make the shelves adjustable by installing what is called *shelf standard* on the upright 1×10s. Shelf standard is sold in hardware stores and is made of strips of slotted steel. Two are fastened to each vertical support. Small clips are set into slots at the same height on either side and a wooden shelf sits on top of the clips.

Shelf standard can be screwed directly to the surfaces of the vertical uprights. But the installation looks better if the shelf standard is recessed into the uprights themselves. Do this by cutting two long recesses into each upright, each recess being about as deep as a strip of shelf standard is thick. The shelf standard then fits into the recess and is largely out of sight. Making such an installation also allows the shelves to come within a fraction of an inch of the sides of the vertical board supports; with the shelf standard not recessed, each shelf end could come no closer to the surface of the uprights than the thickness of the shelf standards themselves. For a fee, your lumber yard may be able to make these recess cuts for you.

Built-In Benches

An alcove or a gable dormer is an ideal place for a bench that also serves as a storage area. You can make it with 2×3s or 2×4s as the framing and plywood as the covering. Plywood also serves as a lid and raises by means of a long hinge, called a piano hinge, along the lid's back edge.

The framing should be firmly fastened to studs behind the wallboard or plaster of the walls using lag screws. A good height for such a bench is between 17" and 22".

To make a built-in bench and storage area, proceed as follows:

1. Determine the height for the bench. Draw a line across the back wall for the back supporting 2×. Cut a 2× to length, and attach it to the studs of the walls with lag screws.

2. Draw level lines out from the back supporting 2× along the side walls for the side wall supports. Attach them to the side wall studs with lag screws; then toenail or screw the ends of the side supports into the ends of the back support.

3. Determine the size of the lid and the location for the back edge of the lid. You'll need framing to support the lid. Install a 2× parallel with the back support between the two side supports where you want the back edge of the lid to be. Use screws or framing connectors, or toenail this lid support to the two side wall supports.

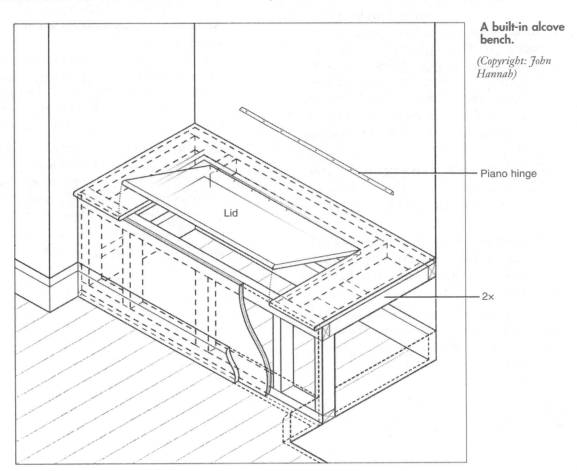

A built-in alcove bench.

(Copyright: John Hannah)

Piano hinge

Lid

2×

4. Cut a support to fit across the front, lapping over the fronts of the side wall supports. Fasten this front support to the ends of the side walls supports.

5. Cut a 2× to serve as a vertical center support. Run it from the floor up to the center of the front support. Screw or toenail it to the front support and to the floor. Alternatively, you can use a type of connector called an angle iron, a right-angle piece of steel with two holes on each arm for joining two pieces of wood that are at right angles to one another. These are smaller than regular framing connectors and are used more in cabinetmaking than house framing.

6. Cut additional vertical supports left and right of center vertical support dividing the space in front into four equal distances.

7. Run supports from the front support to the lid support installed in step 3 so that they will support the left and right edges of the lid.

8. Cut ¾" plywood for the front, top, and lid. You may want the lid and the plywood left and right of the lid to overlap the vertical plywood by an inch.

9. Screw the plywood covering and front to the 2×4 supports. Attach a piano hinge to the lid support. Using only two or three screws, temporarily attach the lid to the piano hinge. See how much the lid projects in front of the horizontal plywood to its left and right because of the piano hinge. Remove the lid and trim either its front or back to eliminate this projection.

10. Cover the front edge of the lid and the plywood to its left and right with molding especially made to cover plywood edges. A common type is called half round; you can glue and tack it to the plywood edges with small finishing nails.

The Least You Need to Know

- You can recess a built-in cabinet in a wall just as medicine cabinets are used in bathrooms.

- Think about what might be behind the surface of a wall before you begin to remove it.

- You can make a book case look built-in by running baseboard and crown molding across it at top and bottom.

- You can make a built-in alcove bench by using simple framing techniques and covering the framing with plywood.

Appendix A

Glossary

2× Pronounced "two-by," this term refers to dimensional lumber that long ago was 2" thick but for the last century has been $1^1/_2$" thick. A 2×4 is 2× material. So are a 2×6 and a 2×8.

3-4-5 triangle method A means of checking if a right angle is truly 90°. It will be if the end of one leg from the angle 3' long and the end of another 4' long are exactly 5' apart.

ampere A measure of the electricity required by an electric motor. A circular saw might draw 9 or 10 amperes. The higher the number, the more powerful the saw. But most household circuits are built to deliver only 15 amperes. If you are running a circular saw drawing 10 amperes when an appliance plugged into another outlet on the circuit tries to draw 6 amperes, the fuse will blow or the circuit breaker trip. If you think you are going to be drawing lots of amperes through a circuit, make it a 20-ampere circuit. A short name for ampere is amp.

anchor A piece of steel used to fasten a piece of lumber to masonry.

arbor Part of a circular saw onto the end of which is slipped the hole at the center of a circular saw blade. A retaining nut threads into the arbor and holds the blade tight.

awl A hard and sharp pointed metal rod with a handle. It is used to mark wood for cuts or to make dimples useful in starting screws or nails.

balloon framing An older framing style in which the exterior wall studs rise two stories from the foundation.

band joist A piece of dimensional lumber the same size as the floor joists but running along the perimeter of a floor. Also called a rim joist. A band joist that is perpendicular to other joists is sometimes called a header joist.

base plate Bottom plate of a circular saw which rests on the piece being cut. The saw's blade protrudes through a slot in the base plate. Sometimes called the "shoe."

beam   A heavy-duty framing member that supports other structural pieces, mainly floor joists. Beams are normally made of 2×10s or 2×12s glued and nailed together. Also called a girder.

bearing wall   A wall that carries the weight of the building down to the ground.

bevel cut   A cut across a piece of wood at an angle to the edge.

bird's mouth cut   The cut of a rafter where it meets the top of a supporting wall. Also called the bird's mouth.

block plane   A small plane you can operate with one hand.

blocking   Pieces of wood placed between framing members either to stabilize and tie them together or to provide nailing surfaces for sheathing or wallboard.

body   The longer and wider arm of a framing square. It is sometimes called the blade.

bottom plate   *See* sole plate.

box, to box   The act of nailing framing members around an obstruction, such as a beam or duct, to give nailing surface to wallboard that then covers over the obstruction.

box nails   Nails that have more slender shanks than common nails. They tend not to split wood as much as common nails.

boxed eaves   An eaves treatment where a fascia is nailed to the ends of the rafters and a soffit to the underside of the rafters or to the underside of lookouts.

break line   A line on an architectural drawing that shortens the drawing but indicates the object or area goes on as before.

bridging   Slender pieces of wood or steel set at a slant between floor joists to stabilize them.

building codes   Local ordinances that carry the weight of law and that describe standards certain constructions must meet. There are codes for framing, electrical work, plumbing, etc.

building permit   A permit issued by the local building department when it sees that the plans meet the local building codes.

building inspection   An inspection by a building inspector employed by the local building department to assure the department that the construction is following the approved plans and meeting the requirements of the building codes.

building line   A term used in rafter layout that corresponds with the line of the outside of the wall that will support the lower end of a rafter.

cantilevered   A framing member that is attached at one end and supported somewhere along its middle length but not fastened or supported at its other end is said to be cantilevered.

carbide-tipped blade   This is a circular saw blade whose teeth are each tipped with a tough carbon steel cap. These blades are tougher than the normal steel blades that come with a new circular saw. A carbide-tipped blade can cut through nails and so is especially welcome in renovation work where you might be cutting through lumber that has nails in it.

carriage   The framing member at the sides of stairs holding the treads and risers.

cat's paw   A short piece of curved bar steel with a notch at one end for extracting nails whose heads have been hammered flush or below the surface of the piece of wood it is in.

C-clamp   The body is shaped like a C and a screw jaw threads up through one end to press any piece within the C to the other end. A very effective and tight clamp, but the threading mechanism often makes it slow to use. C-clamps come in sizes only a few inches high to ones with jaws 8 or 9 inches wide.

cement nail   A nail with a coating of resin or vinyl that gives it greater holding power in wood. Also called a "sinker."

center line   A line on an architectural drawing that indicates the center of an object. A center line can also be drawn on a piece of wood to indicate its center.

chalk line   A string inside a steel housing that contains colored chalk. Used for marking a long straight line on wood.

chase   A boxed enclosure around a duct allowing it to be covered over with wallboard.

chuck   The cylindrical metal piece at the front of a drill which clamps down on the shank of a drill bit.

chuck key   The tool that often comes with a drill and is used to tighten and loosen the chuck's grip on a drill bit.

circuit breaker panel   An electrical panel in the home that contains circuit breakers. See *electrical panel*. Circuit breakers are more convenient than fuses because when they are "tripped"—that is shut themselves off because of a malfunction in the circuit—they can be turned back to "on" once the malfunction has been fixed.

circular saw   A portable, electric-powered saw. An old name, from a manufacturer, was SkilsSaw, which can still be heard around framing sites.

claw   The back portion of the head of a hammer. The claw of a framing hammer is relatively straight so it can be wedged between two pieces of lumber in order to pry them apart. The claw of a claw hammer is more curved to better extract nails half driven into wood.

claw hammer   A lightweight hammer with a curved claw, which is mainly used in finish carpentry.

cleat   A short piece of wood that supports or anchors another.

clinching   A type of nail joinery where nails penetrate both boards. Then the protruding shanks of the nails are hammered flat.

codes   *See* building codes.

collar ties   Faming members that connect pairs of rafters on opposite side of the roof ridge, stabilizing the roof structure.

combination cut   A cut across a piece of wood that combines a bevel cut and a miter cut.

combination square   A hand tool that has a straight edge marked in inches fitted to a body that has a section running at a right angle to the straight edge. Another section runs at a 45-degree angle to the straight edge.

common nails   The nails most used in framing. Common nails have substantial heads so a hammer does not slip off and substantial shanks so they do not bend.

compass   Also called dividers, this tool has a sharp leg on one side and a pencil on the other. The legs adjust in distance apart and can be locked in position. Used for "scribing," that is, marking the distance between lengths of material.

chord   A perimeter piece of a truss. A triangular truss has a long lower chord and two shorter upper chords that meet in the middle and form a peak.

cripple stud   A stud running from a header over a door or window to the top plate; or a stud running from the sole plate up to the rough sill of a window opening.

crown   The edge of a piece of lumber that rises.

cutoff saw   *See* power miter saw.

d   A designation meaning "penny," which stands for a size of nail. A 16d nail is a 16-penny nail.

dead load   The weight of the empty building bearing down to the ground.

decking   Another name for subflooring.

detail drawing   An architectural drawing which shows the detail of some element not clearly understandable from the floorplan or other kind of drawing. Normally the scale is larger.

dimension line   A line on an architectural drawing that indicates the height, length, or thickness of an object.

dimension lumber   A common name for lumber that goes by such names as 2×4, 2×6, 2×8, 2×10, and so on. These are the normal studs, joists, and rafters of house framing.

duct chase   An enclosure of 2×4s that encompasses heating or cooling ducts.

drywall   Panels of plaster-like material fastened to studs and finished to make a paintable wall. Also called wallboard.

drywall screw   Also called a zip screw, drive screw, general purpose screw, or bugle head. Originally invented to attach drywall to studs, drywall screws became popular for attaching plywood to joists and other sorts of joinery. Generally, no pilot hole is needed, and they can be applied with a screw gun or variable speed drill. They have good holding power.

eaves   The area where the roof overhangs the wall below.

electrical panel   The box or panel in the home where the circuit breakers or fuses are located. The various electrical circuits running through the house and to an outside wall for an outside outlet all run through the electrical panel. An electrical panel may contain circuit breakers or fuses. Either device stops electricity flowing through a circuit when there is a short circuit on the circuit or other malfunction.

engineered lumber   Lumber made from parts of wood rather than solid wood. Trusses and wood I-beams are examples. In some respects they are stronger than solid wood pieces and make a job go faster.

equal-diameters method   A means of checking that a rectangle has precise right angles. It does if the diagonals between opposite corners are equal in length.

expansion shield   A soft metal sleeve used as part of an anchor for fastening a piece of lumber to masonry. Also called a jacket.

face nailing   Driving a nail perpendicular into a piece of wood.

fascia   A board nailed to the ends of rafters.

finish carpentry   Finish carpentry, sometimes called trim carpentry, is the work of placing door and window trim, baseboard, and like pieces of wood in a house. The wood pieces are more delicate than studs and joists and are left exposed for painting or staining.

fire blocking   Horizontal framing members as wide as the vertical framing members of a wall nailed in place to stop the rise of heat and flames inside a wall.

flat bar   A flat piece of steel curved at both ends used for extracting nails and prying apart two pieces of nailed wood.

floorplans   These drawings show the outline of a building and all its principal components. The view is from overhead.

flush   In carpentry, flush means "at the same level as." If a nail head is flush with the wood, the nail head is resting at the surface of the wood. Flush can also mean aligned with or one exactly atop another.

footings or footers   Concrete bases on which foundation walls are built. Footings also are required to support piers rising from the foundation level.

framing anchor   A general purpose framing connector for right angle joints.

framing carpentry   The skill of erecting the "bones of a house," generally, the parts not seen but covered with wall board, flooring, ceiling material, and the like. Framing carpentry works with wall studs, joists, beams, rafters, and plywood. Also called rough carpentry.

framing connector   A piece of stamped steel that facilitates and strengthens wood-to-wood joinery. Some framing connectors are joist hangers, rafter ties, framing anchors, and truss plates.

framing plan   An architectural drawing showing the exact positions of studs, joists, or rafters.

framing hammer   The general hammer for framing, it weighs between 20 and 24 ounces and normally has a straight claw.

framing connector A piece of machine-punched steel used to help reinforce a joint between two or more pieces of lumber.

framing square An L-shaped flat steel or aluminum rule with two arms, one called the body and one called the tongue. It is marked in inches and contains tables for mathematical calculations.

frost line The depth in the soil at any particular locality to which freezing temperatures do not penetrate. Foundation footings must be set below the frost line.

furring strips Long thin pieces of wood generally 1 1/2" wide used for nailing to the edges of studs, joists, or rafters to elevate the position of their edges.

fuse box An electrical panel in the home that contains fuses. *See* electrical panel. A fuse "blows" when a malfunction occurs on the circuit it controls. Unlike circuit breakers, fuses cannot be reset to "on." "Blown" fuses must be discarded and replaced.

girder *See* beam.

grading Lumber is graded at the mill where it is cut. Lumber for light framing is normally designated construction, standard, or utility. Two other categories are stud—good for general framing—and structural light framing—designating pieces that can bear greater stress.

grade stamp An inked designation on pieces of lumber which shows the mill where it was manufactured, the grading agency, the moisture content, the species, and the lumber grade.

grain (of wood) The way the growth rings run in a piece of wood. Pieces of lumber have their long dimensions going *with the grain*. When you cut across this dimension, you are cutting *against or across the grain*.

Ground Fault Circuit Interrupter (GFCI) An electronic-electrical device that fits into an outlet or into the home's circuit breaker box and shuts off electricity in a fraction of a second if there is a short circuit or other trouble. Any circuit being used for outdoors or in damp locations must be protected by a GFCI in the outlet or at the circuit breaker.

gusset A steel or plywood plate used for holding together elements of a truss.

hack saw A saw for cutting through light metal such as nails, bolts, and copper tubing.

hand-grip clamps A kind of bar clamp that tightens with a hand gripping motion.

header A piece of dimensional lumber running perpendicular to others. A name often used for the wide piece running over a door or window opening. Also used for the framing members at the narrow ends of openings in floor framing.

header joist A joist that runs perpendicular between two trimmer joists and defines the edges of a floor opening. Also used for the name of the band joist that runs perpendicular to the regular joists.

heartwood The dead cells at the center of a tree's trunk. Often it is darker than the sapwood and is stronger and more durable.

hand sledge hammer A hand sledge hammer is a small sledge hammer with a short handle, suitable for swinging with just one hand. It is often used to "persuade" a piece of framing to move properly into place.

hammer drill A heavy-duty drill, often with a grip for both hands, that moves its chuck rapidly forward and backward, thus "hammering" the drill bit against the material being drilled. Such a tool is rentable as well as available for purchase.

hardwood Generally, the wood of deciduous trees. For example, maple, ash, walnut and oak.

J-bolt A bolt shaped like a J with threads only at the straight end. Used for anchoring framed house walls to a foundation, the J portion of the bolt is sunk in the fresh concrete of the foundation top and the bottom plate of the wall is fitted over the threaded end. Nuts and washers tighten down on the bottom plate.

jack stud   The stud next to a king stud near a door or window opening that runs from the sole plate up to the bottom of the header. Also called a trimmer stud.

jig   A device, often made by framers themselves, for aiding repetitive tasks. A common jig is one made 4' or 8' long for making straight cuts in plywood. It is a straight edge allowing a circular saw to ride on it and is clamped to a 4" ×8" panel when needed for a cut.

joist   A piece of 2× material holding up a floor. A joist could be a 2×6, 2×8, 2×10, or larger depending on the span it has to cover and the projected weight from above.

joist hanger   A framing connector that is U-shaped and supports a joist.

kerf   A groove made by a saw blade in a piece of wood.

keyhole saw   A narrow blade attached to a wooden handle. The narrowest portion of the blade is at the tip. This saw is meant for starting cuts in the middle of a piece of wood rather than an edge or for cutting in confined locations.

kickback   The action of a power saw against your hand if, when cutting, the blade gets pinched by the wood on either side of the cut. A kickback can throw you off balance. Kickbacks are prevented by proper support for the piece of wood being cut.

king stud   The stud next to a window or door opening that runs all the way from the sole plate to the top plate.

knee wall   A short wall rising from the floor to a sloping ceiling.

lag screw or lag bolt   A very large screw that has a hexagonal head so that it can be turned with a common wrench or socket wrench. Used for attaching large pieces of dimensional lumber to other large pieces or for making beams.

laying out   Marking for the positions of joists, studs, or rafters.

leader line   A line on an architectural drawing that identifies an object or calls attention to a note.

ledger   Name given to a piece of lumber attached to a house and from which rafters or joists extend.

level   Absolutely horizontal. The word is also the name for an instrument called a spirit level that determines if a piece of wood, decking, etc., is level.

live load   The weight of objects brought into a building and added to the dead load.

load   A term for the stresses a building needs to resist in order not to collapse or sag.

lookout   A piece, generally of 2×4, running from the house wall to the end of a rafter.

lookout ledger   A horizontal board fastened to the house wall to support one end of the lookouts.

miter box   Once a necessity for any carpenter, a miter box has largely, though not entirely, been replaced by a power miter saw, also called a cutoff saw or chop saw. A miter box typically was three pieces of wood joined in the shape of a U with slots cut into the vertical walls to guide a saw blade for making 90° and 45° cuts through a piece of wood laid onto the horizontal bottom of the box. These were replaced by metal miter boxes that were less boxes than a cutting table and a pivot arm holding a saw. The pivot arm set the angle and the saw descended to make the angled cut. These manual miter boxes are still good for precise work on small pieces; larger lumber can be cut on a power miter saw.

miter cut   A cut across a piece of wood at an angle to the board face.

nail set   A hardened cylinder of steel with a squared head for striking with a hammer and a narrow tip for applying to the head of a nail. It is used for making a nail head flush with the wood into which it is driven or driving it slightly below the surface.

new construction   A term meaning the construction of a new home or new room space, thus for a certain time open to the weather.

nominal size   The nominal size of a 2×4 is 2" wide and 4" broad. Pieces of dimensional lumber are always called by their nominal sizes. But their real sizes are always smaller. A 2×4 is really $1\frac{1}{2}$" wide and $3\frac{1}{2}$" broad. A 2×8 is really $1\frac{1}{2}$" wide and $7\frac{1}{4}$" broad.

non-bearing wall   A wall that bears no weight from above but just divides space.

object line   A line on an architectural plan that outlines an object.

on center   Abbreviated O.C. The term means to separate joists, studs, or rafters by the spacing indicated. 16 O.C. means separate the pieces 16 inches apart, one after another.

open eaves   An eaves treatment where only a fascia is nailed to the ends of the rafters.

Oriented Strand Board (OSB)   Similar to plywood, the layers are made of strands or chips of wood oriented in a single direction. Layers whose chips are oriented in different directions are laid one atop another, giving strength akin to that of plywood.

outrigger   A 2×6 set flat running from a pair of rafters across notches in rake rafters and supporting a pair of gable overhang rafters.

overhang cut   The cut at the lower end of a rafter, generally perpendicular to the ground and parallel to the house wall.

particle board   Similar to plywood but mainly composed of a composite of glue and wood fibers. This can come in 4"×8" sheets or smaller pieces similar to *dimension lumber*.

penny   A designation for a nail size and abbreviated "d." A 16d nail is $3\frac{1}{2}$" long.

pilot hole   A hole drilled in advance of placing a screw or even sometimes a nail. Its main purpose is to create a channel through the wood so the screw or nail does not split the wood.

pitch   A word used to describe the slope of a rafter. *See* rise and run.

plainsawn   A method for cutting lumber out of a log. Most framing lumber is cut in this way. Compared to quartersawn, more lumber is reaped from a log, but the pieces are more prone to warpage.

platform framing   A conventional form of framing in which the studs for exterior walls are supported on individual floors. Also called western framing.

plywood   4"×8" manufactured panels of five or seven layers (plies) of wood.

plumb   Absolutely vertical.

plumb bob   A long string with a heavy weight attached. The nonstring end of the plumb bob comes to a sharp point. A plumb bob is used to locate a point, as on a floor, directly under another point, as the underside of a ceiling joist.

plunge cut   A cut with a circular saw through the middle of a plywood panel, for example, to make a hole for ducting.

pneumatic nailer   A nailing or stapling tool powered by compressed air. It requires an air compressor and a hose connected to the nailer. Used considerably by professionals to speed nailing, it is expensive for amateurs. Drills, grinders, and sanders can also be run with compressed air.

pocket (in a foundation wall)   A broad recessed area facing toward the interior and into which fits the end of a beam that holds up the floor.

pocket cut   A cut that notches a piece of wood.

pocket or sliding door   A door that slides into a recess in a wall rather than swinging into a room on hinges, often very useful for small bathrooms.

point load   The weight on floor and framing below a particularly heavy object.

post cap A framing connector that ties the top of a post to a beam.

pry bar A curved metal bar used for prying apart two pieces of lumber or removing a nail by gripping its head and prying it up.

power miter saw A electric-powered saw elevated above a platform. The operator's hand guides the saw down over the piece to be cut. It can be set to cut the piece at an angle. Also called a chop saw and a cutoff saw.

pump jacks Brackets attached to 4×4 posts rising near the outside of a house wall in order to make a platform for workers and materials.

quartersawn A method for cutting lumber out of a log. This method, as opposed to plainsawn, leaves the lumber with the grain showing in a more attractive pattern and makes the lumber less prone to warpage. But there is more wastage, so the lumber is more expensive. Quartersawing is normally reserved for hardwoods.

rafter A piece of dimensional lumber holding up a roof. These might be 2×6s, 2×8s, or larger.

rafter tie A framing connector that reinforces the joint between a rafter end and the wall top it rests on.

rake rafter A rafter at or near the end of a ridge beam whose lower end rests on the wall perpendicular to the ridge beam. Gable studs run below the rake rafters.

rasp A handheld piece of steel with sharp teeth for roughly shaving a piece of wood that is too long or wide to fit where needed.

reciprocating saw A motorized keyhole saw whose motor is mounted behind the blade and causes the blade to move rapidly back and forth in a line. Practically essential for demolition work in advance of remodeling, it is also good where a circular saw cannot reach owing to the motor being mounted to the side of the blade.

rim joist *See* band joist.

ridge The horizontal framing member of a roof at its highest point and to which the upper ends of rafters are attached.

ridge cut The cut at the upper end of a rafter for fitting against a ridge.

rip cut A cut along the grain, rather than across the grain. With lumber, this means cutting along its length rather than across it. It is a more difficult cut than a cross cut, and also more dangerous when using a circular saw.

rise A vertical distance. An important term in the construction of stairways and roofs. In roofing, the ratio of rise over run is called the pitch.

risers The vertical parts of stairways.

run A horizontal distance. An important term in the construction of stairways and roofs.

rough sill or sill A horizontal framing member at the bottom of a window opening.

sapwood Sap-carrying wood between the bark of the tree and the heartwood.

sawhorse A four-legged 2'-high structure with a narrow top used to support material for sawing, drilling, and other tasks. It can be made from scrap lumber or bought from home improvement stores.

scab joint A butt joint reinforced with a piece of wood nailed across the joint to the two pieces of joining wood.

schedule Information in the form of a chart or table. A materials schedule coming with a project's plans indicates elements, such as doors and windows, and their locations. A nailing schedule indicates what nails and how many to use for given situations.

scribing Done with a compass. Holding the end of the non-pencil leg against a length of material and the pencil-end leg on another adjacent, you pull the compass along. The pencil end draws a line in exact profile of the material under the nonpencil leg. Cutting along the pencil line leaves a piece of material that fits snugly against the first.

section drawing   An architectural drawing showing a right angle "cut" through some other element in a floorplan. A section drawing might show how a vertical wall is built.

section line   A line on an architectural drawing that indicates a section view on another page or location.

shear load   The force of wind or earthquake to move a building sideways.

sheathing   Structural material that is fastened to studs, joists, or rafters. Normally this is plywood or a plywood equivalent.

shim   A wedge-shaped piece of wood placed under another piece of wood to hold the top piece in an elevated position.

short saw   A hand saw, sometimes called a toolbox saw, that is shorter than ordinary hand saws.

sill or sill plate   The horizontal piece of dimensional lumber. A sill plate is a piece of lumber that is bolted to the top of the house foundation.

sledge hammer   A long-handled very heavy-headed hammer. It is often used to knock a piece of framing into place, said to "persuade" the piece into place.

sliding T-bevel   A handle and a sliding piece of steel that can be locked at any angle to the handle. It is used for duplicating an angle onto a piece of wood to be cut.

soffit   Sheathing that is attached to the underside of rafters or to the underside of lookouts.

softwood   Generally, the wood of evergreen trees.

sole plate   The horizontal bottom piece of a framed wall. Also called a bottom plate.

spread load   The force of rafters bearing down on side walls and attempting to spread them apart.

spring clamps   Small, low pressure clamps for holding pieces in place or applying pressure to two pieces being glued together.

square-edged   Said of plywood that is not tongue-and-groove. The edges are squared and cannot interlock.

staggered joints   A technique of avoiding joints between pieces of wood being next to or near one another. Staggering joints gives better strength to a system of wood pieces.

step-off method   A way of marking the length and cuts of a rafter or stair stringer by moving a framing square along the rafter or stringer length. It does not require the use of mathematical tables.

stud   A vertical piece of wood. Usually a 2×4 in a framed wall.

stud finder   A hand tool used for finding studs or joists behind finish wall or ceiling material.

Sturd-I-Floor   A designation for plywood panels that can be used as subflooring and underlayment. Similar grades for plywood are "sheathing" and "siding."

subfloor   The first layer of flooring, which is fastened to the joists. It may be plywood or a plywood equivalent such as Oriented Strand Board (OSB). Also called sheathing and decking.

tail (of a rafter)   If a portion of a rafter at its lower end extends beyond the outside of the wall that supports the rafter, this portion is called the tail.

tail joist   A joist that runs from a header joist to a beam or sill plate.

toenailing   Nailing through the end of one board into an adjoining board. Much toenailing of 2x material is with 10d nails.

tongue   The thinner and shorter arm of a framing square.

tongue-and-groove   Term applied to wood that has a groove on one side and a protruding tongue on the other. A tongue can slip into the groove of an adjoining piece. Tongue-and-groove is common in flooring and in plywood that is meant to be used for subflooring and roof sheathing. An abbreviation is T&G.

tool apron A canvas apron with a couple of nail pouches and perhaps a loop for a hammer and used for light work and for protecting clothing.

tool belt A leather or synthetic belt hooked at the back for carrying common framing carpentry tools and supplies such as a hammer, measuring tape, utility knife, and nails.

tool bucket A 5-gallon bucket with a nylon bib running around the outside. The bib has pockets for tools, such as screwdrivers and chisels; inside the bucket may be carried trays of nails and a power drill.

top plate The horizontal 2×4 at the top of a framed wall.

trade Lingo for one of the "building trades." These include the skills of electrical work, plumbing, heating and cooling work, tile setting, concrete pouring, floor installing, and the like.

trade plan The "blueprint" plan showing the layout for one of the trades such as electrical, plumbing, or heating and cooling.

treads The horizontal pieces of a stairway.

triangular square A piece of heavy-duty aluminum or plastic in the shape of a triangle used in marking cuts. Also called a speed square (T) and a rafter angle square. A flanged side holds to a wood edge so that marks can be made along adjacent edges. Right angle and 45° marks can be made speedily. Some people use a triangular square to guide their cuts with a circular saw.

trim carpentry *See* finish carpentry.

trimmer joist A joist defining a opening in a floor and that runs parallel to regular joists.

truss A configuration of parts of wood engineered to support a roof.

truss plate A flat framing connector for where two or more pieces of lumber come together, often used on trusses. Also called a gusset.

T-strap A framing connector for right-angle joints.

unit rise For rafters: The number of inches a rafter rises per unit run (12") of the rafter. For stairs: The number of inches one stair rises.

unit run For rafters: 12 inches of horizontal spanning distance of a rafter. For stairs: the horizontal distance of one stair.

utility knife A triangular blade that retracts into a steel housing handle. Spare blades are stored in the handle.

wedge anchors Anchors whose ends expand in masonry holes when the upper screw is tightened.

wood I-beam A form of engineered lumber that takes the place of a solid joist.

veneer grades Grades for the surfaces of plywood sheets.

waferboard Similar to Oriented Strand Board (OSB), but the strands are not directionally oriented, hence waferboard is not as strong as OSB.

web members Pieces of 2×4 that run between a truss's lower chord and upper chords, helping to give the truss strength.

wedge anchors A kind of masonry anchor that uses a wedge near the bottom of the bolt's sleeve. The wedge expands as the bolt is turned and grips the assembly to the sides of the walls.

western framing *See* platform framing.

wet wall A framed wall for a bathroom that is often wider than a regular 2×4 wall in order to accommodate wide waste pipes.

workbench About the height of a sawhorse, but with a wider working surface, sometimes fitted with a tool tray. Homemade ones are often used as step stools. Ones bought from stores are often collapsible and have vices or clamps attached.

Resources

Organizations

APA—The Engineered Wood Association. ("APA" stems from its former name, the American Plywood Association.)
www.apawood.org.

National Association of Home Builders
www.nahb.org

Western Wood Products Association
www.wwpa.org

Northeastern Lumber Manufacturers Association
www.nelma.org

Magazines

Build It

Fine Homebuilding

Homebuilding and Renovation

Old House Journal

This Old House

Traditional Building Magazine

Books

Black & Decker. *Carpentry Essentials*. Cowles Creative Publishing, 1996.

Black & Decker. *Complete Guide to Home Carpentry*. Creative Publishing International 2000.

Editors of Journal of Light Construction. *Essential Guide to Framing*. Hanley Wood, 2005.

Editors of Fine Homebuilding. *Framing*. Taunton Press, 2005.

Frier, John L. and Hutchings, *Gilbert R. Guide to Residential Carpentry*. McMillan, 1990.

Jones, Jack P. *House Framing*. McGraw-Hill, 1995.

Grizzle, Roger. *Basic Carpentry Techniques*. Ortho Books, 1997.

Haun, Larry. *Carpentry*. Taunton Press, 1999.

Lewis, Gaspar. *Carpentry*. Delmar Publishers, 1995.

Miller, Mark R., and Miller Rex. *Miller's Guide to Framing and Roofing*. McGraw-Hill, 2005.

Peters, Rick. *Framing Basics*. Sterling Publishing, 2000.

Smith, Ronald and Honkala, Ted. *Carpentry and Light Construction*. Regents Prentice Hall, 1994.

Spier, John. *Building with Engineered Lumber*. Taunton Press, 2006.

Wagner, John D. *House Framing*. Creative Homeowner, 2005.

How-to Websites

www.taunton.com/finehomebuilding (under "Articles" on the left side, click "Framing")

www.thisoldhouse.com

www.housetips.com

www.hometime.com

Tools Websites

www.stanleytools.com

www.sears.com (click "Tools" in the tabs at the top)

Index